SANTA ANA PUBLIC LIBRARY

D1118735

THE SECRET LIFE OF
CATS

THE SECRET LIFE OF

CATS

EVERYTHING YOUR CAT WOULD WANT YOU TO KNOW

CLAIRE BESSANT

JB

JOHN BLAKE

Published by John Blake Publishing Ltd,
3 Bramber Court, 2 Bramber Road,
London W14 9PB, England

www.blake.co.uk

First published in hardback in 2006

13-digit ISBN 978 1 84454 304 5

ISBN 1 84454 304 8

British Library Cataloguing-in-Publication Data:

A catalogue record for this book is available from the British Library.

Design by www.envydesign.co.uk

Printed in Great Britain by William Clowes Ltd, Beccles, Suffolk

1 3 5 7 9 10 8 6 4 2

Papers used by John Blake Publishing are natural, recyclable products made from wood
grown in sustainable forests. The manufacturing processes conform to the
environmental regulations of the country of origin.

Every attempt has been made to contact the relevant copyright-holders, but some were
unobtainable. We would be grateful if the appropriate people could contact us.

For Mum and Dad
with love and thanks for all your support

Contents

Introduction xi

1 The Perfect Pet 1

The Time Factor 3
The Responsibility Factor 4
The Nurture Factor 5
The Companionship Factor 5
The Female Factor 6
The One-to-one Factor 7
The Guilt Factor 8
The House-proud Factor 8
The Feline Factor 9
The Cat-flap Factor 10
The Cost Factor 11
The Age Factor 11
The Acceptance Factor 12
The Cat – A Perfect Pet 12

2 How it all Began 15

'Domesticated'? 17

3 The Natural Cat 21

Living Together 23
Group Living 25
Communicating 26
Long-distance Communication 29
Communicating at Close Quarters 32

4 What Makes a Cat? 37

The Perfect Design 38

5 The Hunter 49

How Cats Hunt 51

6 Cat Talk 55

Smell Talk 55
Body Talk 56
Talk Talk 69

7 Living With Us 79

What is it About Cats? 79
Making Comparisons 81
Meeting, Greeting and Talking 84
Sleep and Catnaps 87
The Joy of Touch 89
Grooming 91
Feeding 94
A Clean Job 100

8 Intelligence and Training 105

Measuring Intelligence 106
Releasing the Potential 110
Training Techniques 110
Rewards 115
Punishment? 116
Acts of God 117
Who Trains Whom? 118
Fetch! 119

9 What Cats Want 123

10 The Intensity of the Cat-Human Relationship 149

What Makes us Close to our Cats? 149
How People Approach Cats 154
Bribery 155
Competition 155
Do we want Independent Cats? 158
Cleanliness 159
Non-destructive 160
Companionship 162
To Be Loved 163
Playful 165
Friendly 166
To Fit in with our Lives 166
To Hunt or not to Hunt 169
No Sexual Behaviour 170
Fitting in with our Beliefs 170
Individuality 172
Beauty 174
What We Don't Want 174

11 How to Make a Cat Happy 177

Company 178
Safety 180
Health 184
Fitness 187

12 Stress and Health 189

Improving Security with scents 193
Overattached Cats 193
Rescued Cats 194
Nervous Cats 195
Aggression 196
Eating and Stress 198
Night Calling 200
Health and Stress 201
High Blood Pressure 202
Lower Urinary Tract Disease 203

Glucose Levels 205
Skin Problems 205
Immune Changes 206

13 Getting the Balance Right 209

Understanding and Respect 209
Choosing the Right Cat 211
Buying a Pedigree Cat 212
Taking on a Moggie 215
Providing Some Consistency to
The Changeover 217
How Can All of this Help? 217
Getting Another Cat 218

Making Introductions 220
Too Many Cats? 223
Indoor Only Cats 224
Bringing Outdoor
Behaviour Inside 229
Changes in Behaviour in Cats 231
Pheremones – A Useful Tool 232
Help in the Veterinary Surgery 234
Conclusion 235

14 A to Z – Tips for Common Feline Problems 239

Introduction

DO YOU KNOW what makes your cat tick – what motivates it to behave as it does? With behaviours developed and honed over millions of years to produce a highly skilled hunter and adaptable survivor, how has the cat managed to slip into the role of man's top companion without actually compromising any of its instincts? What goes on beneath that beautiful exterior – would understanding the secret life of the cat enable us to make sure it is happy living alongside us?

Actually, we put a great deal of pressure on our pet cats in our modern lives, trying to keep a largely asocial animal with others of its kind, often without access to outside or with it having any understanding of its motivations. We live in cities where the density of cats must cause them great stress and we expect them to take on our human frailties of needing to be needed. We are breeding cats which have inherited problems, are failing to socialize them in early life and expect them to live with however many other cats we decide we want to have around. Our attitudes and demands are a real challenge to the adaptability of the cat and it is a credit to its flexibility that so few problems do occur and most cats and people live very contentedly together.

This book is a combination of two of my favourite books – *Cat Whisperer* and *What Cats Want*. It attempts to explain what a cat really is, how it behaves and why it does what it does. Our modern lives are a real challenge to the cat and sometimes I fear for how far we can actually push it. A cat cannot say what it wants. I have attempted to interpret its behaviours and actions to deduce what it might want in this life which is now ever more closely linked to ours.

Go back to basics, understand what a fantastic creature the cat is, how it might think and give it the respect it deserves.

1

The Perfect Pet

SOCIAL, VOCALLY CENTRED biped meets top-of-the-chain solitary scent-communicating predator. It's love at first sight for the biped and the two form a non-jealous, mature, mutually rewarding and respectful relationship in which the predator maintains its independence (and may even be allowed to have other relationships) and the biped takes the supporting role. Sounds too good to be true – can such a mismatched relationship last? Well, not only has it lasted, it seems to be getting stronger! Man (or perhaps more often, woman) meets cat and the fascination continues. The mystery in the relationship has kept the flames alight.

In days gone past, it was not wholly socially acceptable to be so smitten by an animal in such a way. The working dog was held in high regard because it had a role and thus humanity had a reason to lavish it with attention and affection and was not just being 'soft'. The cat had no real role (save that of ad hoc vermin control) and was seen as something of little value that lived alongside us rather than with us. For men especially, acknowledging affection for a cat was seen as rather odd. In the Middle Ages, women who liked cats were seen as witches and, until recently, a cat that was loved was explained away, rather condescendingly, as a 'child substitute'.

How times and attitudes have changed. The cat, long considered a second-class citizen to the dog in terms of a place by the fire, has quietly moved from living outside, pushed the dog out of the way and even had the cheek to take over the master's best chair with the softest cushions! There are more pet cats in the UK than pet dogs – 7.5 million cats compared to 6.1 million dogs. These cats live in about 5 million homes – thus, the average cat-owning home has one-and-a-half cats. And, whereas people tend to keep just one dog, many households have multiple cats (over one-fifth of people who keep dogs keep more than one, whereas over one-third of cat owners have more than one feline) – but more of this later.

It is now acceptable to heap love and sentiment on our animals – indeed, the old-fashioned and rather more structured role of the working dog, which is kept outside, is rather frowned upon by pet lovers – a pet's place is seen to be central to the family unit. Today, unless you are seen to behave lovingly to your animal you are frowned upon! Cats have done well out of this change of attitude and, as will be discussed later, their adaptability has enabled them to take full advantage of it.

How has the cat made this transition from low-value rodent-controller to prized companion in such a relatively short period of time? Has the cat done anything different? The answer is that the cat hasn't, but that humanity has changed considerably. The cat has merely moved into the role opened up to it by our changing lifestyles and attitudes and blossomed there. What factors have contributed to this?

THE TIME FACTOR

Our lives have never been so busy. People are working harder and longer hours; expectations of dedication to work (demonstrated by longer, unpaid working hours) have increased. Although there is a small voice of concern raised about family values and the need for time for parents to spend with their children, pressure of work usually means that people stay there long after official office hours. Those working for themselves also have to put in long hours to ensure they take up all opportunities and are available to the people who are still in their offices! It's a vicious circle. Indeed, far from living with a shorter working week with time for hobbies – as predicted twenty years ago – today our working lives are characterised by the need to prove our dedication and to give up more of our free time.

Thirty to forty years ago there was also a dramatic difference in the home – women still usually stayed home to care for husband, children and house in whichever combination they occurred. Today, both partners in a relationship usually work, simply to pay for mortgages and the other expenses of life. Not that childcare is an easy option – most women will tell you that they go to work for a rest. However, being at home does allow a person to organise those dull chores such as doing the shopping, putting clothes in the washing machine and paying the bills. These days such things have to be fitted in late at night or at the weekend, and most of the latter can be taken up by domestic duties or children's activities. There is little time to relax and little time for any unorganised activity; simply chilling out has become a luxury option. The cat requires little formal time – eg for walking – and so can be opportunistic and snatch small bits of our time here and there.

THE RESPONSIBILITY FACTOR

Mankind's traditional best friend, the dog, is having a hard time fitting into our busy schedules. As a pack animal, its instincts cry out for it to be part of a group, where it feels more secure. It can be stressed by being left alone all day and this may lead it to embark on destructive activity. Because we are legally responsible for our dogs' activities, we also have to know where they are and have control over them all the time: an uncontrolled dog can be a nuisance and, at worst, a danger to the public. Even a controlled dog can foul the pavement or cause noise pollution by barking all day in a house or garden. Thus, there is great pressure on owners to provide an environment in which the dog is happy and to ensure that it is well behaved and safe around other people and animals. In the countryside, a loose dog can do great damage to livestock. Dogs seldom come to us perfectly trained or behaved – like children, they need time and some expertise to be taught what is acceptable and what is not; how to fit into the group around them. They also need access to exercise areas.

And because we are legally responsible for the behaviour of our dogs, if they cause harm or damage we may have to pay the consequences. We are not responsible for what our cats get up to – if a cat was to break into a pigeon loft and kill some of the birds there, it would be up to the owner of the loft to build it more strongly to prevent the cat getting in. Sometimes this can work against the cat. For example, in the UK if you hit a dog while driving your car you are legally required to report the incident – not so with a cat. Under the law, a dog should not be out on its own and, in our cities and towns, dog wardens are employed to ensure that any dog found wandering is taken off the streets. Thus, while a cat may be seen as less important in the eyes of the law, this means that less control is required and there is less onus on owners to control their cats.

THE NURTURE FACTOR

The number of people who have the time, space and knowledge to keep a dog are decreasing. Yet whatever it is that makes us like to keep pets – perhaps we might call it the 'nurture factor' – has not disappeared. We like to care for something; we like to be welcomed home by something that in turn responds to us unconditionally. It is not pleasant to go home after a long day in the office to an empty house. Being met by a pet that is delighted to see you and welcome you gives you a lift. Enter the cat – clean, independent, unlikely to get lonely, good on companionship and low on maintenance – the answer to our prayers. Moreover, it is unlikely to cause our neighbours and friends much (if any) nuisance or danger.

THE COMPANIONSHIP FACTOR

Cats make excellent companions. Most are happy to mooch around the house with their owners, having a sleep on or near them and generally joining in by sitting on the newspaper that someone is attempting to read, filling the computer with hairs as they lounge on top or pottering with us in the garden. Stroking a purring cat can be wonderfully relaxing and great therapy.

There have been many studies on the benefits of dog ownership – dog owners have lower blood pressure, less depression and recover from illness more quickly than those without canine companions. Some of this may be due to the exercise that is part and parcel of owning a dog – and which, of course, is missing from this list of feline factors. Cat owners are spared the need to go out in all weathers and pound the footpaths and moors and can look forward to a warm cuddle in front of the fire instead of a cold excursion in the winter. Admittedly, they do miss out on the contact with strangers that usually accompanies a walk with a dog – all sorts of people stop and talk to you, feeling they can approach and make conversation if it starts with a comment to or about the dog. There are even schemes in practice whereby owners of temperament-tested dogs are taken into hospitals and homes to visit the patients; undoubtedly, some people obtain great therapeutic benefit from meeting and patting dogs. There is a similar scheme for cats, but it does take a rather special cat to enjoy going off its own territory and meeting strangers in a strange place. Cats usually want to take their time to assess a person and decide if they want to make contact. Cat companionship is of a rather more personal nature than the sociable companionship characteristic of dog owning.

THE FEMALE FACTOR

Women's role in our society has changed even more rapidly than that of cats! Women now juggle home and work and are equal decision makers within the home. The male-orientated household, in which the man would probably have chosen a pet to fit the perhaps more male role of the dog, is vanishing rapidly. For whatever reason, women like cats. Moreover, they are 'allowed' to like cats and to form strong relationships with them, and tend to choose them in preference to the dog – one possible major reason for this being that cats are easier to keep.

THE ONE-TO-ONE FACTOR

But it is not only women who like cats. Men have had a hard time being allowed to say they love their cats and, often, men prefer the more controllable, non-questioning loyalty and obedience of the dog. And perhaps because they have not owned a cat, their assumptions about the cats are based on viewing at a distance – the cat may seem independent and aloof; it will probably not run up to strangers and ask for attention the way a dog will, and thus close encounters with cats may have been few and far between. However, the convert, as is often the case, can be the strongest advocate of the cat. Many self-confessed male canine lovers might never have chosen to take on a cat, but for some reason a cat may have come into their lives, either accidentally or because it arrived with a new partner or via a child. They may initially view the cat as non-loyal and rather too independent but will usually find themselves gradually won over by its intelligence, its grace and that same feeling of 'specialness' we all get when the cat runs to greet us or deems to grace us as its choice of soft lap. These men are the first to become distressed if the cat is ill, and the most upset when it is lost.

They also get to study the cat in comparison to the dog and, quite frankly, the cat often makes the dog look rather a fool, falling over itself to please its owner or hanging around waiting for a word or pat. The cat seems immensely cool, calm and collected seen alongside its canine cousin. Indeed, in the cat/dog relationship, it is usually the cat that is in charge. Many times a cat will simply sit and stare at a dog, which will not catch its eye, and will sit or even lie down to try and avoid the feline attention! Of course, some cats and dogs become the best of friends – the lack of inter-species competition allows them to enjoy each other without fear of losing position!

THE GUILT FACTOR

Guilt provides another strong reason for the popularity of cats. These days, people have many calls on their time – they can't manage to do everything, and feel guilty about those things they cannot fit in. One's partner does not get enough of one's time; one's children do not even get that 'quality' time which is supposed to be allotted to them and thus make parents feel better and, to crown it all, the dog is unhappy because it doesn't receive enough attention – more guilt. A dog that has been left too long may soil in the house, howl, bark or chew up the furniture because it feels distressed at being left alone. Such behaviour not only causes dog owners to worry about annoying the neighbours, but makes owners feel very guilty about leaving the dog alone for too long.

The cat, on the other hand, is more often than not very happy to be left alone and will get on with its own life without too much worry. Because cats will usually eat in a fairly measured fashion, they can be left food to eat as they wish; they can go outside if they need to or be provided with a litter tray and thus are not crossing their legs if their owner is stuck on the 17.30 train outside Waterloo for two hours. Cats are content without too much input. An owner can alleviate any small worry that they might get lonely by getting two kittens together so they have company when they are left alone. Two cats are seldom much more work than one and they provide at least twice the fun.

THE HOUSE-PROUD FACTOR

Because people are working longer hours and money is perhaps not as readily available as it was in the late eighties and early nineties, we do not actually have a great deal of free time. Our entertainment is often centred around the house – home-entertainment centres with mini-cinema screens, DVDs, videos, Sky television, etc. are all aimed at those who don't go out all the time, but have home-based entertainment or relaxation. Our televisions have been swamped by a glut of house-design programmes over the past few years and, as a consequence, we are all much more interested in what our rooms look like and how to get the best from them. One such programme, *House Doctor*, which features a female Californian house expert who will give a house a make-over in order to help it to sell, has majored on this lady's frankness about the fact that dogs make a house smell and can thus make finding a buyer problematic. Even the cleanest and youngest of dogs can smell pretty bad if it gets wet – and the older and damper the dog, the worse the situation becomes. While country dog owners may have a boot room or an outdoor kennel for the dog, at least until it dries out, most homes have to contend with a damp dog in the kitchen, and wiping up the muddy paw prints and wiping down the mud spatters all over the walls. Cats do leave hairs around and if you have a very fluffy type of cat this can be a problem. Thankfully, cats don't smell (unless you don't clean out the litter tray regularly). They also look great draped over the new throw on the settee, or lying on the Habitat rug.

THE FELINE FACTOR

Even the scruffiest battleworn tomcat has a certain grace – but the healthy, young supple cat has an elegant beauty of form and movement that is hard to beat. Luckily, we have not tried, or have not been able if we have tried, to change the feline form too much. Some pedigree cats may vary in how much hair they have, or in their body form from slim to more stocky in shape, but the feline form, the beautiful eye colour, coat colour or pattern and the fluidity of movement and grace remain. It is a joy to have such beauty in our homes.

THE CAT-FLAP FACTOR

The cat-flap is second only to the litter tray in making cat-keeping easy. It removes the need to control or be at the beck and call of our cats; they can be in or out as they please without needing a middle man. Modern cat-flaps do allow us some control if we want it – to shut out the world or to keep cats in at night or during potentially stressful occasions, such as fireworks night. Sometimes

flaps can make it all too easy to let any cat in the neighbourhood visit, but, in terms of boosting the popularity of cats as pets, it has had a great effect.

THE COST FACTOR

For most people, obtaining a cat costs very little. Only about 10 per cent of cats in the UK are pedigree cats and have a purchase cost associated with them – usually several hundred pounds. The remaining owners obtain their cats from a variety of sources, from going to a rescue shelter, to taking on a kitten from a friend's cat or simply having one turn up on the doorstep. In many cases, cats cost little or nothing to acquire. Kittens are often 'free to a good home' from people who have not realised that their female kitten is no longer a kitten – the local tom knows immediately of course, but by the time the owners notice it is too late!

However, whether you have a moggie or a pedigree, the cost of keeping it is the same – vaccinations, worm and flea treatment, insurance, food and litter – all cats have the same requirements and this is not an insubstantial cost.

THE AGE FACTOR

The cat is also a long-lived pet. In general, the larger the animal, the longer it lives – mice live shorter lives than rabbits, and dogs outlive rabbits. However, in general, cats will outlive dogs. Interestingly, within the different pedigree dog breeds the reverse is usually the norm – the bigger the breed, the shorter the life. This has probably more to do with the extremes we have gone to in breeding than what would naturally happen if dogs were allowed to breed together to form that medium-sized black-and-brown mongrel we still see from time to time. Within dogs, too, the more active breeds usually live longer – the Jack Russell and the collie being particularly well known for their longevity. The average age for a dog is probably about twelve years; for cats it is thought to be about fourteen years. Anecdotally some breeds are said to live longer than others – the Siamese and Burmese often live into their late teens or twenties. Perhaps it is because cats are active animals, or because they know how to relax when they are not being active. Whatever the reason, it means they are with us for a long time – sometimes as long as our children – and become very special companions in our lives.

THE ACCEPTANCE FACTOR

We do not feel the need to change our cat's behaviour to fit in with what society expects; in contrast, we tend to feel a responsibility to ensure that our dogs behave in a socially acceptable way. Our relationship with cats is rather different and we are usually very happy for them to have their own very different personalities and even accept behaviour that may not please. This also makes the cat easy on the conscience, as we don't feel we have to be watching out for them all the time.

THE CAT – A PERFECT PET

To sum it up in a couple of sentences: the cat is a clever, beautiful animal that provides great companionship while retaining an independent and graceful self-respect that makes us feel honoured to be with it. Aside from that, it is clean, quiet and doesn't hurt anyone. What more could we want?

Thus, through no effort of its own, aside from behaving as it always has, the cat has found itself fitting a role for which it has not actually even auditioned. We are the makers of the cat-shaped hole – the cat, with its great adaptability, has happily slotted in.

2

How It All Began

TO CONSIDER WHAT comes later in the book in terms of what cats need or want, it is very useful to understand how the cat has come to be in this position alongside humanity – after all, why not a ferret or a racoon? How has the cat become 'domesticated'?

HOW IT ALL BEGAN...

About 4,000 years ago, the ancient Egyptians – a strong and inventive race – began to store grain; these stores enabled the Egyptians to spread their harvest across the year. Of course, the availability of grain also attracted animals such as rats and mice, which also benefited from this year-round availability of food. No doubt they ate and bred very successfully. Luckily for the Egyptians, there were predators that fed on these rodents and kept the numbers down. Among these were North African wildcats – a breed of sandy-coloured cats with some darker stripy markings on their legs and tails. They would have been slightly larger than our domestic cats and no doubt initially very timid.

Researchers believe that we are lucky that the African wildcat (*Felis silvestris lybica*) seemed to be able to get over its shyness and start to live close to mankind. An abundance of prey would have meant that the wildcats could feed and stay healthy and thus reproduce successfully. Perhaps the Egyptians started to capture some of the kittens and bring them up in or near their homes – the kittens must have been (like all kittens) very appealing. The Egyptians had many generations to play with – they could choose the friendliest or the prettiest and keep them – inevitably, these would have bred and been kept close to hand. The European wildcat, even if hand-reared or handled at an early age, will revert to its wild behaviour as it grows – it is highly sensitive to danger and reacts quickly – ensuring it will survive to live another day. It may be, therefore, that the African wildcat had certain genetic traits that allowed it the possibility of adapting to domesticity.

Research has revealed that during this time of 'domestication' the cat's brain became smaller. The areas of cats' brains that kept them 'jumpy' – those areas sensitive to sound and movement – are actually smaller today. This makes evolutionary sense: for cats to live with humans, they have to become willing to stay with us while we crash and bang around as we go about our daily lives. The calmer cats would have been able to do this. Indeed, the size of the cats' adrenal glands have also reduced over the millennia. The adrenal glands produce the hormone adrenaline – the hormone responsible for what we call the 'fight or flight' response. Less adrenaline would mean that cats were not so reactive and so less likely to run away.

Those cats that started to live closer to the Egyptians not only had to overcome a fear of man and all the activities that go on in a town or city, but also had to be able to live close to other cats. Wildcats are usually strongly territorial and live very solitary lives, only coming together with other cats for mating. After the young are reared, they move on and the parent cats live alone again. The reasons for this are probably based on availability of food. A female would have an area from which she could gain enough food to survive herself and, during the breeding season, feed a litter of kittens. Another cat in the area would severely reduce her chance of success. By making use of the abundance of food around the Egyptian settlements, the restrictions on food availability were removed – cats could live closer together if they were able to adapt to this type of behaviour and not automatically maintain exclusive territories. Again, the cats that were able to do this would have benefited from the food availability.

To sum up, during this period cats became more friendly towards man; they became physically smaller; their brains became smaller, and they became less reactive. Other changes in the appearance of cats may have begun with their domestication in ancient Egypt. The original African wildcat has an agouti coat – like a wild rabbit's coat, it is made of hairs that have stripes of different colours across them – ideal for camouflage. Having begun to keep cats, did the Egyptians then start to breed from those with slightly different coat patterns or mutations in colour which arose, to breed cats for an aesthetically attractive appearance?

'DOMESTICATED'?

We may marvel at the ability of the African wildcat to adapt and be adapted by humanity to 'domestication' but, despite this huge change to its lifestyle and reactivity, the cat has remained relatively unchanged by mankind. Unlike cattle or sheep, which can be said to be fully domesticated, the cat has walked a thin line between domesticity and wildness – perhaps it can be said to have met us halfway to domestication. Our pet cat, *Felis catus*, still retains the ability to live a completely feral lifestyle if it wants to, or has to – the biological independence to live with us or without us and survive.

Let us look for a moment at that other animal we have domesticated as a pet: the dog. Humanity has been able to take the dog and breed it for a multitude of different tasks, including companionship, retrieval, fighting, running or hunting. Alongside the requirement for the task came changes in body size and shape that enabled the dog to undertake whichever task was required – a small body for going down rabbit holes or a large muscular body for protection or fighting; a lithe, agile body for running miles and herding sheep or long legs and a lightweight body for running fast. With the body changes came changes in temperament. However, any developments had to allow for the fact that the dog must live peacefully with man without causing danger to him or his family. Thus, the dog has been changed and moulded to fit human requirements – it ranges in size from the tiny Chihuahua to the huge mastiff or Irish wolfhound.

We haven't been able to do the same for cats – or perhaps we just haven't tried because we have not been able to make cats do our bidding. They have been genetically adaptable enough to change from wildcat to domesticated cat, from *Felis sylvestris* to *Felis catus*, but there adaptability has ended. Man has been able to twiddle with the genes for coat colour and length and to some extent for body shape – consider our breeds of snub-nosed longhaired Persian with a stocky body compared to the slim, long-legged, quite fragile-looking Siamese. These are quite different but still roughly the same size and exhibit basically the same behaviour. They do not show the wide variation in behaviour seen between, say, a Labrador and a terrier, or a greyhound and a King Charles spaniel.

Thus the cat has been able to make the best of its association with man while maintaining much of its self-sufficiency and physically changing very little.

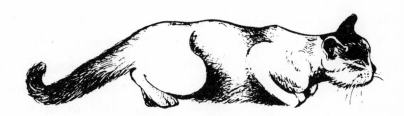

3

The Natural Cat

TO SET THE scene against which to look at our pet cat in our homes and living according to our lifestyles, we need first to look at the natural cat – how it behaves and the ways in which it interacts with its environment without people. In order to see how we fit in with the cat, we need to look at what motivates cats and how they behave without the benefit of human helpers. How do they interact with other cats, how do they like to live and what do they avoid? To do this, we need to look at the behaviour of feral cats or wild-living domestic cats. At this point, it is worth taking time to define the different terms we use when we talk about the different guises of *Felis catus* when it associates with man.

Feral cats are domestic cats gone wild. True ferals will act like wild animals – they will not accept handling and will be terrified if trapped. They can live alongside humans and scavenge available food, but adult ferals will seldom, if ever, make happy, confident pets – they should be respected as wild animals.

Semi-feral cats are cats that have probably had some contact with people previously; perhaps they were strays that have grouped together around a food source or have joined other true ferals. Many may be tameable and, if they receive particular attention, may be happy to become house cats again.

Farm cats could probably be grouped with ferals or semi-ferals. However, we have long given them a grouping of their own. They are as we imagine cats to have been – drinking milk off the cobbles, in the parlour and chasing rats around the farmyard. Of course, times have changed and soft brown cows don't spend too much time these days in wooden barns chewing contentedly with shafts of sun shining through the broken slats while the farm cats play in the warm straw. However, there are still many cats on farms and they do help to keep rodents at bay around grain silos. They live alongside the farm inhabitants and may be fed or even come into the house; however, they often live independently from humans, although they will be familiar, and may even be friendly, with the people there.

Pet cats are familiar to all of us and we expect to live with a cat that will enjoy sharing our lives and will choose to stay with us in our homes. The cat will probably have a relatively free existence and be able to come and go as it pleases. We consider the pet cat to be part of the family and will take it with us if we move, put it in a cattery when we go on holiday and care for it if it is sick. However, should most cats have to, they could survive in a semi-feral state.

There are a couple of subcategories of pet cats that differ from the 'original' pet cat in the way they are kept and what they are capable of doing. Some cats are now kept totally indoors because their owners cannot or will not let them out. These indoor cats, almost by definition, have a closer relationship with their owners because they are dependent on them for everything – food, toilet facilities and entertainment. If they were to get outside they might panic initially but would adapt quite quickly.

Among the pedigree cats there are several breeds that may not do so well if they had to live the wild life. The pedigree Persian has been bred with such a thick, long undercoat that it cannot actually groom itself adequately. If its owners do not groom it regularly, the coat will become matted and form clumps that the meticulous cat would probably find most uncomfortable and stressful. The Persian also has a very flat face, which may make it difficult for the cat to groom and hunt to kill, so it might not fare well if it had to return to a wild existence. Likewise, the hairless Sphynx would not survive a UK winter if it is forced to fend for itself.

LIVING TOGETHER

In order to understand our cats it would be useful first of all to look at how cats live together. Changes in their ancestors allowed cats to live more closely together. How far have those changes gone in our pet cats?

The European wildcat – a wild felid that likes to keep itself to itself and has a territory to match – may live in densities of between one and three cats per km². However, groups of cats that live around a source of food, such as a dump, or a dock or hotel, or who are regular feeders, may reach a density of 100 cats per km². On farms where they are also fed, cats can live at densities of 5 to 100 per km². In city areas they have been known to have a density of as many as 2,000 per km².

In a group of feral cats, the density of cats in a certain area may also be affected by the availability of shelter – certainly it is the female cats that form the basis of these groups and they will need some form of den or hidey hole in which to bring up their young.

Female territories thus depend on food and shelter. Male territories depend on females!

The range of female cats is determined by food abundance and distribution – they need just enough space to give them access to food all year round and to raise their kittens. Variation in the size of the female territory will depend on whether this food is concentrated in one place or is spread over a large area.

The range of breeding males is about three times that of females – it changes throughout the year, depending on where the breeding females are and on the time of year. Non-breeding males have a smaller territory – probably about the same as that of females.

If females have to live on natural prey they usually have a solitary lifestyle – there is only enough food available to allow one cat to live and reproduce. However, if there is a source of food such as a dump or dustbins near by, then groups of cats can live quite closely together. Usually these groups are comprised of related female cats and their offspring. Recently born female kittens may stay around while young males are pushed out to move on elsewhere. These younger males may not breed for several years – the large, fiercer breeding males will not allow this. Breeding males will move between groups of females. Unlike lions, the males do not seem to form bands of brothers, but stick to a fairly solitary lifestyle.

How did the African wildcat ancestor of our domestic cat overcome its strong instincts of being solitary and come to live in groups? The theory is that, as long as the food source is good enough and is situated in one area, then cats can start to come together. Indeed, they can now be so close that females will share the care of kittens and defend their den together – co-operative defence of kittens will benefit them all. Perhaps this is why the females that do group together are related: there is benefit in supporting all the kittens because they have similar genes and are therefore worth protecting. Females from outside the group will be chased off. Males are sent away and only a few will reach breeding status. Strange males, however, will be accepted more readily than strange females. This is understandable, as new females will compete for food and shelter especially if they have kittens.

Male territories actually overlap each other; they cannot defend a huge area all the time. Most breeding males adopt a roaming mating tactic between groups or solitary females. The same pattern is seen in wild felids. Breeding males roam more than subordinate males. Thus, group living depends on human help – food availability in large lumps – and stable groups based on related females.

GROUP LIVING

Let's look a little more closely at these feline groups. Even solitary-living wild female felines will actually spend about 80 per cent of their time in a group – of their own making – with their kittens.

To reiterate:

- Domestic cats will form groups if there is enough food around – groups consist of related females and generations of their female kittens. These will be aggressive to any other female cats which are not related to them.
- Breeding males will come and go from group to group and young male kittens will be driven off to wander into their own territories.
- Unlike lions, they do not seem to join up and form gangs of young males, but go their own solitary ways.
- The breeding males have little contact with kittens and will be hostile and aggressive to other adult males – if the group

is small they will also be aggressive to juvenile males, perhaps because they are more of a threat in a small group.

• Female cats may give birth together and share the suckling and care of kittens.

Researchers have studied many groups of cats and have found that male kittens have stronger interactions with their male littermates than with older male kittens. Likewise, female kittens seem to prefer their littermates to their older sisters. Is this to do with the fact that they have been with them during the socialisation period (see chapter 10) and so have stronger bonds?

COMMUNICATING

By looking at the way cats leave signals for each other and communicate by various means in different situations, we can perhaps understand some of the signals they leave for us. We may also be able to unravel the reasons for some of their behavioural patterns, especially those which we may see as problems (such as indoor spraying) by ascertaining the circumstances in which these behaviours occur in the wild-living cat.

In the way they communicate, our domestic cats can once again be compared to their solitary-living feline cousins. They also need separate consideration because they live at much greater densities than these wildcats and can choose to live in groups (like lions), albeit without the hunting co-operation. Thus, they communicate not just with long-distance signals, but at much closer range and have perhaps developed ways of doing this that are absent in their wilder relatives.

When animals live closely to one another they have to learn to tolerate each other and have some way of communicating to avoid conflict and thus injury. Dogs are pack-living animals – they need a pack around them to feel secure and have a behavioural repertoire that allows them to fit into a slot within the pack and to appease, submit or dominate as befits their status or place (or desired place) in the pack. Thus, although there may be a great deal of grumbling or cringing going on, there is little outright aggression and the pack works well together. For this, dogs have the ability to perform a wide range of body language in order to work together and prevent injury. Dog groups do have a hierarchy, and the rules of status prevent them hurting each other unnecessarily and save energy by having a structure whereby the group knows how to act and doesn't need to make an issue out of each decision.

The only group-living cats that co-operate during hunting are lions; they also live in groups and manage to live seemingly in harmony. However, these are female groups with cubs. The male lives alongside the females until it is ousted by a younger or fitter rival; males do not have to live alongside each other in harmony. Young males will form small groups when they are of an age to be pushed out of the pride.

Our domestic cats fit into both these camps and have a variety of signals that help them to communicate with other cats.

For the solitary-living cat, most communication is directed at keeping other cats away – scent messages can be left that will last for several hours or even days, although the endurance and success of the signal may depend on the weather not washing it away or blowing it in the wrong direction. Another problem that can occur is that circumstances may change more quickly than the message. It's a bit like sending a letter second class to say you will be in on a certain date: during the time it takes to get to its destination you find that something urgent has come up and you will need to change the instructions – thank goodness for the phone or e-mail to override the original message. For wild solitary-living cats it may not be easy to change the message quickly.

As we have seen, the level of food available will often be the deciding factor as to whether cats live solitary lives or in groups. Cats will defend their territories and try to push away other cats so they do not put added pressure on food resources or take over precious shelters where cats can keep their kittens safely. Males too will repel other males. However, defence is not necessarily the same as out-and-out war – male cats can fight very fiercely and have the weapons to cause great damage. That said, they will have gone through a large number of signals and threats before a confrontation finally takes place. There are many opportunities to back down – cats don't submit in the way dogs do, but they can remove themselves from the conflict situation. If you can manage to scare off your opponent, you do not have to risk physical injury, which can be fatal if wounds become infected. Cats do not have the social stratification of the dog in terms of dominance and submission in order to fit in with a group that must work as a whole for hunting and group living. In the feline world, peace is maintained by threat and compromise, not for the benefit of a group but for the good of the individual. Group living also adds complications – not only do individuals have a personal scent, but members of a group will have a group scent that marks them as part of the team. Cats without this marker are considered outsiders. Cats could be termed non-obligatory social animals and can interact in a friendly way if they want to. They do not live in organised groups – some cats may be more intolerant, oppressive or domineering than others, but it is not an organised agreement that all the cats have accepted.

There are, of course, circumstances when even the most solitary of animals wants to make contact and this is vital to the survival of the species. In this case the message in the signal changes and male cats will soon track down a female in oestrus (heat) that wants to be found.

Cats use several methods of long-distance communication to let other cats know about their reproductive state or to tell them to keep away. They use urine and faeces as well as glandular secretions from various other parts of the body that not only reassure them in their own territory, but tell other cats about their presence. Loud vocal communications that carry over distance are only made during times when males and females want to get together or when males are keeping other males from getting to the females they wish to get to! The calling of the female in season and the caterwauling of the male carry over a long distance. Most other vocal communication is also aimed at keeping other cats away and is used in much closer quarters in conjunction with body language – the communication between queens (mother cats) and their kittens being an exception. Close-quarter communication is also extremely scent-based for the cat and is used in combination with body language.

LONG-DISTANCE COMMUNICATION

Cats are equipped with an excellent sense of smell and can even concentrate scents by drawing air into a special organ in the roof of the mouth called Jacobson's organ – the grimacing look on the cat's face (in which it raises its upper lip and holds its mouth slightly open) is called the Flehmen response and can also be seen in horses and deer. With specific movements of its lip and tongue the cat pushes the air into the organ in a series of short breaths. This allows cats to concentrate the molecules in the air inside the organ and get much more information about it. In this way cats move in a

FLEHMEN

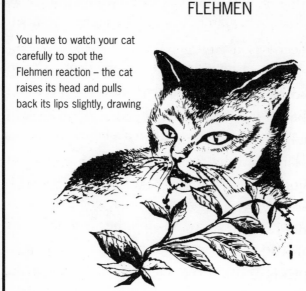

You have to watch your cat carefully to spot the Flehmen reaction – the cat raises its head and pulls back its lips slightly, drawing air into a special organ in the roof of its mouth to taste/smell the air. About 50 per cent of cats react in the same way when they smell the catnip plant. Catnip is thought to affect the same chemical pathways as LSD in man, although the effect is short-lived, harmless and non-addictive in cats. It is often put in cats' toys to encourage the rubbing, rolling and mewing reaction it also elicits.

world rich in scents from which they constantly glean information.

Among many creatures, from insects to mammals, there is a means of communication whereby a chemical (called a pheromone) produced by one animal will trigger a reaction in another. The term pheromone comes from the Greek 'pheros', meaning 'far', and 'horman', meaning 'to excite'. Tiny amounts of these pheromones will elicit a certain behaviour from a distance in animals of the same species. Pheromones have a role in sexual communication and it is in this aspect that we often see our cats reacting to them. If you watch a male cat in the garden after another cat has been through, you will notice that it samples the areas that the cat has marked or sprayed and often you will see the characteristic Flehmen response – if the mark has been left by a female cat in season then the response will be marked. We think of the scents left by the cat from glands on its face, paws, back and tail areas as pheromones.

Urine can be used most effectively as a long-distance message –

indeed, we believe that the reason most cats will dig a hole and cover the urine they deposit is to try and not leave a message that they are there. If a queen has kittens near by she doesn't want other predators hanging around waiting to make a meal of them. By covering the urine, scents are contained in the soil and prevented from escaping into the air, thereby preventing others from knowing there are cats around. This may work very well for solitary cats where territories are large and the smell of the urine stands a good chance of decomposing in the ground without being discovered by another animal. However, for our pet cats, which live very closely with others, it may not be terribly successful.

Urine can also be used as a red flag in terms of catching attention. Instead of squatting to bury and hide the scent, cats can deposit urine on to a vertical surface at cat-face height, leaving it to blow further afield. To deposit the urine in this way – i.e. to spray it backwards – cats take up a standing position and paddle their back feet up and down while quivering their tail. A small volume of urine (about 1ml) is squirted backwards. Toms spray most frequently and even more frequently if there is a female in season in the vicinity.

Added to urine are secretions from the anal glands and, as the urine degrades and bacteria start to break it down, it produces that exceptionally strong scent of tomcat urine which is so distinctive and can't be missed. It seems that the spray contains amino acids that are degraded by the bacteria to produce sulphide containing compounds which are distinctive to tomcat spray. Apparently, the smelliness of the spray may be an indication of the male's health. In order to produce lots of these amino acids that degrade to produce the smell, the cat must have ingested plenty in the first place from a good diet – i.e. the cat is likely to be strong and healthy if its urine is good and smelly! On a still day, tomcat urine can be detected by another cat from more than 12m away.

Researchers and observers of feline behaviour are unsure whether cats use faeces as a means of leaving a message or not. Most cats in their own territory will dig a hole, deposit the faeces and cover it up; we are still unsure as to whether it does so to mask the scents it holds or perhaps just as good housekeeping to ensure the health of their core area. However, many carnivores do leave faeces in prominent places (a habit known as 'middening') as a message of some sort to others. Cats can do this too.

Cats may also leave scratches and scent marks along pathways they regularly use. These scents are a way of organising the cat's territory – they are termed spacing pheromones and they aim to let other cats know where the no-go core areas are and where there can be some sharing of walkways. The scratches help mark the area with a visual signal should the pheromones become washed away.

Aside from this, long-distance signals will include those which can be heard over a distance – these are the sounds produced between cats trying to attract each other, such as the calling of the female in season, or caterwauling of tomcats letting the females know they are around and keeping each other at bay while in pursuit of females. These are all known as 'strained intensity sounds' produced when the cat is ready for mating or fighting in what we might term an emotionally charged state.

In summary, most long-distance signals are aimed at keeping other cats away unless it is time for mating, during which females will call loudly and repeatedly for males to come to them.

COMMUNICATING AT CLOSE QUARTERS

For wildcats that have solitary lifestyles, long-distance communications are used for most of their interactions with other adult animals, save for mating. Obviously, there is close communication with kittens. Our pet cats, like lions, can also be group-living animals and have a repertoire of scent and visual signals that allows them to let other cats know what they want. Vocal communications are seldom used, except with kittens (and, of course, with people – but more of that later).

Scratching or clawing, usually carried out on vertical wooden posts or trees, seems to have three roles for cats. It pulls the old blunt covering layer off the nail, revealing a sharp new point underneath; it leaves a visual signal of the cat's presence; and it leaves a scent message with secretions from the glands between the pads on the underside of the paw. Cats that are 'dominant' or feel themselves to be of a higher ranking than other cats will scratch in the presence of the latter – again, perhaps as a sign of which cat wants to control the area.

Scents also play a large role in close-quarter communication. The cat has various glands on its skin that produce secretions personal to that cat. These are situated under the chin, at the corners of the mouth, on the temples either side of the forehead, at the base of the tail and along the tail.

Cats will rub these areas on twigs and vertical objects to leave messages perhaps for themselves and for other cats. Although we can see and smell nothing, other cats will be very interested in these spots when 'bunting' (the rubbing of scent) has taken place. Tomcats will be very interested in the scents left by female cats in season, so this type of information must be conveyed by the scents.

Cats also rub each other and exchange odours, giving them an individual odour to which is attached a group smell comprising them and the other members. The head will smell more of the individual, with the tail and sides having more of the group's scent.

Interestingly, such facial scents are thought to be left for the benefit of the cat itself – scientists have termed them familiarisation pheromones. The theory is that the cat will go from area to area which it has marked in this way and the pheromones will mean something to that particular cat and make it feel secure and relaxed in that place.

Most of the cat's visual communication is, by definition, at fairly close quarters, because other cats need to see it. Thus, if they do get this close, many will be signals of conflict – cats with hair raised and standing sideways to make themselves appear larger, other cats crouched down with ears flattened to convey withdrawal and non-provocation, etc. How much of this is bluff and what subtle signals are moving between cats in conflict are issues that are probably lost on us.

It would be interesting to see if there were any types of interaction or communication, or what scientists call 'signals', which group-living cats such as our domestic cats use in comparison to solitary-living cats (which our cats can be too) which only come into visual and tactile communication with other cats for mating and, of course, during the rearing of kittens. In the excellent new version of Turner and Bateson's book *The Domestic Cat: The Biology of its Behaviour*, the authors bring together all the scientific work that has been done in this area to try and ascertain if 'domestication' of our *Felis catus* has made it behave differently. It is a fascinating read for anybody interested in research into feline behaviour.

That body posture we cat owners like so much – the 'tail-up' approach – is, it seems, only to be seen in our pet cats and in lions, not in those species of cats with solitary existences. In other wildcats, the tail-up posture is only seen when they are spraying urine. Thus, perhaps it is some form of communication to tell other cats that this is a friendly approach – something only necessary for cats living in a group situation and aimed at avoiding conflict when approaching. Another behavioural trait seen in both our domestic cats and lions is the act of rubbing against one another. Often in this situation, the cat doing the rubbing seems to be wanting to placate the one on the receiving end of the attention.

Allogrooming – a term used to describe cats grooming each other – is usually interpreted by us as a sign of affection, but it may not actually be so. Researchers have found more assertive cats groom less assertive cats and the act often ends in some form of aggression – the groomer may turn the lick into a bite! Perhaps it has a much more sinister purpose, and is a way of one cat asserting itself over the other.

Other body language, such as rolling, can be a sexual come-on from females of most species of wildcats, but it does not seem to have been recorded between males as well. In our domestic cats, it is usually seen when an immature male rolls in front of a mature one – perhaps in some form of submission – again, something developed to cut down aggression where there are groups of cats living together. Rubbing of the body and cats grooming each other is almost exclusively a sexual behaviour in wild felids; in our domesticated cats it is also a greeting, although, interestingly, rubbing can develop in solitary cats that are kept in groups in zoos, so perhaps solitary-living cats just don't have the time together as adults to develop trusting relationships that can result in rubbing.

Thus, our domestic cats, although descended from solitary-living cats, have adapted to be able to live in groups, if there is enough food and shelter. They use plenty of long-distance signals but also have a repertoire of communication signals that they can also use at closer quarters and which may have developed from living in groups around a source of food. We can learn from this that, although they are descendants of wildcats that had very little interaction with other cats, today's domestic cats have adapted to be able to live with other cats if they wish or need to.

4

What Makes a Cat?

PEOPLE FIND CATS visually pleasing and this may have been the initial impetus for the Egyptians to take them into their homes and speed up the 'domestication' process. They may have taken the pretty ones, perhaps those with stronger tabby stripes on their legs or a lighter coat, and kept them together, producing kittens with slightly new or stronger coat patterns. As cats lived alongside man and mutations in colour arose and were incorporated, a range of coat colours and patterns would have developed. Of course, we are still working on this process with our pedigree cats and are still developing new colours and patterns. While we have changed coat length and colour, the cats are still fundamentally the same shape and size as their ancestors – there are breed differences but individual differences still span these too and the degree of difference in size between the largest and the smallest would be only slightly over a factor of one. This may be because we have only been concentrating on breeding cats actively for about a hundred years or because the cat is less amenable to change when compared to, say, the dog, which has been bred into a range of sizes and shapes which vary much more considerably – from smallest to largest is a factor of nearer three figures in centimetres. Most of these changes have accompanied a change in function – for example, some dogs have been bred to run, while others may have been bred to go down holes or to scare off wolves.

Most of the cat's genes are responsible for its exceptional physiology; only a few of its genes account for its coat colour or length. Our relationship with cats began because of their vermin-killing ability but the importance of this has diminished to almost nothing (indeed now it is often seen as a negative part of the cat's behaviour), while other aspects of the relationship have developed further.

We have not tried to change what a cat does and so have not altered its looks greatly. We have also not altered its behaviour a great deal and across the breeds one cat is still very much the same as any other in terms of its instincts and abilities. In contrast, a Labrador is compelled to retrieve everything in the house at all times and a terrier is on the hunt for anything that moves; the cat is the same the world over and very similar in most ways to its wild ancestor *Felis silvestris lybica*.

THE PERFECT DESIGN?

If looks are linked to function, what does a cat do to have warranted its present form? I began to think of how a group of specialist designers would pool their expertise and put together a machine to do what a cat does, and it really made me think of how amazingly clever the feline machine is. So what would be the specification that Team Feline would have to achieve?

All animals must be able to survive – to find enough food to get through the year and to reproduce and raise offspring to a stage at which they can carry on the process themselves.

For the cat specifically, there are more clues as to where to start. The cat is an obligate carnivore – it must have meat in its diet to survive, because it cannot synthesise or detoxify certain chemicals that other animals can use to their benefit. It cannot survive on vegetable matter – thus, there is a necessity for hunting trips to be very successful. The cat uses top-quality fuel but must be able to refuel regularly.

Prey such as rats, mice and other small rodents are likely to be active during dawn and dusk, when light is low. These animals can scuttle away into the undergrowth very quickly, thereby disappearing from view and evading capture. Cats need to be stealthy to get near enough for a final powerful dash to grab the prey. The grab must be successful and the prey immobilised quickly or else it will get away – the predator won't get a second chance.

The cat must be able to hunt on its own, not as part of a team like, for example, the wolf or the lion. No back-up here or the use of numbers to create an ambush: one animal must get close enough to another (which will be on guard the whole time) and be able to get hold of it and despatch it on its own.

Perhaps Team Feline looked at the dog as a model to start with, but realised that the cat design must be superior – it must be self-sufficient and it must be stealthy; it must be supple but deadly. Indeed, in order to get to where the prey is the body of this animal must be capable of fairly unique feats of flexibility and power. So Team Feline worked on a design that incorporates a long flexible spine with rounded vertebrae for ease of turning, a tail that can be used for balance, highly mobile joints and ligament and muscle attachments adapted for ease of movement. They kept the clavicle (collarbone) slim and, rather than attaching it to the shoulder, as it is in humans, they let it float in muscle, freeing up movement (and making it easy for a cat to carry out tasks such as walking along narrow ledges). They reduced the shoulder blades to allow the cat to swing its shoulder along with its leg, again adding to the length and the fluidity of movement without compromising power. The cat also walks on its toes – the pads are the equivalent of our toes plus the part of the foot in front of the ball. The extra length allows them to get a long stride, touch the ground lightly and move on again. They made the hindquarters powerful to push the body forward and the front quarters to assist in stopping movement. The body can move from a walk pattern to a run and then to a gallop in which the back legs hit the ground together and push off; the spine bows and lengthens and allows for greater stride length. When it comes to a large leap, the cat can jump five to six times its own length.

All of this would allow the body to get to the prey and pounce on it – but what then? Imagine a small animal running for its life: it is extremely fast and can change direction in an instant – trying to grab with just jaws would be clumsy. Wolves manage it, but then they have the bonus of having several jaws coming at the prey in different directions as the pack closes in. The cat needs to make a successful grab almost immediately. Of course, Team Feline will need to add weapons to the front feet to allow the cat to grab the prey and hang on to it – claws (the sharper the better) would be excellent. However, claws would make silent movement much more difficult and the constant wear and tear from walking on them would blunt them quickly – like the claws of a dog, which help give it grip for the chase but which are not much use for anything else. Team Feline were not to be put off – they came up with a brilliant design: a set of razor-sharp weapons that are normally kept sheathed and sharp but can be brought into play the instant they are needed. While the cat is walking or resting the claws are tucked away in the pads, but when required the muscles and tendons of the foot pull the end bone of the toe forward and this automatically pushes the claw out and straightens it so that it is firm and strong. The nails of the claws are backward facing, so that when they hook into the prey they prevent it escaping. Brilliant enough, but a dog with retractable claws would still not be good enough. The cat must be able to use these weapons in a flexible way, not just be straight legged. Thus the cat has a flexible 'wrist' that allows it to turn its paw for hunting, getting its prey to its mouth and additionally useful for grooming, climbing, etc. Indeed, these built-in crampons are also ideal for climbing and help the cat to follow prey or to escape from danger. When they are tucked away, the cat walks on cushioned pads that give it a light silent step.

So the flexible forelegs and claws can be used to grasp the prey, get it to the mouth and pass it into a strong jaw with powerful teeth – in particular, long and pointed canine teeth. These are used with extraordinary fineness rather than brute force – they slide between the neck vertebrae and sever the spinal cord very cleanly and quickly, with accurate precision.

Team Feline should be very satisfied thus far – the body of the cat is lithe, supple and strong; it can move silently, has a powerful leap and can catch prey with its retractable claws. It is not designed for long sprints or running prey down, but for stealth and surprise. So far so good. But how to find the prey?

Some sort of radar system built to respond to the appropriate kind of prey would be excellent. What could it home in on? Small animals make rustling noises as they move around in the undergrowth; they also make sonic and ultrasonic squeaks. If these could be picked up, that would give a starting point. Team Feline thought about the ear of the cat – it must be able to hear sounds in the range made by the prey, much of it in the human ultrasonic range. In fact, they gave the cat one of the largest hearing ranges in the animal kingdom (surpassed only by the dolphin and the horse) and spanning 0.5 octaves – a range of frequencies from 30 to 50,000 hertz. So that the cat can hear when there is prey in the field – the area of the field is rather large and the prey is rather tiny and the cat is not built for running long distances – the team added a couple of radar dishes, similar to those used to gather information from the stars, right on top of the cat's head. These ears, with large ear flaps called pinnae, are controlled by more than twelve muscles and can swivel independently through 180 degrees. Internal ridges or corrugations channel and amplify the sound down into the internal ear. By calculating the difference in the time taken to reach each ear, an internal computer can pinpoint the source of the sound very accurately – the cat will be able to distinguish between sounds 8cm apart at 2m or 40cm apart at 20m, accurate enough to get the cat near so that it can see the prey before pouncing.

One of the specifications Team Feline had at the start of the challenge was to ensure that the cat could function in the low light available when its prey is on the move. Thus, another specialist review would be necessary to tackle the problem. For humans twilight is a very difficult time to see: colours become very muted and definition is lost – brown mice would melt away into the grey undergrowth without too much trouble. We struggle to see human-sized animals in this light.

This will have been one of the team's greatest challenges – the eye would have to fit on to quite a small head and be designed to make the best of low light levels. So the designers made the eye itself quite large in proportion to the head (another feline feature humans find very attractive) and gave it a pupil that can open to about three times the width the human eye can. This lets in as much light as possible on to the retina, the sensitive layer of cells at the back of the eye that conveys signals to the brain. They packed in more rods – the specialised cells that respond to light – at the expense of cones, the cells that are responsible for colour sight. Thus, the cat sees much better in low light but will have sacrificed some ability to see colour – it will probably be able to see muted blues and greens, but not reds.

Then they fitted the turbo system. Using the principle of re-routing exhaust gases through the engine in a car to use again, a special reflective layer of cells called the *tapetum lucidum* reflects light that has not been absorbed by the eye first time around and gives the retina a second chance to use it. The reflective layer can be seen when a cat is caught in car headlights or in the flash from a camera and looks silvery green. Team Feline should have patented it – it made someone a fortune when applied to devices placed in the middle of the road to aid night driving! This maximum efficiency gives the cat immensely better night vision than humans. Not content with this, the designers added some cells that are very sensitive to movement, allowing the cat to pinpoint its prey very quickly.

The only problem with this brilliant system is that its sensitivity may cause problems in the strong light of day – especially for a desert-dwelling animal that is active during the daytime too. Other designs, such as the bush baby, have large and very sensitive eyes but are purely nocturnal – they do not have to deal with the full glare of the daytime sun. So the designers added a safety feature: the ability to shut down the system when the light is bright. The beautifully coloured protective shield that surrounds the light-sensitive pupil can be drawn right across, leaving only a thin slit to let the light through – this is the pupil. A second set of much stronger shutters (the eyelids) can then shut down horizontally for maximum protection. Indeed, Team Feline were so proud of their stunning design that they added a third eyelid that can be drawn across the eye in times of danger to it. This third eyelid is hidden away and seldom seen, occasionally being raised halfway when a cat is not well.

These beautiful precision instruments are positioned at the front of the skull and give the cat a wide field of vision – a combination of the fields used by animals that hunt and those that are hunted (which, of course, can include the cat itself). The cat focuses best at a distance of 2–6m, the distance from its prey it must reach before it makes that final and all-important strike.

Thus, the cat has good eyesight in the day and well into what we would term darkness. However, when it is truly dark even the cat will have difficulty seeing. If it is following a sound and moving through the undergrowth, how can it avoid the danger of obstacles in the way? Could Team Feline come up with something else innovative? Being exceptionally inventive, they came up with a very simple system that acts like a sensory force-field around the cat but is especially concentrated around all that sophisticated equipment on the head! A series of long, firm but flexible hairs protrude around the head and on the elbows, with smaller hairs over the body on the coat. These are exceptionally sensitive to movement. Called vibrissae, or (in the case of those around the mouth) whiskers, they are sensitive to a movement of 5 nanometres – that is, about one two-thousandth of the width of a human hair! Any tiny movement causes bundles of nerves around the base of the hair to send information to the brain or other sensory systems so that the cat can react quickly to avoid obstacles. Indeed, so sensitive are these hairs that they will probably be able to feel eddies of air around obstacles and give the cat a detection system that doesn't even rely on touch.

Another little problem that faced the team was to consider how to get the sharp teeth into position for the nape or killing bite without dropping the prey (which would scamper off immediately and become lost in the undergrowth, resulting in a lost meal). As it gets very close to its prey, a cat will need a different means of being aware of where it is. Step in the whiskers and sensitive hairs again – make the whiskers mobile and they can be held flat on the face or almost straight out in front and used as sense organs. As the cat pounces and grabs the prey and brings it to its mouth, the whiskers are thrown forward and act as another hand to let the cat know what is happening at close quarters. An additional row of sensitive hairs along the upper lip also tell the cat about the position of the prey in its mouth – which way the fur or feathers are lying – and hence where the neck is. This intimate knowledge allows the cat to kill the prey easily.

The team certainly outdid itself with ideas and innovative design in tackling the bodywork and the main sensors. They produced something that was not only functional, but also very beautiful – the Ferrari of the animal world. However, in order to pull it all together and make it work, they needed a central control unit that could receive all of the incoming information from the sensors and send out information on what to do next. The area set aside for this is not overly large – it can't be too heavy because otherwise the cat will be handicapped in its movement. They used the basic mammalian brain as a template but tweaked it to give some bits more space than others. They had a huge volume of sensory input to deal with: information from the eyes, the ears and the other touch sensors. With all of this information coming in from the outside world they opted to devote more working power to an area called the cerebellum, which processes these complex continual signals.

In order to hunt successfully, the cat must be able to hold its head (and, by implication, its eyes) level and steady to keep the prey in sight as it moves forward, and to be able to calculate accurately how and when to strike. Thus, a very sensitive sense of balance was a must. The organ of balance, the *vestibular apparatus*, is situated in the inner ear. Consisting of three fluid-filled semi-circular canals and lined with millions of tiny hairs, the nerve attachments pick up signals from the hairs as the fluid moves in response to movements of the cat's head. This system is common to mammals; however, the cat has taken it to Formula 1 racing precision. A continual monitoring system that responds automatically to changes in position allows the cat to adapt its position continually and thus maintain its sense of balance seemingly without effort.

But that's not all. Team Feline also developed a self-righting system so that if the cat fell from a height it could automatically turn around in mid-air and fall on its feet. As it falls, an automatic sequence of events is put into action that turns the cat so that its head is horizontal and upright and then brings its body around. The back of the body then swings around too and the cat can land on all fours. Of course, cats do fall awkwardly and if they fall from great heights they will injure themselves. The cat can land unscathed from most tree-height falls, however.

The self-righting sequence is an example of a process that involves automatic responses to signals coming from the vestibular system. Because the cat has to be a successful hunter and thus react very quickly, it has many such automatic responses. You may think that the nervous system works quickly enough via the ordinary system whereby messages come from the outside and into the brain and another is sent out in response. This method uses a little 'thinking' time, however, and sometimes this involves too much delay – in a fall, the cat would have hit the deck awkwardly with only milliseconds of delay. Under this automatic system, the information goes directly from the sensor to the muscles and puts into motion a series of pre-programmed movements, making the system lightning fast and giving the cat an edge over both its competitors and its prey.

So Team Feline did a fantastic job. They produced the ultimate predator, the earth-bound equivalent of the shark, and one at which we should marvel. It is also adaptable to being affectionate with us, which puts it leaps and bounds ahead of the fish!

Millions of years of evolution have brought the cat to this point, and into the human sphere as well. Team Feline designed a super-animal, the equivalent of a Formula 1 racer. No sensible town car this. If we had wanted Team Feline to design an animal that was purely capable of sitting on our laps and purring, and moving itself to the food bowl a couple of times a day, I doubt it would have ended up looking like a cat. Perhaps we should bear this in mind when we want to change fundamental things about our cats – to make them vegetarian, for example, or to stop them hunting. Our beautiful cats look and act as they do because of their superbly efficient design.

5

The Hunter

NO STUDY OF the cat would be complete without a look at how it hunts – in the context of this book it will give us a better understanding of how all of that amazing feline equipment is put to work and how the animal spends its time when hunting.

The 'domestication' of the cat is based on its hunting abilities – it took advantage of a concentration of rodents around stores of grain. The cat is still valued for its hunting abilities in some places, but today, in most cat-owning homes in the UK and other western countries, this is probably the least appreciated of the cat's talents. There are two reasons for this lack of appreciation: first, most people do not understand the fantastic design of the cat and its prowess in hunting; second, most owners these days don't actually want their cat to hunt. To be a little more accurate, most don't mind if the cat kills rats or mice (though they would prefer them not to bring their prey indoors, especially if it is not dead), but don't want to see their pet feline killing birds or other small and furry animals. Our expectations for our cats these days are not only that they live alongside us and our other pets but also that they live peacefully alongside our birds and small mammals.

We have all seen pictures of cats sitting with mice climbing all over them or birds perched on their heads nibbling their ears. While their owners may swear that the cat will not harm its small companion because it has known it since birth, I for one would not want to lay even a small bet on it. It is argued that if the cat grows up with these smaller creatures – potential dinner, after all – it will know they are part of the family group and not harm them. I still wouldn't leave them alone together. Stimulate a cat to follow movement of the right size in the right direction and it will automatically go into a predatory sequence and will have that bite-size morsel in its mouth before even the cat knows it. Millions of years of evolution have created a near-perfect hunter and much of the cat's success lies in the development of automatic or reflex responses that don't even require thinking time. A cat is fast – fast enough to catch a flying bird or a scampering mouse – and, of course, it is clever. I am not the first parent to rush around the local pet shops looking for a certain colour of hamster to replace the one that has just been extracted from its clip-together tubing tunnel complex by a shrewd pet cat!

Cats may have to survive through hunting alone if they are not in the vicinity of man and his food, either indirectly via scavenging or by being fed directly. Cats that have been fed may or may not hunt. The control centre for hunting is different to that for hunger. Therefore, turning off the hunger control does not necessarily turn off the desire to hunt. No doubt a hungry cat will be a keener hunter, but a full cat may also continue to pursue its prey. Cats will still hunt on a full stomach, perhaps because they usually survive on frequent small meals and so need to keep alert for opportunities. Cats given free access to food will eat between seven and twenty small meals a day.

HOW CATS HUNT

Most of us are unaware of the strategies our cats use to hunt – they simply go out through the cat-flap and reappear some time later, perhaps carrying a small body of some sort. We may simply find presents on the bed or in the cat's bowl, or come down to the kitchen in the morning and find it awash with feathers.

The cat must be able to hear and identify the sounds of its prey from quite a distance away, to be able to pinpoint the likely position of the prey and then get close enough to it to grab it quickly. From a very young age the cat begins to learn how to interpret all the messages coming to it from its ears, eyes and other sensory organs. It must learn how to approach different kinds of prey and how to get close enough to be effective in its final pounce. It is not built for pursuit, so stealth and prediction are important.

Cats do employ different hunting strategies, both generally and individually. Some cats move around looking for prey or listening for what they might just come across – this is called the M strategy (M standing for 'mobile'!). As owners, we are probably not aware that cats are even listening as we watch them in the garden. However, we have probably seen our cats undertaking the second approach, the S strategy, where S stands for 'sitting and waiting'. How often have you looked out and seen the cat sitting and gazing into space, seemingly just daydreaming the afternoon away. If you looked more closely, you would probably find a small burrow or a tiny pathway or run that is frequently used by one of the garden's little inhabitants. The cat will position itself outside the burrow and sit silently and patiently, staring at a likely spot until something comes out or until the cat itself becomes bored and moves on to a more likely spot. If something does come out, it will wait until it has moved a little distance from the burrow entrance before moving forward and pouncing to prevent it going back in.

Cats can employ both these techniques together (they are not bothered by scientists' neat classifications!) depending on the type of prey they are after. Birds on a bird table may require a sit-and-wait strategy; birds feeding off the ground may require a very careful M approach, as birds can see all around them and are constantly checking for danger. The cat must use all of its movement-control systems to glide over the ground without attracting attention with sharp or large movements. It may slip in a couple of runs if the bird hops out of sight and then freeze again – similar to the children's game 1-2-3 Red Light – stopping still if the subject of its gaze turns around to look in that direction.

Some cats don't bother to hunt birds; others become expert at this 3D hunt. Apparently, cats have a natural period of inactivity – a waiting moment – just before they pounce. This is not conducive to bird hunting, because the upwardly mobile prey will often fly away at this point.

When we looked at the cat's senses and its physical attributes and automatic control sequences for hunting, it became clear just how much finesse went into the hunting sequence – down to being able to position the prey precisely enough to slip a canine tooth between the vertebrae at the nape of the neck and sever the spinal cord, causing instant death.

As owners, we would probably not dislike the cat doing all this killing so much if we knew that every animal died very quickly and painlessly. Unfortunately, not all cats kill all prey immediately. Some may still be learning their technique and these, probably younger cats, may play with the prey before it dies. Researchers have found that, although both sexes of cat will bring home prey, females will do this more frequently than males. This is understandable, because queens will bring home prey for kittens to eat or for them to practise their hunting techniques on once they have reached a certain age. Male cats have nothing to do with kittens so perhaps they are just bringing it into the den for safekeeping.

Why do cats play with prey? Different research has suggested that the act of hunting fills the cat with tension. When it kills it is still 'hyped up' and needs to release this tension, which it does by playing. Researchers who carried out one study of tigers in captivity found that, if they made the tigers 'hunt' for their food by placing it at the top of a pole and making the big cats climb up and work to get it, the tigers would bring it down but then leave it for a while before they ate it. The theory is that they had to calm down from the adrenaline rush that accompanied the hunt and catch before they could eat the food.

Female cats with kittens have been found to be much more efficient hunters than females without kittens – no doubt the motivation of four or five hungry mouths to feed, either by producing milk or by bringing home prey, serves to speed up hunts and make more successes of each attempt. Apparently, female cats with kittens are able to hear higher sounds than other cats. Perhaps this is so that they can pick up any distress cries of the kittens, but it may also be because they need to hear the sounds of small animals.

Younger pet cats too are very enthusiastic about hunting. When we first let them outdoors they start to bring in insects and worms, which they have successfully sneaked up on and caught. They then progress to voles and mice as they become more confident and able to use their skills. From about a year on, they will hunt very enthusiastically and owners of young cats that like to hunt often despair in the first couple of years because of the number of small creatures their pets bring in. However, this enthusiasm does not usually persist at the same level after about three years. Some cats do keep it up, but many become less enthusiastic and prefer to sleep in the sun or watch the birds through the window when it is cold or wet outside.

Cats seem to enjoy hunting and they are certainly highly motivated to partake in this activity. Their natural abilities are honed with practice and patience. We need to make sure that we do not underestimate cats' need to hunt and be aware that we need to amuse the totally indoor cat which does not have the great outdoors as a playground for this innate activity.

6

Cat Talk

THE CAT, ARMED with all its super senses, does not merely use them to catch its daily meals. They allow it to enjoy a rich and complex life, communicating with other cats and with us using body language, vocalisation and scent. We can, with a little observation, understand some of the cat's body language (although the subtleties are probably lost on us) and interpret the intonations of its calls, miaows and purrs. The third medium, that of scent, is all but lost to us – unless we are 'lucky' enough to get a whiff of good old tomcat spray! But it is the sense of smell which is the most powerful of all the cat's senses and an integral part of every moment of its life.

SMELL TALK

A blind defenceless new-born kitten uses its well-developed senses of smell, touch and warmth detection to guide itself to its mother's nipple. Using scent, it comes to know its own particular nipple, to which it will try to return at each feed. The queen knows her young by their smell and by her scent on them and the importance of scent as a mode of communication is established. We have already seen how important scent communication is to cats (see chapter three) – what about other forms of communication?

BODY TALK

Cats are known for their independence and their solitary hunting techniques. Unlike their canine cousins, they do not co-operate to hunt or group together for protection and therefore don't have the social rules of the pack. However, they do mix with other cats, not only for the purposes of mating or raising kittens, but for what we would call more 'sociable' interaction. They have a complex body language – scientists have noted twenty-five different visual signals used in sixteen combinations; no doubt many of the cat's more subtle nuances pass unnoted. But if we can master the recognition and translation of a cat's basic expressions, then we are well on the way to understanding what our cats are feeling and meaning to 'say'.

Most encounters between strange cats occur outside, and in high-density suburban or urban environments cats will meet many others within a small area. The most dramatic body language occurs during encounters between rival males and the most obvious between cats during courtship. Since most pet cats are neutered and we rarely watch them outdoors, most of us have to be content to observe the less extreme interactions between cats, between cats and other animals, and between cats and ourselves.

Some of the most appealing aspects of a cat's behavioural repertoire are displayed during play. Kittens, and even adults, will put on for us a playful pantomime, which includes hunting, fighting or courtship – in fact, the whole gamut of behaviour. The play-acting can be likened to tribal dances where wars and courtships are re-enacted as a learning, as well as a social, process. In most cases, cats that share a home get on well together and interactions are friendly and calm. Where there is friction, you have a much better chance of seeing the cat's entire repertoire!

Of course, most feline confrontations do not end in fights – even when they are between rival toms. The aim of language is to put your message across, avoid – or at least not prolong – confrontation and prevent injury. An aggressor will put on a full display to try to make the other cat get the message and run away without resort to tooth and claw. Quite often cats will simply have a long staring match (with a few vocal insults thrown in), which is sufficient for them to decide who comes out on top. The dominant aggressor may merely walk away from the loser, sit down and look in a different direction or even groom, and human observers will be totally unaware that anything has gone on at all.

In this chapter, body language has initially been divided into head (eyes, ears, whiskers and mouth) and body (tail, position, size and angle). As regards positions, however, since some expressions of fear and anger can be very similar, the signs from individual 'components' may be conflicting and easily misread. To get the whole story, the entire body must be taken into account, as the examples will show. Isolating one feature may also be misleading because signals often change rapidly as the cat's mood and mind alters.

Looking at head position, ears, eyes and whiskers can tell us a lot about what the cat is feeling. The many muscles of the cat's face give it the ability to display a wide range of expressions, while the position of the head itself can give some clue as to whether the cat is trying to invite contact or attempting to become invisible. When the head is stretched forward, the cat is trying to encourage touch or to see another cat's facial expressions or those of its owner – the best example of this is when you come home and your cat wants to greet you and to be fed! If in conflict, an assertive animal may raise its head, but an aggressive one may lower it. An inferior cat may also lower its head but, if fearful and defensively aggressive, may raise it! A lack of interest is indicated by keeping the head down, pulling in the chin and turning sideways to prevent eye contact. Obviously it is very difficult, if not highly confusing, to try to guess the cat's mood by looking only at the position of its head, but by considering its body at the same time we can gain enough clues for an educated guess.

EYES

Eye contact is one of the most important aspects of human communication, and in cats too it plays an important role, but we must realise that, in the same way that a tooth-baring chimpanzee is not smiling but is actually showing fear, prolonged eye contact between cats is not a friendly action as it is in humans. Staring is certainly an assertive behaviour among cats, and rivals will try to out-stare each other to resolve conflicts. When a cat realises it is being watched or stared at, often it will stop in mid-groom or wake and look up. Although it may then continue with what it was doing, it does so in what we would call a 'self-conscious' manner until the observer has looked away also. We too can sometimes get that unnerving feeling of 'being watched', but cats are obviously particularly sensitive to observation.

At the other extreme, cats are often described as 'day-dreaming'

EYES

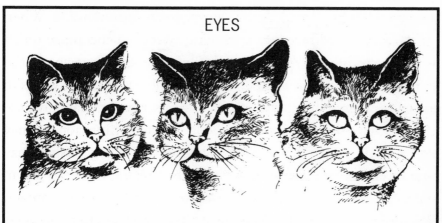

Left: Dilated pupils can be a sign of fear or excitement. Pricked ears indicate that the cat is aroused through interest, not fear.

Centre: A relaxed cat watching the world go by. The pupils dilate or constrict according to the available light and degree of arousal.

Right: Alert and ready for action in the daytime, the cat is cautious but not fearful. At night the pupils will be more dilated.

or gazing into space because they sit quietly, appearing not to be looking at anything in particular. This is because cats take in a great deal of information through the edges of their eyes, whereas we view more through the central portion and so look directly at things around us. Cats tend to use this peripheral vision unless they need to 'fix' their eyes on something, such as a moving target.

The eyes are good indicators of mood in cats. A narrowing or widening of the eye can display interest, anger or fear, in the same way as it does in man. The size of the pupil is not only governed by the amount of available light, but by the cat's emotions. Pupils may dilate because of either fear or aggressive excitement and, in less dramatic circumstances, when the cat sees its dinner bowl being filled, or becomes excited or aroused by the sight of a friendly cat.

When a cat is happy and relaxed, the pupils will be as dilated or constricted as the available light demands – the less light there is, the wider the pupil and the blacker the eye seems. A relaxed cat will probably not have its eyes wide open but the eyelids may appear heavy and it may blink slowly as a sign of contentment. Blinking is a reassuring signal between cats and breaks that aggressive stare which makes them feel so uncomfortable.

A fearful cat will often have dilated pupils and, as the fear increases, it may get an almost 'boggle-eyed' look with pupils completely dilated and eyes wide open. On the other hand, an angry cat that is asserting itself, but feeling confident in its position, may have pupils constricted to a slit. Of course, there's a huge range of degrees in the dilation of the pupil, depending on the intensity of fear, anger or excitement the cat is feeling, and on the amount of available light, and so it is best for us to look at the eyes in combination with the ears.

EARS

The ears are one of the cat's most important instruments of communication. Between twenty and thirty muscles control their movement and they can swivel through 180 degrees and move independently of each other, around, up and down.

In some of the larger members of the cat family pale markings on the back of otherwise dark ears accentuate their position during offensive or defensive encounters, making their owner's message not only easier to see but also leaving little margin for error in translating its message. Some wildcats, such as the bobcat, have a much shorter-than-average tail and so are deprived of one of their methods of communication. To compensate for their lack of tail, they have developed tufts on their ears which accentuate their position and give them more opportunity for communication. In

FACE

Above: A relaxed cat with perked ears and whiskers. The dilation of the pupil depends on the light.

Above: A cat which is annoyed will turn its ears back, while its pupils constrict and its whiskers bristle forward.

Above: Dilated pupils and flattened ears indicate a fearful cat. Its whiskers may be pulled back.

Left: When playing or hunting, ears are pricked, pupils dilated and whiskers thrust forward.

Right: A contented cat will half-close its eyes, relax its whiskers and doze off in a warm spot.

our domestic cats, the Abyssinian also has little tufts on the tops of its ears.

A happy, relaxed cat will usually sit with its ears facing forward but tilted slightly back. When its attention is caught by a noise or movement, its ears will be pulled more upright and become more 'pricked' as the muscles in the forehead pull them in. It's rather like us wrinkling our brow when we concentrate. If the ears begin to twitch or swivel, the cat is probably feeling anxious or unsure of a noise or situation.

As anxiety increases, the cat moves its ears slightly back and down into a more flattened position. My two young cats exhibited this ear-dipping beautifully when a new bumptious puppy approached their basket where they luxuriated by the wood burner. As he got within their flight distance (the distance they need between them and him in order to get away successfully), their ears flattened until they were lying almost parallel to the top of their heads, which they lowered into the basket hoping the puppy would then lose sight of them and go away. This is a perfect example of a defence reaction where the cat tries to disappear by making itself as small and unprovoking of attack as possible. When my old moggie was faced with the same problem of trying to rid himself from the pup's attention, he used the more 'active' approach of attacking before he was attacked. He set himself in a position where he could corner the pup and then frightened him with a startling hiss, arched his back, fluffed up his tail to make himself 'large' and started a battle of wits with a good stare. His tensed ears swivelled so that the inside surfaces were directed to the side and the backs visible from the front. His hackles went up and he waited until the pup bounced into range before having a swipe at his nose. The pup got a shock and was put in his place, and indeed the interaction was repeated many times over the weeks while the pup learned about life – both of them even seemed to enjoy the mock battle. The cat always won, of course!

WHISKERS

Whiskers too can indicate mood and are much more mobile than we realise. When relaxed, they are held slightly to the side, but as the cat's interest increases they come forward in front of the muzzle. A fearful cat will pull its whiskers right back alongside its cheeks –

WHISKERS

Above: When a cat is relaxed or indifferent to what is going on around it its whiskers stand out on either side of its face. However, watch a cat yawn and you will see the range of movement the whiskers are actually capable of, from lying flat against its face to fanning out and round in front of its nose and mouth. A cat on the defensive, as shown here, will hold its whiskers back, close to its face. Its ears will also be held back and down and its pupils may be dilated in fear.

Above: An inquisitive cat may fan its whiskers forward using them almost like a third hand (or paw) to feel what is immediately ahead of it. Whiskers are used to see/feel in the dark when the cat moves through the undergrowth or negotiates small gaps.

making its face as small and unthreatening as possible in the hope of avoiding conflict.

The whiskers accentuate the muscle movements around the mouth, and in fat-faced toms (in neutered cats removal of the primary male hormones means that the fuller face does not develop) close observation may reveal cheek muscles pulling down the cheek ruffs when the cat is excited or fearful. Wildcats have fuller faces or extra hair, as in the lion's mane.

MOUTH

The cat does not use its mouth in aggressive confrontation as the dog does – a cat's open-mouthed hiss and snarl is brought on by a feeling of threat. Licking of the lips may be a sign of anxiety, although sitting with the tongue hanging or sticking out seems to be a sign of relaxation or contentment, often giving the cat that amusing 'simple' look.

When humans yawn for reasons of tiredness or boredom, they can start off a chain reaction of yawning that is almost impossible to stifle in whoever sees them. Yawning is not contagious in cats, nor is it a sign of boredom; it is more a signal of reassurance and contentment and often accompanies a languid stretch after they have awoken from sleep.

TAIL

The tail is used for communication as well as balance. When hunting, the cat holds its tail in a streamlined manner behind until it is required as balance for the final rush. It may also announce the cat's interest and concentration with a twitching movement as it corners its prey. However, the tail comes to the fore as a tool of communication when the cat interacts with other cats or with people. It has a whole range of movements, from side to side, and up and down, in speeds ranging from a graceful slow sweep to a thrashing whip. The tail can change from a sleek coil folded around the cat when it is asleep to an erect bristling brush when the cat is frightened.

A relaxed, confident and alert cat walking through its territory will merely let its tail follow behind until it meets another cat or finds a point of interest such as a spraying or scratching post. If it decides to spray, then the typical tail-up posture and foot-treading motion quickly follow as the post is anointed with urine. When it sees a known friendly cat or its owner, the cat will often quickly flick its tail into a vertical position, pulled slightly forward over its back and kinked down a little at the tip. This position allows a friend – cat, or person (if they so wish!) – to investigate the exposed region under the tail where a recognisable scent will confirm that the cat is a part of the group. The greeting is often accompanied by a murmur or chirrup. Kittens greeting their mother will run up with their tails in the air and proceed to let them drop over their mother's rump and rub over the top of her tail in an

TAIL

Above: Typical greeting posture to a friend. The tail is held high with the tip slightly bent forward.

Above: When walking the tail is held relaxed behind the cat at a slightly downward angle.

When not being used for communication the tail is used for balance during jumping and climbing.

Left: The best time to see an 'inverted-u' shaped tail is when cats or kittens are at play – usually during that mad half hour when they chase each other around the house. The cats seem to enjoy that mixture of high excitement and fear which children also love. The hair on the tail may also be fluffed up like a bottle-brush.

attempt to solicit some of the food she has brought to the den. Adult cats will do the same with their human owner, rubbing and wiping their tails around legs, hands or even plates in the hope of being fed or fussed over.

Cats at rest, but preparing for action, may watch what they are about to get involved with and sweep their tails haphazardly from side to side. It's almost as if they're mulling over the idea and deciding whether to go ahead or not. As the cat becomes more alert, the tail may swish faster and in a wider arc. This can be the first sign of anger, or it may be intended simply to tantalise or encourage another cat to join in a bout of play. Violent thrashing indicates high excitement or imminent aggression – a signal not easily missed. A wagging tail in a cat means the complete opposite to that of the cheerful, friendly dog: it is a sign that the cat is in some state of emotional conflict.

If a cat feels itself to be seriously threatened by an attacker, it may become so defensive that the hairs on its tail become erect and it bristles like a bottle-brush. Held straight in the air, it can be fluffed up to at least double its size and this pilot-erection is used for display when the animal is defending itself and trying to look as large as possible. Cats in conflict may also hold their tails at a strange angle like an inverted capital 'L' – that is, the tail continues the line of the back before bending and pointing straight down to the ground. This can also be seen in kittens at play, as can the inverted 'U' tail. When kittens or cats play chase or when they have that explosion of energy during a 'mad half-hour' when they rush around the house bounding over anything in their paths, be it people, dogs or chairs; they often hold their tails in this upside-down horseshoe shape which, when all the hair is erected, makes the madcaps look as if they have 'the wind under their tail'.

POSTURES

Making yourself look bigger than you actually are is a trick employed by many animals for defence and attack. Often conflict is successfully avoided and the rival backs off when the bluff is convincing enough. Cats too use this ploy and also straighten their legs to look taller if on the attack. As the cat's hind legs are longer than the forelegs, its body slopes down towards the head from the higher rear end. An aggressive attacking cat will erect the hair along its spine and tail like a ridge, again making it look more impressive.

By contrast, a very frightened cat that is cornered or desperately trying to deter an attacker will erect the hair not just along its back but also over its whole body. It positions itself side-on to its aggressor, with its back arched to make itself appear as big as possible, in the hope that its attacker will think twice about proceeding against a larger foe. Having stalled the attack, the potential victim cat may then move sideways with a crab-like motion towards a safer area, keeping its eye on the foe in case even this slow retreat stimulates a sudden attack.

A submissive frightened cat may shrink into a crouch and try to look as small and unthreatening as possible in order not to provoke attack or draw attention. It is the opposite posture to a big defensive display and is often practised by a less confident cat that simply wants to be left alone to live a quiet life. It may then roll over on to its back with its head turned to face its attacker as an ameliorative, appeasing gesture. This is not quite the same as the submissive belly-up posture in the dog, which, from such a position, is very unlikely to fight back. The appeasing cat has been pushed as far as it will go in its attempt to avoid conflict and is as ready as it can be with teeth and claws to defend itself to the end if provoked or attacked further.

POSTURES

Above: During hunting and stalking the tail can often indicate interest by wagging slightly at the end.

During the rush and pounce the tail is used to balance the body and help ensure an accurate strike.

Above: As the cat grows more defensive the hair on its body bristles even more and its tail is held arched over its back.

Left: The amplitude of horizontal swing of the tail can indicate the degree of agitation the cat is feeling. From a gentle twitch at the tip denoting interest, it can build to a wide fast sweep when the cat is highly aroused, perhaps at seeing a rival in its garden.

Right: The 'Inverted-L' tail is often seen in a cat which is the aggressor in a conflict. Its back is slightly arched and its fur bristles along its spine and on its tail. The front paw is often raised.

Above: A defensive cat will stand with its back arched and its body at an angle to its aggressor. The hair on its body and tail bristles.

Of course, cats roll over in play, and sometimes also when they greet us. Many don't at all mind having their stomachs tickled, and some clearly enjoy it. Females in season will roll in front of males to solicit their attention. In summer, cats enjoy a dust or sand bath as much as the birds do, and they roll over and over on a warm sunny path, usually keeping a keen look-out in case a passing cat or dog catches them in that most vulnerable of positions.

TALK TALK

Not much research time has been spent trying to fathom the intricacies of the feline vocabulary and those who have studied the subject have categorised the sounds in different ways, but it is probably best to look at them in the context of our interactions with our pet.

Listening to the many different sounds and intonations a cat employs in communicating with us requires more than a little concentration. We usually react instinctively when the cat 'talks' to us, not listening to it as much as looking for visual clues as to the source of the cat's desires – does it want a cuddle, its dinner or just a reassuring chat? The clever cat makes it easier for us by going to the empty food bowl or to the door, or paws the latch on the window if it wants to be let out. If you are really keen to differentiate between the sounds your cat makes, tape them using a portable recorder and then talk yourself about what the cat seems to want. Listening to the recording later, without the benefit of the cat's body language and movement clues, may enable you to identify the more common feline expressions, calls or requests or the particular ones your cat uses with you.

Cats do have their own individual repertoires of sounds and actions. Not only that, they are probably much better attuned to ours than we are to theirs. They adapt what they say to how we respond, almost as if they have trained us to react to certain sounds. If we respond in a positive way to a certain mew, they are likely to use it again and the resulting success ensures that their vocal repertoire for use with people, or perhaps one individual in the family, expands as we cotton on. Often they have 'words' for speaking to us that they do not use with other cats or even with other people in our family.

The different breeds not only have varying leanings towards vocal conversation (Siamese cats and other Orientals are known for their chatty natures), but they also place a different emphasis on the sounds or pronounce them differently (as with human regional accents perhaps) and we can often tell our own cat's voice from others'. They may also make additional characteristic sounds identifiable with the particular breed, such as certain chirrup or clicking sounds, just as different breeds of dog sound different when they bark. When Bean, one of our Siamese kittens, disappeared, I combed the area calling her name until, at about six o'clock in the morning, I heard a cry emanating from a neighbour's shed. There was no mistaking her voice coming from the far corner under an old table. She replied with increasing vigour and desperation every time I called, allowing me to pinpoint her exact location. Her rescue was due entirely to the fact that she is a talkative little soul.

About sixteen different vocalisations have been identified in cats, though no doubt there are many more which are either too subtle for us to differentiate from others, or are in the 'ultrasonic' range. These latter sounds are ones that are beyond our hearing abilities but are certainly not 'ultra' to the cat, which is sensitive to much higher frequencies of sound.

When kittens are very small, their mother uses only a small range of vocal sounds with them. By regularly going into the kittens' nursery, we can learn more about cat communication while it is kept simple. The queen uses certain sounds to express distress, greeting or danger and each kitten has its own distress call to gain her attention. By the time they are twelve weeks old, the kittens will have mastered the entire repertoire and, unlike human babies, who must hear and repeat sounds in order to learn our language, even a deaf kitten will use all the available vocalisations of cat conversation.

Cats can vocalise and breathe in and out at the same time.

Hence, they can produce sounds in a slightly different manner from ours. The cat's tongue plays a less important role in forming the different sounds, which are made further back in the throat by pushing air at different speeds over the vocal cords stretched across the voice box. Shifts in the phonetic quality of the noises are achieved by changing the tension in the throat and mouth muscles. Much of the vocalisation is for short-range communication, except of course with those most blatant of all cat sounds – calling and caterwauling during courtship or the warning angry cries of rival toms squaring up over territory disputes.

PURRING

The purr could be said to epitomise the cat and it is one of the reasons we enjoy our feline companions so much – they tell us very audibly when they are contented. It's a tonic to our emotions to hear our cats purr – like being regularly told that we are loved by our partners or family.

All cats purr at the same frequency – 25 cycles per second – irrespective of age, sex or breed.

They begin to purr when they are tiny kittens, and because purring does not interfere with nursing it can continue as a reassurance between mother and kitten that all is well. The mother may also purr as she enters the nest to let the kittens know that she is home and there is no danger. Older kittens will also keep their little engines going if trying to get adult cats to play – probably like a child trying to ingratiate itself while begging Dad to 'please, please play football with me'.

More dominant kittens also purr when they want to initiate play with a more submissive litter mate – a case of 'Don't run away; trust me, I'm friendly, and I'm not going to beat you up this time ... honest!' Adult cats also purr to one another in the same reassuring way, and they may also use purring for self-reassurance when in pain or to placate any potential nearby aggressor. This is because purring is associated with a feeling of well-being and the cat may be using it to back itself up when in pain or fear – like, in a crisis, you might chat to yourself or sing in order to keep your morale high and to distract yourself from the dangerous reality of the situation.

Just how a purr is actually produced in the body is still much of a mystery and theories abound. One suggests it is created by a vibrating of the false vocal cords which are positioned next to the vocal cords. Another holds that turbulence in the bloodstream sets up a vibration in the chest and windpipe and resonates in the sinus cavities of the skull to produce the noise we call a purr. A third theory suggests it is caused by out-of-phase contraction in the muscles of the larynx and diaphragm.

But, however it is produced, like the tail wagging of the dog, which has a similar meaning, purring can vary in intensity and enthusiasm. Cats can keep up their purring rhythm for hours, the sound varying in loudness from the rough purr with a distinctive 'beat' to the smooth, drowsy or almost bored purr with indistinguishable beats that suggest it will probably draw to an end relatively soon. A higher-pitched purr is also often used when the cat is eagerly seeking attention or has spotted something it thinks might give it pleasure.

SOUNDS OF WELCOME

The whole greeting behaviour of the cat – tail up, striding forward watching your face, rubbing and purring – is crowned by its call of welcome. It is a special short mew or a sequence of chirrups which lets you know just how pleased the cat is to see you. Each cat may have a special 'welcome noise' and may even vary it with members of its household, some of whom may receive no welcome at all if they are not favoured! Coming home is a great opportunity to make the time and effort to talk to your cat. It is excited to see you and wants to interact – so make the best of it. If you do not respond, it may gradually become less enthusiastic about its interactions with you too. Nothing is nicer than having an independent loving animal choose to rush up to you and want to 'talk'. Use it as one of those times to unwind. Ask the cat how its day was and your warm tones will encourage it to tell you just what it's been up to.

The chirrup that sounds like a rolled miaow is often used by a queen calling her kittens or a cat making a friendly approach to another cat or person. My two Siamese cats used to make a certain 'rrr' sound when Bullet my moggie came in through the cat-flap and they rushed to greet him. Cats also have an acknowledgement murmur – a short inhaled purring tone that drops in pitch – as well as a coaxing murmur that they use to encourage the owner to give them something they want.

Professor Paul Leyhausen, who studied cat behaviour intensively for many years, noticed the various 'gargling'-type sounds a mother cat made when she brought prey for her kittens. She seemed to make one noise that signified a mouse and another, more of a cry, when bringing in a rat. He questioned whether the cat was in effect using 'words' which corresponded to the types of prey, so that the kittens knew what she was bringing in. Although an injured mouse could be approached without risk, a rat might well be more dangerous to a small kitten, and indeed the kittens did show much more caution on the utterance of the mother's 'rat sound'.

Leyhausen suggested that a cat's ability to convey meaning and our ability to interpret it have been underestimated and that the subject merits much more study.

THE MEANING OF 'MIAOW'

The miaow, mew or meow has many variations and is uttered with an open mouth which closes on the 'ow' to make what seems to us like a distinct word. Miaows of many types are used to request us to get the food out, open doors, give attention; they are also used to beg and demand, or even to complain.

If we break the 'word' miaow into syllables – 'me-ah-oo-ow' – it is apparent that the cat can vary the length of each component or emphasise one or more to make different sounds with different meanings. If the 'ah' component is not stressed, the cat sounds 'pathetic' or disappointed. If it lengthens the 'ow' element too, the situation sounds absolutely hopeless. We often hear these plea sounds when the cat is shut out of a room it wants to be in, or when the Sunday chicken is on the table and it has not been offered any. If you look as though you might be giving in, the sound becomes 'happier' and lighter and may be interspersed with purring to encourage you not to change your mind – it's called manipulation!

When plea turns to beg (in a dignified cat manner, of course), many cats repeat the 'ow' at the end, closing the mouth slowly and drawing out the message. Adding emphasis can turn the plea into a demand, often used when owners are a little too slow in filling the feeding bowl. Often the short higher-pitched mews emphasise how desperate the cat is to put its point across. Sometimes it sounds as though the cat is merely using the middle 'ah' sound – a favourite tactic of my two Siamese when they are desperate to come into the warm after venturing outside on a frosty morning. The cat uses the highly pitched noises – the ones its mother acted on so promptly when it was a kitten – to gain our attention. In fact, the first miaow the cat uttered was probably when it wandered from the nest and had to call for help.

Cats often approach and get our attention with a tap of the paw while issuing a 'silent miaow'! It has been suggested they use this most persuasive of pleas with those who don't usually give in to their needs, or to a dominant individual in the house, when asking for attention or food. It's a good ploy and it usually works since that tapping paw and half-heard whisper are hard to resist. Of course, the sound is not 'silent' to other cats but it's too high for our less sensitive ears really to detect. Bullet uses the same ploy with me when he wants a lap to climb on to in the evening, so perhaps it is more of an intimate plea used with certain people who have a close relationship with him.

HISSING, SPITTING AND GROWLING

Hissing, spitting and growling are used by the cat to warn or threaten, noises we seldom hear in our indoor relationship with our pet.

Hissing is used as a warning and is produced by the cat opening its mouth, drawing back the upper lip so that the face is wrinkled, and arching the tongue to expel air extremely fast. If you are close enough, you can feel the stream of air rushing past. This is probably the reason why, unlike horses, cats don't like humans to hiss at them by blowing up their noses or on their faces. Producing a hiss affects the sight, hearing and, if close enough, the sense of touch, and the message behind the hiss is very effective. A hiss can be used effectively to let cats know when they are doing something you don't like. A quick 'sssss' as the cat goes to leap up on to the work surface, jump on to the cooker or scratch the furniture usually gets the message across in more than adequate 'felinese' without your having to resort to shouting or physical intervention.

Cats spit both voluntarily at an approaching opponent and almost involuntarily if they get a sudden shock. The spit is usually sudden and violent and often accompanied by both forepaws hitting the ground with a thud in the same way that rabbits thump the ground with their back feet. This is normally a bluff to surprise the opponent into stepping back and to allow the spitter to make a break for freedom.

Growling is usually a more aggressive act, which can progress to a raised-lip snarling if the perpetrator is attacking a rival. My cats growl quietly if one of them has managed to purloin a tasty bit of chicken and the other two have come to investigate and try to grab it. The low guttural growl from the pilferer usually convinces the other cats that their normally friendly companion actually means it this time and, while possession is nine-tenths of the law, the snarl is the remaining one-tenth that deters any nagging doubts in the challengers.

CALLS AND CRIES

Many of the higher-strained noises are reserved by cats for other cats. These sounds are higher than we can hear and have effects on the feline ear and brain that we can't imagine. Within this repertoire, some sounds are made with the mouth open, as with the tomcat caterwaul or the anger wail aimed at another cat on the territory.

Another dramatic cry is the screech of distress, which can also be made by females after mating and is an accentuation of the last syllable of 'miaow' – the cartoon character Tom of Tom and Jerry tends to use this one quite a lot! At the moment of ejaculation, the female releases a loud piercing cry followed by an almost explosive separation and she turns on the male. It is thought to be caused by the stimulus of the male's penis, which is covered with spines at its tip, and the sensation may be painful – it certainly sounds so.

Trying to catch the cat to place it in its basket – a sure sign, as far as the cat is concerned, that it is heading for the vet or a cattery – is often difficult and may cause a cry of protest or refusal aimed directly at the heart of the owner. It is upsetting to hear and you need to grit your teeth and adopt the attitude 'it's for your own good!' to stick to your purpose. Keep chatting and reassuring the cat that everything is fine – it will help to convince you as much as it. Things usually get even more heart-rending when it's time for the cat's annual vaccination at the veterinary surgery. There, cats usually take one of two actions: either they shrink into the submissive crouched posture and utter little mews of protest or they become cats out of hell, striking anybody within reach. If your cat opts for the former tactic, you can be helpful and reassuring and even hold it firmly and comfortably while the vet gives the injection or does the examination, talking quietly all the time and instilling confidence with your calm presence (no matter if you are only outwardly calm). If your cat is panic-stricken and resorts to aggression, then it will probably not be reassured by anything and it is best to let the veterinary nurse hold it in a safe firm grip, which may not look very comfortable for the cat but does ensure that the whole procedure is over and done with quickly and with minimum fuss. Once it's safely back in its basket, you can talk to it, and when you arrive home spoil it a little until its indignation passes.

TEETH CHATTERING

Teeth chattering is not really a communication noise. It is often produced when a cat sees something it wants but can't get to, such as a fly high on the wall or a bird on the other side of the window.

Perhaps the cat is voicing its frustration by chattering its teeth, like we might shout through gritted teeth. With its mouth slightly open, the lips are pulled back and the jaws open and close rapidly. The noise is a combination of lip smacking and teeth chattering as the cat gets more and more excited. The cat may also emit small bleating/nickering-type noises as its teeth chatter.

Our understanding of feline vocal communication could be said to be still in its infancy. The more we study the cat the more we find we don't know. Not only are we making guesses about the sounds we can hear, but we also have very little idea how much the cat uses its ability to hear in frequencies higher than we can sense in order to make its feelings clear.

7

Living with Us

THE PREVIOUS CHAPTERS have looked at what a cat is and how it lives when it is left to its own devices, how it behaves as it does and even why it looks like it does. Now we add in another element: people. Indeed, when we look at the domestic cat, it is difficult to cut out the human factor – without us providing centres where food is concentrated and available all year round (artificial situations for a wildcat), the domestic cat may never have come into being. So, in a way, it is false to look at the natural domestic cat without considering people too. It is useful to see how it behaves and interacts with its own kind, however, and to compare how these behaviours are used in its relationship with mankind.

WHAT IS IT ABOUT CATS?

Many people have tried to analyse the relationship between cats and humans. Cats are often dismissed as child substitutes. This puts the onus for the relationship on the person rather than on the cat and therefore is somewhat condescending. The attitude probably began at a time when it was not quite so acceptable to be 'soppy' about one's animals, and provided an excuse for it for the women involved – and invariably it would be women rather than men who regarded cats so affectionately. Moreover, the cat is regarded by some people as a complete parasite, living alongside us and simply taking everything it can get – food, warmth and protection – and never doing anything it is told to do or giving anything in return.

Perhaps some of us *do* treat our cats like children. Indeed, with people delaying having children until later in life and many even deciding not to have children at all, and with the growing number of people choosing to live alone and families not living as close to one another as they once did, perhaps cats are filling a family void and a need to care and nurture. In turn, we want something to respond to our nurturing instincts.

For some, the appeal of the cat lies in its physical grace and beauty, while others are attracted by the cat's independent nature. Many people want to live alongside an animal on an equal basis with mutual respect; the cat fits this scenario well. The dog has a pack mentality – for a peaceful life, its position within this family pack must be subordinate to that of the human inhabitants. The dog has to do as it is told; it cannot try to take over the house or become aggressive if people step out of line! No such problems with a cat. Respect its choices and it won't ride roughshod all over you – and, even if it does, it will be wearing velvet slippers!

Perhaps more of a clue to the nature of the relationship between humans and cats lies in the way they behave with us. It is worth reflecting for a moment on the ways their behaviour with humans is similar to their interaction with other cats and, perhaps more interestingly, on what features are unique to the cat/person relationship.

MAKING COMPARISONS

Cats that live closely alongside humans are usually confident with us – they don't raise their hackles in fear and they don't sit in postures that keep the body small and protected, as they would if they felt threatened. They walk confidently to us and often greet us with the 'tail-up' response discussed earlier. It is a signal of acceptance and perhaps even a greeting. Kittens greet their mother in this way. The posture also makes the ano-genital area available for investigation and cleaning by the mother. From this, perhaps we can conclude that our cats see us as part of their group, something to be confident with and to be welcomed.

Another familiar cat behaviour is to rub around us with their heads and bodies; in fact, cat/human rubbing happens more often and with more intensity than cat/cat rubbing. In this way, they are picking up some of our scents and also depositing their scent on us – building up a group scent to establish where they belong and who belongs in the group. In groups of feral cats this behaviour is initiated by cats of 'lower rank' to cats of 'higher rank' – kittens rub

RUBBING

Cats rub themselves around objects in the house and garden as well as people and other animals, not simply to satisfy their need for touch but also to leave subtle smell markers. Glands around the chin and lips and at the base of the tail secrete a personal odour which the cat uses to anoint its territory and its friends, creating a group and area smell.

their mothers and females rub males. Do they perhaps see us as superior members of their social group? Alternatively, have they learned to use rubbing as an attention-getting signal?

Several aspects of feline behaviour point to a maternal type of relationship. Cats retain behavioural patterns with us that are exhibited mainly during kittenhood. Kittens purr almost from birth – they purr as they suck, perhaps to let their mother know everything is fine. The queen will purr as she enters her den – possibly in order to tell her young that they are safe and to encourage them to join in. We still don't really know whether it is a communication of contentment or of safety, or a way of encouraging greater interaction. Interestingly, cats will sometimes purr when they are extremely ill or in pain. It is possible that they do so in an effort to try to reassure themselves, or to bring on a more relaxed state of mind, or perhaps as a signal of a need for reassurance. For humans, this unique feline sound is very rewarding and is taken as a sign that the cat is happy.

Another kitten behaviour humans love is the kneading action that cats undertake on our laps or when they are sitting on a soft woolly blanket. They push their feet forward with a sort of rhythmic action, similar to that of kneading bread, and usually push their claws in and out at the same time. This is truly a kitten behaviour, as it is executed to stimulate the flow of milk to the nipple while sucking. For a cat, kneading and purring on our laps is similar to a return to that warm and contented position snuggled next to their mother, protected and with a meal imminent or already in the tummy – a position of no responsibility, no fear and lots of contentment: sheer bliss! So, we are probably right to be delighted when our cats behave this way on our laps, although such kneading can be quite painful. This neoteny (a term for baby behaviours carried over into adult life) is a sign that our cats are very relaxed with us, relaxed enough to 'return' to a very vulnerable place and time in their lives when they were not able to be the independent creatures they have become as adults.

Cats also let us stroke them, a form of behaviour they have to learn to accept. They were groomed by their mother initially out of necessity, as kittens cannot evacuate the bladder or bowel without maternal stimulation when they are first born. They seem to enjoy being groomed around those areas that contain scent glands – the head and face and base of the tail. Is the spreading and mixing of scents encouraged by making the touching of these areas a pleasurable experience?

The most interesting facet of our relationship with our cats is our vocal communication with them. We live in an environment and culture that centres around verbal communication. In groups in the wild, adult cats are rarely vocal with each other. They sometimes revert to high-intensity sounds outlined in the previous chapter – yowling, calling and caterwauling or even spitting and hissing – but rarely make that most feline of sounds, the miaow, with each other.

Perhaps it is simply that cats use forms of behaviour with us that they usually display only with other cats that do not pose a threat to them. For kittens, this would be their mother at those times when they are dependent on her for nourishment and protection. For adult cats, it may be other cats with whom they are relaxed – often related cats. Our cats may feel they can also exhibit such behaviour in our presence and retain their juvenile characteristics.

It is the use of vocal communication that is the most intriguing aspect of our relationship with the cat, however, and which demonstrates a dramatic shift from the animal's usual behaviour with other cats. How, and why, has this come about? Has the clever cat found that it can get itself noticed by responding to this very noisy human? A miaow to bring attention elicits a query as to what the cat wants, or the offer of food. Responding to the human response brings even more attention and this positive reinforcement creates and cements the bond. If cats were able to form human words with those feline vocal cords, I am sure these highly adaptable creatures would be clever enough to work out a way of doing so.

When cats live with us, they can really get under our skin and they seem to make it their business to have their nose or a paw in everything that goes on. They appear from nowhere to watch over the DIY; they lie on the clean ironing or sit in the middle of a newspaper when we are reading; they scramble the wool or string we're using, or merely sit on our laps when we're trying to write a letter. Over the years, we come to be at ease with our cats – we learn their likes, dislikes and habits, and they learn ours.

We can gain even more insight into their behaviour by understanding some of the motivations behind everyday happenings and habits. For example, why is touch so important to cats; how should a cat be greeted or a new cat approached; is there a best place to position a cat-litter tray; how much sleep does a cat need, or just prefer?

MEETING, GREETING AND TALKING

The key's in the lock after a long day at the office. As the door swings open, the cat miaows and runs forward, its tail up in that typical greeting posture. As the cat hops with its front feet in mid-air and rubs against your shins, the tension slips away – you're home. Guided by its internal clock, the cat has probably been waiting for the sound of your particular car and your known step on the path when you arrive.

Chirruping and purring, it'll weave between your legs, rubbing its head and flanks against you, anointing you with its smell and the essence of home. The typical greeting behaviour between cats that know and like each other is to walk forward, tail up and slightly bent forward at the tip – ready to meet face to face, to sniff and touch noses, rub heads and lick ears and then to sniff under the tail. Some cats bow their heads slightly before rubbing heads, and they may do this with us too, adding other purrs and postures designed just for 'their people' and stretching upwards to be tickled and stroked. They may also throw themselves on to the floor and roll over.

On coming home to our cat, we chat as we would to another human. For certain, the house does not have an empty feel – this small body with the big personality makes sure of that. Often the cat will be shouting for its supper, running to and fro between you and the food cupboard until the hint is taken and, in its impatience, standing on its hind legs to scrape at the door with its front paws. As we chat away, the cat hears our warm tones but probably only recognises the odd word such as 'dinner' or its name, but is probably trying to encourage us to prepare its dinner as much as we are encouraging a reaction to our conversation.

Communicating with our own cats to help them feel confident and secure is easy, but how should a cat that's strange to us or slightly nervous be encouraged? Paws are often used as weapons if cat meetings are not friendly, so perhaps it is best to keep hands out of the way initially. Because friendly cats greet head to head, it is best to get down to the cat's level to begin with and also to approach face to face. Watch the cat but don't stare – this is a threatening behaviour between cats, often a tactic for testing strength and will-power in rivals. Half close your eyes and blink, as this will reassure the cat. Twitching of the ears is a sign of anxiety in the cat, so slow down and relax if you see signs of fear. Let the cat come forward and sniff and then introduce your hand slowly at cat-shoulder height, not like a bolt from above. The cat will probably stretch its face forward a little once it is sure that your intentions are friendly. Then rub its head and chin to interact more, and maybe even make a purring sound yourself. Confident people-loving cats soon get into the swing of a good fuss and tickle with everyone; others need more time and patience and some may never really relax with anyone but their owners.

Just why cats always seem to go for the lap of the one non-cat-lover in a room is a mystery. Some cat experts suggest that it's because people nervous of cats do not stare at them but sit still, blink and look away, hoping not to attract attention. The cat may see this as a sign of friendliness. Conversely, the cat may be deterred by a cat lover approaching too quickly or trying to entice it into a willing lap by calling and staring to attract attention. Perhaps the person who doesn't want the cat near is also inadvertently giving off certain vibrations or smells that are actually attractive to the cat.

There are certainly 'cat people' to whom cats, even those nervous of mankind in general, will be attracted and whom they will approach with confidence and friendliness, often to their owner's surprise and delight. These people often do not need to make friendly overtures or may not even own cats themselves: they merely have to sit back and let the cats find them. Whether these certain types are the nicest people we know needs a little more study, but why not watch your cat's response and see if it is a good judge of character. Certainly, I was always wary of people my normally very friendly bullmastiff dog seemed to take a dislike to, but I feel warmly disposed to those my cats select to be cuddled by and crooned over. Is a cat person also a person person?

SLEEP AND CATNAPS

Cats are the world's best sleepers, slumbering away 60 per cent of their lives, which means they spend twice as long asleep as most other mammals. A typical day encompasses over fifteen hours of sleeping and dozing, almost six hours washing and playing, while hunting, eating and exploring make up the rest of the day. Lions will sleep a great deal after gulping down a carcass because the food will keep them ticking over for several days. While herbivores have to munch away all day on vegetation in order to meet their energy requirements, a feed of meat is rich in calories and nutrients. The carnivore must exert more energy to catch its meals, but it is also able to rest and digest between them. Domestic cats, being well fed by their owners, also have spare time in which they sleep. Perhaps this investment in rest goes some way to explaining their longevity when compared with other larger mammals like the dog. Of course, if they are hungry or cold, or during courtship and mating, cats are more active. Newborn kittens sleep 90 per cent of the time but this has reduced to adult levels by the time they are four weeks old. Old cats, like old people, sleep or snooze more often. Cats, like us, also slumber more if they are warm, secure and well fed. They often fall in with the daytime pattern of their owners, choosing to sleep when they are alone during the day and being active in the morning and evening when we are around. At weekends, they return to regular periods of short catnaps when they take forty winks, and have periods of deeper sleep when they are safe in the knowledge that we are at hand for friendship and comfort if required.

Cats, being superior sleepers, have been used in several scientific studies of sleep. Their brains show similar electrical activity to humans' during sleep. During the first fifteen to twenty minutes, cats remain fairly tense around the neck and head and are instantly awakened by clicks, squeaks or sudden noises. They then relax and may roll on to their sides for six or seven minutes, and their whiskers, tail and paws may twitch, perhaps in dreaming. Cats do exhibit what we call REM (rapid eye movement), a characteristic of deep sleep in humans. They may return to shallow sleep for a short period before 'dreaming' again. This deep sleep takes up about 15 per cent of their lives, while shallow sleep accounts for about 45 per cent. Kittens do not shallow sleep in their first month of life because the centre in the brain that controls this lighter sleep does not develop fully until they are about five weeks old.

When 'catnapping', cats will settle on any spot and close their eyes while remaining fairly alert. However, before settling into deeper sleep, they need to find a place where they feel secure. After all, this is when they 'switch off' entirely and so they need to be relaxed and safe. (Mind you, we've all had cats which slip from nap to slumber on the back of the sofa and then fall off!) Because the temperature of the body drops during sleep, cats often seek a warm spot in the sun or in the airing cupboard so they feel warm as well as secure.

A napping cat will be well aware that you are around or that you are approaching because its ears will still be on 'radar patrol', scanning for any small sound. The cat that is sound asleep may get quite a shock if awakened by a loud noise or sudden prod, so if you need to waken it treat it as you would wish to be woken yourself – with a gentle whisper, a soft touch and reassurance that everything is OK – and hope that it wakes from deep sleep in a better mood than you do!

Cats are often used in advertising to symbolise warmth, security and comfort within a loving family and are pictured curled up and cosy in front of a roaring fire. One German animal expert studied more than 400 sleeping cats and concluded that he could tell the temperature of the room by the position the cats took up when sleeping. At less than 55°F, the cats curled up with their heads tightly tucked into the body but, as the temperature increased, the cats' body shape opened up. At over 70°F, the cats were uncurled with paws out in front. Cats may end up with their feet in the air or they may lie flat out on their sides if they feel both safe and very warm. Each cat may have its own particular pattern, which its owner will recognise.

Bear in mind the cat's need for security and warmth when you choose a site for its bed because it'll choose its own spot if not satisfied. Height gives security, especially if there are curious young children or puppies around. Cats climb up to where they can safely watch the world and strike out with a paw should danger come from below. They need safe niches or boltholes for a peaceful snooze, which is why many choose a high shelf in an airing cupboard or wardrobe. Don't forget that, however suitable and cosy a basket you offer, your cat will use several napping and resting places, so don't go overboard on an expensive bed. A cardboard box with an old cushion inside or a blanket in a corner of the sofa is ideal.

On waking, cats usually take a moment or two to stretch and restore their circulation to all parts of the body. With an amazing suppleness that would make even a yoga expert green with envy, they stretch their joints and muscles from top to toe, often digging their claws into the carpet for extra anchorage, arching the body and raising their bottoms high into the air to stretch the hind legs and tail. A few yawns later, a quick face-wash… and they are ready for action.

THE JOY OF TOUCH

Touch is very pleasurable for many cats and their pleasure at being groomed by another cat or being stroked by us is obvious. Rubbing enthusiastically and purring in a strong rhythm, they ooze enjoyment. Touch is thought to stimulate the release of chemicals in the brain called endorphins, which give a feeling of pleasure or well-being or can even help overcome pain. The cat is thought to have a very active endorphin system and many vets have commented that when some obviously seriously injured cats are brought in for treatment they do not behave as if in pain. Perhaps this is the reason many manage to drag themselves away after road accidents to somewhere quiet: the painkilling effect allows them to move away to safety without causing further hurt. If stroking also releases these strong psychoactive chemicals, no wonder they purr.

Touch is the primal source of affection, and it is known that a human child, monkey or pup may not thrive, and may even die, in the absence of reassuring and loving touch. The same is undoubtedly true for the kitten; indeed, the very survival of a newborn kitten is dependent on its mother's touch. Without her stimulating licks on the stomach and under the tail, a kitten is unable to open its bladder or bowel. She licks and cleans the kittens regularly, eating the waste to ensure that the bedding area does not become wet, cold and a breeding ground for infection, all of which conditions could reduce the survival chances of the kittens.

Grooming and touch are vital reassurances to the newborn kitten as it cannot see the world or hear very well. Enveloped in its mother's nest, it is dependent on touch and smell to survive. A cat deprived of touch may be withdrawn and fearful and may even groom itself more in an attempt to compensate for this lack of touch from others. Kittens respond to this safety and comfort by purring – a behaviour they maintain in adulthood in their relationship with us, along with other kitten-like behaviours, in the safety and security of our homes.

As mentioned in the previous chapter, another juvenile behaviour which is often continued is kneading. Cats usually purr very enthusiastically as they are stroked on our laps, almost in rhythm with the paddling with their feet as they draw their claws in and out. This behaviour stems back to the kitten's suckling period when kneading on their mother's stomach around the nipples stimulated milk flow. Even though many years old, cats may revert to this behaviour with us, and we should be flattered that they obviously feel sufficiently secure and content to relax and become defenceless kittens on our laps.

GROOMING

Kittens learn to groom themselves, using their barbed tongues like combs, at about three weeks, often before they can walk. It is an instinctive behaviour at which they are proficient by six weeks of age. They need to care for their coats in order to remove loose hair, stimulate new hair growth and prevent matting, and to spread secretions from glands on the skin so that the coat is kept waterproof and their bodies insulated. However, the act of grooming is itself also a way of keeping cool since saliva evaporates off the coat and removes excess heat. Hence, cats groom more in warm weather or after strenuous activity and may lose as much fluid through grooming as they do through urinating.

Most cats have their own routine for grooming. Some spend up to one-third of their waking time pursuing a head-to-toe clean-up; others hardly bother. Most groom symmetrically and systematically, using their forepaws to clean the face and behind the ears, covering each foreleg with saliva before wiping the 'dirty' area several times in a circular motion from back to front. One scientist believes that cats secrete a special 'cleaning fluid', a detergent that cleans the fur. They certainly smell clean and don't seem to give off that dank smell associated with the less fastidious dog.

Contorting that extra-supple body, cats can reach almost all parts by twisting and leaning. But by far the best way to get to those inaccessible places around the ears, the back of the neck and under the chin is to get a friend to help. Friendly cats living together use mutual grooming as an integral part of their social bonding and will approach each other frequently for a wash-over, before returning the favour later on. It is a way of creating a group smell that also includes humans and other animals, such as dogs in the family, which are also rubbed and washed. After we have patted and stroked our cats, they groom and 'taste' our personal scent and incorporate it into the communal scent picture discussed earlier.

Most shorthaired cats are exceptionally proficient self-groomers and need little help from us to keep their coats in top condition.

GROOMING

Up to a third of waking time may be spent grooming. Scratching may help to dislodge parasites behind the ears and under the chin, where even the ultra-supple cat cannot reach with its tongue.

Most cats are very meticulous. They twist and contort their bodies to lick clean almost every part, but must use their forepaws to. wash behind the ears and head.

Covering each foreleg with saliva they wipe the face and behind the ears with a circular motion from back to front, repeating the action many times until they are happy with the result.

However, this is not to say we cannot join in and use grooming and touch, like all cats do, as part of the social bonding. Grooming using a brush or glove should be started as early as possible after weaning or getting a new kitten, thereby continuing the mother's role.

Ensuring that your attempts at grooming are accepted and enjoyed is especially vital in the case of some longhaired cats. Modern Persians are unlikely to survive in the wild because they are unable to keep their coats unmatted and an effective barrier against wet and cold. Also, many longhaired cats are bred with very flattened noses (e.g. the Peke-faced Persian) and probably find it difficult to breathe and groom at the same time, let alone hunt successfully. Many have been bred to have a more docile temperament and so are more tolerant of grooming. If you start young, the cat will be much more likely to accept your role, though whether it ever gets to relish regular brushing is another matter! The worst thing to do is to delay tackling tangles, because it can then become a battle requiring the cat to be pinned down in a vice-like grip and attacked with brush, comb and scissors. The even more drastic scenario of a visit to the vet's for a general anaesthetic and a complete short-back-and-sides (down to the skin) may be necessary if longhairs have not become accustomed to the essential grooming early on. The rule is: start young, and most cats will enjoy it. If you do have a longhaired cat, groom it at least once a day whether it looks as if it needs it or not.

Cats are, of course, very individual in their likes and dislikes and some enjoy being brushed. Most enjoy being stroked and tickled around the head and some really revel in it. Almost all cats dislike their hair being brushed the wrong way, the reason being that it is likely to cause discomfort as their hair grows from the follicles at an angle specifically designed to allow the hair to lie flat on the skin and provide effective protection and warmth. Nerve cells in the skin tell the cat if the hairs are not lying flat – hence, it doesn't enjoy being continually brushed the 'wrong way'. Of course, some cats enjoy being ruffled and tickled all over, and they may roll on to their back to expose their stomach, that vulnerable area which is usually otherwise well protected. Most accept a little tickling before grabbing your hand with their claws and teeth. They appear to be totally relaxed and enjoying themselves one minute, then snap out of the 'trance' and attack the hand quite ferociously. Americans have termed this the 'petting-and-biting syndrome' and it is in fact a basic defensive reflex: the cat first relaxes but then seems suddenly to find itself just a little too vulnerable and it snaps into a defensive display of aggression – often surprising itself as much as you.

But grooming is not just about hygiene and social bonding. It also has another function: to relieve tension. You may notice your cat having a quick groom after a fight or when it is upset. Cats also groom if faced with a dilemma, such as wanting to get out but being unable to open the cat-flap. The conflict in their minds is dealt with by what has been termed 'displacement activity' and is perhaps similar to when we scratch our heads or twiddle with our hair in moments of crisis. Excessive grooming can even occur if the cat is feeling under some form of constant stress – perhaps because it does not get on with another cat in the household, or if it is frustrated and bored. The cat then grooms and grooms to relax itself but can end up with a patchy broken coat or areas of baldness.

FEEDING

Left to fend for themselves, most cats will survive by employing a mixture of three methods: hunting, scavenging and accepting free hand-outs from local kind-hearted people. Depending on how closely the cat has previously lived with people, it may simply take what it can while keeping a safe distance or work its way into the hearts and hearth of a new family and there make the most of all they have to offer.

We can use food to bond with our cats, in this way fitting into the maternal role of food provider. Most pet cats never need to lift a paw to catch their supper; they need only gently nudge their owners when they get peckish. So why do cats still hunt, even when there is food freely available at home?

We have seen that the sensations of hunger and the urge to hunt are controlled by two different parts of the cat's brain and, although a full stomach may remove the urgency of going out to find a meal and make a warm snooze a preferable option, it does not override the desire to hunt. If a full stomach did stop the hunting instinct, we would probably see much less of the play behaviour we so love in our cats. Chasing after string or ping-pong balls or leaping at hanging teasers are all actions motivated by movement and the hunting instinct. Loss of our source of amusement and enjoyment from our playing cats would be sad indeed for most of us, although some owners of very proficient hunters may gladly sacrifice it to forgo the morning presentations of birds, mice, voles, frogs and a host of other victims their pet brings in.

Even old cats will revert to kittenish behaviour when faced with a ball of wool. The play sequences we find so entertaining in our kittens are merely practice for the real job of hunting, learning balance, speed and agility, even though the kittens never need to hunt to feed themselves.

Cats sometimes don't even eat what they catch, which seems to us even more of a waste, but this is characteristic of other carnivores too. Shrews and moles are usually rejected – they obviously do not taste good to cats. Some cats leave the gall bladder and some the small intestine of more palatable prey such as mice or birds, while others may eat the lot, fur, feathers and all. Just why cats bring in their prey is not known for sure. They may want to eat it in the safety of their den where they can relax and enjoy it free from the threat of theft from nearby rivals, or they may want to bring it in for us or other cats as a mother would for her kittens. Others seem to bring things in as 'gifts' for owners – much to their owner's non-delight, especially if the mice are not too badly injured and are able to scurry away to take up residence in the house. In one village called Felmersham, a study of what 70 cats brought home over the period of one year amounted to over 1,000 prey items. Some cats regularly brought in large numbers of prey, others hardly any at all.

So what do our cats like to eat, how often do they want it, and how can we use food to build greater bonds with them? Choice of cat food is often based on human values and we are bombarded with advertising about meaty preparations and new flavours. These are usually geared to what we humans see as appetising. Of course, cans of mouse, sparrow or rat wouldn't be at all acceptable from our point of view, even though they may make the perfect meal for cats.

So can cats actually tell the difference between all the available varieties of food? Cats have a very strong sense of taste and smell, are sensitive to constituents of protein and can 'smell' fats. They are also very sensitive to the taste of water but not to the taste of 'sweet'. Therefore, they probably know if they like a food just by smelling, and have no need actually to taste it. They decide if food is palatable using touch, smell and taste. It's common for them to like 'game' flavours. Many cats are wild about rabbit and pheasant.

Given a choice of two equally palatable foods, a cat is likely to choose the new flavour, which would suggest that cats like a variety of tastes and frequent change. However, if the cat is feeling stressed, it will probably choose the more familiar taste, understandably clinging to the security and reassurance of a known quantity. Of course, each cat has its own preferences and, whether it is for canned, dry or fresh foods, it is best to accustom your cat to a variety of flavours and textures from an early age to ensure that it not only gets a balanced diet, but is also prevented from becoming addicted to any one particular flavour or type of food. The newer all-in-one dry diets which were initially introduced from the USA are made of a balanced combination of proteins and fats, minerals and vitamins from different, but consistent, sources, so variety is not so essential.

Appetite can be affected by how the food is prepared and by the cat's emotional state. Strange noises, new people or even a change of feeding bowl may cause loss of appetite. With their acute sense of taste and smell, cats can very easily find stale food off-putting too. They like food best at 35°C– the body temperature at which their prey would normally be eaten – so don't feed cats with food directly from the fridge as its taste and smell diminish at low temperatures. Placing the food bowl too near the litter tray can also put cats off eating from one or using the other. We would probably react in the same way if our dinner was served up next to the lavatory. A position of safety, a little away from the madding crowd, is usually preferred as the cat can then take a relaxed bite out of the way of thieving dogs or curious children.

It is interesting to note that cats, with their origins in the desert, probably never ate fish as a result of their own hunting (there is only one specialist fish-catching cat species, which lives in India) and, apart from those occasions when they've snatched the odd goldfish from a tank or pond, cats have only ever had fish given to them by humans. The linking of cats and fish seems to have come about after the Second World War, when the fact that fish was a ready and relatively cheap source of protein was used by pet-food manufacturers in their advertising. It was clearly a very successful campaign because the association has remained ever since. That is not to say that cats do not like fish, as many owners can testify.

Although, of course, cats do have their individual likes and dislikes when it comes to food, there is one thing that all cats have in common: they must have meat and cannot be fed on a vegetarian diet. While we and our dogs, being omnivorous, can decide, if we wish, to leave meat out of our diet without doing ourselves any harm (yes, dogs can live happily as vegetarians), a cat cannot survive on a diet without certain constituents, such as taurine, which are only available in meat. Diets advertised as vegetarian may have had taurine and other nutrients vital to the cat added to them. If the diet does not have these additives, it is inadequate and unsuitable for cats anyway. Cats do nibble grass and house plants, although probably as purgatives, vomiting them soon afterwards. Some cats even enjoy vegetables, but vegetables alone are not sufficient to fulfil all the cat's nutritional requirements.

Should cats be fed one large meal a day or several small ones, or should they have food available the whole time? Most dogs gulp down their food because in a pack of wild dogs or wolves there are many mouths to feed and a great deal of competition. In order to keep some semblance of order and avoid injury through fighting over every meal, they have a pack order, which defines when each is allowed to charge in and feed. First, the top dog eats until it has had enough and is then followed by the others, in rank order, until each has had its fill. The bottom dog often has to hang around and hope there will be some left. Cats, being solitary hunters, are generally less voracious and, if food is freely available, will nibble frequently rather than devour at one go. Results of feeding studies show that cats given free choice will eat up to twenty times during a 24-hour period. This appears to mimic natural feeding patterns. Mice, being the domestic cat's most common prey, provide about 30 kilocalories of energy each. An active cat weighing 3.5kg expends approximately 300 kilocalories of energy a day – about ten mice or ten meals a day. However, our cats do not have to catch mice to survive and the needs of most healthy, mature house cats that are not pregnant or lactating can be met, if the cat food is of good quality, by feeding them one meal a day, though they still hunt despite this.

But feeding is about more than just getting enough calories and nutrients: feeding is a very important bond-builder between cat and owner. So, whichever type of food you select, mealtimes can be used as a period of interaction and communication. When the cat asks for food we can respond, and receive a very warm response in return.

When we call at mealtimes, the cat will come running. Many will come running before we call because they have picked up cues from our behaviour that feeding time is approaching. Finding the tin-opener, washing its bowl or the click of a certain cupboard door are all clues and the cat usually appears eagerly, out of the blue. A conversation of miaows and replies goes on throughout the bowl-filling procedure and the cat will rub and mark its owner and even the food bowl to give encouragement and prevent distractions that might delay the process. After a quick sniff to check out the menu, the cat then tucks in to the food, its soliciting, appealing behaviour now forgotten and the owner no longer required!

While a cat can be fed enough in one or two meals or provided with dry food to eat ad lib, behaviourists advise that, especially in the first year you own the cat, you feed it little and often. Interacting over each small meal enables you to bond very closely with your cat and continue the original relationship that it had with its mother. At feeding times, both you and your cat make an effort to interact and so you can easily take over and reinforce that maternal role in the cat's life and maintain your friendship. This is the essence of the owner's successful relationship with the cat and it is one of the main reasons why they can relax and enjoy our companionship. Once these bonds have been established, cats can be fed ad lib or larger, less frequent meals.

There are considerable variations in the size of cats, even within breeds, so it is not easy to determine an optimum weight. If you think your cat is overweight, one indication to look for is an 'apron' of skin and fat which hangs just beneath its belly – it may swing as it walks along! Often cats, especially the Orientals, may not put on weight all over, but instead carry the 'extra' slung below. Your vet will be able to advise you if a diet is necessary and how to go about weight reduction in a safe and practical way. Obesity seems to be on the increase in cats as well as people, perhaps because they too are getting less exercise.

A CLEAN JOB!

The cat is inherently clean in its habits. Not only does it spend up to a third of its waking time grooming, but also its toilet habits are usually immaculate as well as modest, and this is another reason that cats are such successful pets. The cat will usually choose a spot that is protected on as many sides as possible, such as a quiet corner of the garden or under a hedge, where it can safely adopt that most vulnerable of squatting positions. It will dig the soil, having chosen a patch where it is fairly soft (new seed-beds are a favourite), defecate or urinate in the hole and, after sniffing the area, fill in the hole with soil. Conveniently for us, it's all done outside and not usually in our own garden, and it's not even something we need to think about. However, a cat-litter industry worth millions per year indicates that many people do have to consider what happens at 'the other end' and they put a lot of effort into carrying bags of litter home for the cat to have somewhere to relieve itself.

Cats may use a litter tray indoors for only a short while, such as when they are too young and unvaccinated, and would be vulnerable to infection outdoors; or when they are too ill, or have just become too old and frail to go out on patrol. Many cats are now kept permanently indoors in cities because of the outdoor dangers of traffic. Others, such as the Siamese and many such single-coated breeds, don't like putting their noses outside in any type of cold weather, let alone trying to dig in frozen ground. They prefer to use a litter tray indoors most of the time. Others, like most moggies, goes out come hell or high water and wouldn't dream of using an indoor tray.

When we take kittens on at between six and twelve weeks of age (or when they are over twelve weeks old in the case of pedigrees), they usually have no problems using a litter tray and we pride ourselves on our success in litter-training them. In fact, all the work has already been done for us by their mother and, provided the kitten knows where the tray is and can get into it, everything usually goes smoothly for the new kitten owner. Tiny kittens learn from birth never to soil their bed. To begin with, they are unable to urinate or defecate without stimulation of the abdomen and genital area by their mother's tongue. This reflex action of the kittens can remain operational until they are about five weeks old, though most can urinate and defecate voluntarily by three weeks. As the kittens start to wander and explore outside the nest, their mother continues to look after their toilet needs. She carries them away from the nest, training them for life that the nest must not be soiled. Good mothers teach their kittens well, and each generation teaches the next.

As the kittens play, they paw at the ground, explore the litter and learn about things around them. They instinctively rake and scratch in soft loose material. They also learn a great deal from watching and imitating their mother, and soon associate the smell of the litter tray with toilet activities. By the time they are weaned at about six weeks old, the kittens have formed the habit of using the litter themselves. This association usually transfers well to using soil outdoors at a later date when the kitten's vaccinations are completed.

It may seem that we have little part to play. Placing the kitten on the litter after it has fed or just woken up, when it is most likely to need to relieve itself, is usually enough to ensure that its enquiring little mind associates the two functions. But we should have a thought for just where we place the litter tray and what we put in it. Cats usually try to find a sheltered quiet spot to 'go to the toilet', so an open tray in a passageway or by the dog's bed may not be well received and, indeed, be boycotted by a more nervous cat. Placed in a corner, a tray covered with a box (with a cat-sized hole cut in one end, of course) or a ready-made covered tray may make the cat feel more secure and content to use it. A cover will also prevent the mess created by an 'over-enthusiastic digger' intent on moving most of the litter out and over the side of the tray.

Cats like to be able to dig, and so newspaper in the tray, as is sometimes used to house-train puppies, is not advisable. Also, the type of litter offered is more important to some cats than to others. Being originally semi-desert creatures, cats will enthusiastically use sand or fine grain material if it is available – as most builders will know on their return to cement-making after a weekend to find added bonuses in their sand pile! Many parents too find the kids' sandpit is frequently used by local cats. You can use this preference to your own advantage if you have recently dug the garden, as the sand will be highly attractive to the entire cat population of the street. A pile of sand in the corner of the garden will probably be even more irresistible than newly dug soil and you may save the seed-beds from the ravages of local cats. I say probably because, typically, there is always one cat that breaks the rules. In his book *Travels with Tchaikovsky, a Tale of a Cat*, about his worldwide travels with his cat Tchaikovsky, Ray Hudson recounts how Tchaikovsky had to be given a litter tray in the middle of the desert because he wouldn't use the sand. So much for the influence of Egyptian ancestors!

Litter for kittens must be disease-free and this cannot be guaranteed with sand unless a sterilised variety is used, sometimes available from aquatic shops. The most commonly used litters are made from Fuller's earth, a granulated dry clay substance which forms clumps when wet. Other litters include the pelleted wood-chip types, which are much lighter to carry, and some finer-grain clay granules. Cats which live permanently indoors may have much softer pads than their outdoor relatives who have hardened up their pads on concrete walkways and through long nights spent on the tiles. Indoor cats may find the larger pelleted types of litter a bit uncomfortable to stand on and prefer the fine-grain varieties.

The type of litter determines how often you need to attend to it. Some require frequent replacement; others 'clump' allowing solids and even liquid waste to be lifted out with a scoop, which leaves the remaining litter available for further use. Removal of waste needs to be done regularly, before the 'clump' is raked around by the cat at the next use. Most litter needs picking over at least once a day in order to prevent excessive soiling (which puts the cat off using the tray), while allowing it to retain the smell of a latrine and so keeping up the cat's toilet association with it. This is particularly important when bonding a new kitten to the litter.

Cats are usually very fastidious and 'accidents' are rare. Giving this mundane but necessary practicality, some thought from the cat's point of view can help the cat feel more relaxed and prevent problems occurring. If they do occur, it is usually because of illness or some upset and tackling the problem is covered in more detail in chapter twelve.

This chapter has looked at the relationship between cats and humans, but in real life the cat living with us is seldom alone. Most of us live in urban or suburban settings with an average of one and a half cats in every cat-owning household. Therefore, if cats live with us, they must also live closely with other cats, something that can be a complicating factor, as we shall see later.

8

Intelligence and training

ARE CATS INTELLIGENT? Are they more intelligent than dogs because of their ability to live independently if necessary, or should they be judged to be less intelligent because they don't respond to what we ask them to do? In order to answer these questions, we must first decide what intelligence is. Is it the sum total of intellectual skill or knowledge, or is it the ability to learn new things, to associate ideas, or to distinguish one thing from another? Perhaps it is more the ability to adapt to changing circumstances and put them to best advantage. It's certainly a fairly complicated matter where humans are concerned, but what of the intellect of animals?

The ability and willingness of dogs to respond to our training instructions is often used as an example of how clever they are. Those which respond quickly or which we have directed to serve our needs, such as guide dogs for blind people or sniffer dogs hunting out drugs or criminals, are classed as intelligent. But dogs we regard as 'thick' may not be slow to learn, they simply may not be motivated to do as we ask. Hounds, such as beagles or bassets, may be extremely bright when it comes to following a trail left hours earlier by a solitary fox running over hill and dale, but to train one to come back when called is almost impossible – yet it is one of the simplest things to teach most dogs.

What, then, of the cat? Historically our relationship has not been a direct and co-operative working one as it has been with the dog. While cats can be useful for vermin control, we have never trained them to hunt; we have merely put them in place and let the animal's natural behaviour work for us. So it would be difficult to categorise cats in the same way as we have done with dogs. Of course, many people have known 'supercats' which can open doors, bring in slippers, obey commands and generally act in what seems to be direct communication with their owners as well as 'thinking for themselves'. Perhaps intelligence would be better defined, in this context, as an ability to communicate, not just within the same species but with another species altogether – such as man – and the cat can certainly do that. And if brain size has anything to do with brainpower, then the cat is on a par with primates and dolphins because, relative to its body size, the cat has a brain larger than all mammals except these two.

MEASURING 'INTELLIGENCE'

How do we measure a cat's intelligence, other than by amassing and analysing anecdotal information of what certain cats have and haven't done? We have to try to devise tests that will reveal just how the cat's mind works. Using these tests, we can to some extent compare different animals but, again, many problems arise. A certain test of dexterity may suit a monkey well – it may have the required thought pathway and action already in its repertoire – but it might be less appropriate for a cat or dog that has never had to attempt such a task before. As a result, the cat or dog appears slower and less understanding of what is required of it. In fact, the animal's thought processes may have had to take large leaps to manage so well or at all and it is actually showing greater aptitude than the monkey. So a badly designed test may actually illustrate the opposite of what is happening. The whole exercise is fraught with 'ifs' and 'buts'. It's like trying to compare the skills of a carpenter with those of a computer programmer. Each has special skills which are not directly comparable or even measurable, but which in no way make one 'better' than the other.

Cats have been found to be able to learn a sequence or chain of responses to enable them to escape from a confined space. They subsequently used what they 'learned' to get out of other similar situations – we would say that this ability shows 'intelligence'.

In another experiment, a dog or cat had to remember and choose a box on which a light came on in order to get a reward. Researchers found that dogs were only capable of remembering which box lit up for up to about five minutes after the light had gone out. Cats, on the other hand, went to the correct box up to sixteen hours later – an ability to remember which ranked better than even monkeys and orang-utans in that test. If cats can form concepts, as they seemed to do with the box and the light, they may have the key elements of real intellectual ability. Their ability to link the light with the reward or to find their way out of a maze or set of obstacles is an example of what scientists call trial-and-error learning. The cat learns to perform certain types or sequences of behaviour that provide the reward of a solution to a problem, such as being shut in, or a benefit to it, such as a tidbit reward. Because the behaviour is rewarded, and the reward is given quickly enough for the cat to link it with the behaviour and not with something which has happened between the two actions, the cat learns to associate the two and is more likely to repeat that action or performance in the future.

Pavlov's salivating dogs are the result of a behavioural experiment with which we are all familiar, and an example of what is called classical conditioning, the association of one happening with the likely occurrence of another. Pavlov rang a bell just prior to blowing food powder into the dogs' mouths and, after a few such experiences, the dogs salivated merely at the sound of the bell, in anticipation of the food. Our cats do exactly the same thing when, in a flash, they appear from nowhere at the sound of the cupboard that holds their food being opened, or the clatter of their dish on the floor. We too associate certain sounds, voices or music with past events – even those that happened twenty or thirty years ago. Amazingly enough, it is our sense of smell, though poor in comparison with that of most other animals, that most strongly evokes associations with other times or places. No doubt, cats with their superior sense of smell and good memories can recognise and associate smells and happenings and thus give a wide berth to those things that resulted in an unpleasant experience.

This conditioned response is vital to the survival of animals as they learn what is dangerous or likely to harm them and what is a sign of a potentially pleasant experience. Once a response has been linked to a certain sound, smell or sight, it stays that way unless it is not reinforced or it becomes associated with something else. Thus, if we move the cat's food to a different cupboard where the door makes a different click as it opens, it will soon stop rushing in every time we open the original cupboard merely to take the coffee out, and instead will begin to associate the position and sound of the new one with its feeding ritual.

As animals grow up, they become familiarised with regular non-threatening features of their world and do not react as strongly as they did when they were learning what is, or might be, dangerous to their survival. Thus, as it grows and learns, the cat's responses to sights and sounds are not quite so dramatic, and each excursion into the garden is no longer crammed with 'new' and exciting objects that needed instant investigation when it was a playful kitten.

If intelligence is measured by adaptability, then the cat should go to the top of the class. As a species, cats can learn to survive in almost every type of environment – desert, jungle or arctic, and with or without man's help. Looking at their lifestyle, we can see that they have the ability to adapt quickly – when they want to, or have to in order to survive. They are not only adaptive but also highly versatile and seem to learn quickly from their experiences. We know that as kittens they learn much by observation. It has also been observed that kittens can become adept at pushing a lever to get food if they see their mothers successfully complete the same task. Cats also learn by association very quickly. The carrying basket is associated with an invariably unpleasant trip to the vet for an injection, if only once a year, and the cat will vanish as soon as the basket is brought out of the loft! The appearance of the anti-flea spray can only mean an imminent assault by that 'spitting foul-smelling horror', another thing the cat will avoid at all costs. My cat gives me the 'run-around-and-vanish' treatment because she observes that I am looking for her in a manner that is different from the one I use when I'm trying to find her before bedtime to put her into the kitchen. How she knows I am armed with a worming tablet I'm not quite sure, but she no doubt senses the 'intent' in my interest in her and is taking appropriate avoiding action.

RELEASING THE POTENTIAL

We know that kittens handled between two and seven weeks of age are much more person-orientated and that they generally develop into more responsive, outgoing and interactive cats if they are given lots of new experiences to react to. Like young children, they take in so much, unafraid and uninhibited by thoughts of their own limitations. It is known that kittens can be weaned and begin to learn to hunt very early if milk becomes unavailable, so even at an early age they can adapt to the situation and learn a new survival strategy. A kitten kept in a non-stimulating environment during this 'sensitive period' may never learn to be inquisitive or how to tackle problems. It simply avoids unfamiliar things and circumstances. So catch 'em young for best results! The same principle is employed in training guide dogs for the blind. They are taken on as puppies by special puppy walkers who introduce them to all types of situations so they encounter as many sights, sounds and contacts with all sorts of people and animals as possible. They live with these puppy walkers in a normal lively family from the age of six weeks, immediately after weaning. In this way, they learn quickly and are able to cope with most situations that arise when they become working dogs and can concentrate on their highly specialised tasks without being frightened into running away – dragging their blind owner behind them.

TRAINING TECHNIQUES

Training is shaping the activity of an animal so that it behaves in the way that is required by the trainer. It can take many forms and be carried out for many different purposes. Sometimes it means teaching 'tricks', such as the simple body postures assumed at the command 'sit', 'stay' or 'beg', or the more complex performances of a circus animal. At other times, such as in litter training, it means teaching an animal an association, whereby the animal learns to perform part of its normal repertoire in a certain place or at a certain time.

Training a cat to walk on a lead is another example. Once accomplished, it allows people who live in urban environments to take their cat out and let it explore without risk of it running under a car or being attacked by local 'wildlife'. Lead training does not only gently familiarise the cat with the sensation of wearing a harness and become used to being attached to its owner with a lead, but it also means introducing the cat to the types of environment where it might later be taken for a stroll. Of course, starting when the cat is a young kitten makes the process a lot easier and the cat will come to see it as normal to go out and walk with its owner.

Some cats, especially if they are fearful, may never take to the harness or to the sensation of being on a lead, whereas confident relaxed cats are less likely to panic and get themselves into tangles and situations that only instil fear of the harness or lead. Try to make the whole exercise calm and enjoyable. Stage one involves accustoming the cat to the harness (a very soft adjustable one is best and much safer than a collar). Stop and take the harness off if the cat gets agitated and put it on again for short periods, perhaps when you feed it so that the harness has good associations. Let the cat wear it around the house and get well used to it before attaching the lead. Never drag the cat around on the lead but allow it to become familiar with the sensation of being attached to you (a lead about two metres long is best for training; any longer and things can get well out of control!). Reward it for taking a few steps with you – you can use food as a bribe to follow. Slowly get it used to walking with you around the house; then, when the partnership is proficient, proceed to the garden.

A cat which has become relaxed about wearing a harness in a quiet room may panic at being taken outside and having to face many new experiences, such as cars, children on skateboards or bicycles, unpredictable dogs or simply loud noises for the first time. Its training should include getting it gently and slowly accustomed to as many as possible of the things it might encounter while out walking. A cat's natural instinct is to flee from danger so you must provide security and safety if you are going to intervene in its ability to escape if it feels the need.

We can all teach a dog to sit or lie down – although, the way many are taught, this is more a credit to the dog than the teacher. But what about cats? Can they be made to 'do as they are told'? Cats are not renowned for their obedience in response to commands and for this reason are popularly supposed to be stupid, defiant or artful. However, they are, in fact, very fast learners under circumstances where their natural response tendencies are exploited. Because with dogs we can get away with breaking all the golden rules of training and they still stay with us and, to an extent, obey our commands, we probably try to employ the same tactics with cats... and fail dismally. But cats most assuredly are not dogs and they view life differently.

The first basic principles of training are the same with all animals, from tigers to elephants, dolphins to horses, but successful training first involves understanding the animal's natural behaviour, for example, how it is likely to react if frightened or what it seems to 'enjoy' and what motivates it to do certain things.

The second principle is that of reward and kindness – punishment and fear actually slow the learning process. You know yourself that if you're nervous you can't think straight, let alone carry out a new task under pressure. The trainers of dolphins, for example, must always be encouraging and ensure their animals want to join in the 'game' of training. If they want the dolphins to leap in the air and over a rope, they don't just put a rope up 10 feet above the water and expect the dolphins to know what to do. They begin by laying the rope on the water and rewarding the dolphins for simply swimming over it. They then raise it slightly and repeat the procedure. This is where one of the most important features of training arises: if the dolphins go under the rope, i.e. they have not understood what is required of them, the rope is immediately lowered and the process is begun again. There is never any punishment – in fact, the animal is never allowed to get it wrong. If the procedure doesn't work, it is because the trainer has gone too far, too fast. So, reward is the only outcome for the dolphin – training is a positive activity.

The same principles can be applied when a cat learns to use a cat-flap. First, you leave the flap wide open and coax the cat through with vocal encouragement and tidbits so it can get used to the concept of being able to gain entry at that point. Then you gradually lower the flap using a prop to keep it up so that the cat has only to push a little and squeeze through the opening. Closing the flap a little more allows the cat to get used to pushing it and eventually it learns to push it open from the shut position. Some modern cat-flaps fit very snugly when shut and need quite a shove to break the draught-proof rubber seal. In this case, the cat will need a bit more encouragement.

If a resident cat already has the ability to use the flap, newcomers often learn much more quickly by watching it in action than from all your coaxing and bribing endeavours. Remembering what has been said about learning by associating actions with results, we realise that a cat loath to use the flap may not be being slow to learn.

It may have got the knack in a very short time, poked its head out and immediately been attacked by a local rival or neighbourhood dog, a result which taught it very quickly never to put itself in that vulnerable position again and made it decide to train you to open the door for it instead! This way it ensures that you are its protection and any rival or other threat in the garden will run away and it can safely go out. So don't blame the cat for its apparent stupidity – its survival may depend on its balanced calculations of risk, not to mention its ability to use you as protector if it feels the need.

There is a method of training called clicker training which has become well known in dog training and which also works for cats. The idea is to indicate to the dog or cat the exact action that has earned the reward. This is done with a clicker – a small plastic box which contains a flexible steel plate which makes a double-click sound when pressed. It is a very distinctive sound and the sound can be made very quickly so that the behaviour you are pinpointing can be marked very accurately. It is much better than a voice and, once the cat has made the association between the click and the reward, even the reward itself becomes less important as the animal understands that the click marks the correct behaviour and the reward will follow. As discussed below, the reward itself must suit the cat and be wanted by the cat – something expensive like chicken or prawns usually suffices!

Having established the marker signal and the reward, you can start to train. Think through what you want to do very clearly and break down the task into small stages. Choose your reward food and break it down into tiny pieces so you can use several bits in one training session. Use the clicker and reward when the cat does the right thing. Never use punishment when training. Even a mild reprimand can be off-putting – reward good behaviour and ignore the behaviour you do not want.

REWARDS

The timing of the reward is vital for success in the learning process. The giving of the reward must be done immediately and consistently after each successfully completed task. Delays of more than a couple of seconds may mean that the animal associates what went immediately before (not necessarily the task in hand) with the reward. Consistent, immediate rewards mean that the animal learns quickly and is keen to do what is required next time.

The other important thing about rewarding is that it must itself be perceived as rewarding – that is, something that the animal wants and enjoys. So, using fish for dolphins or tidbits for dogs is obviously appropriate and brings results. While verbal praise and patting will also work well with dogs, this reward is less welcome to a dolphin. But what about cats? While they may appreciate food if they're hungry, they are not really turned on by tidbits the way most dogs are. At this point, we should consider which are the important motivating factors in our relationship with cats that can be seen as rewarding enough to be used in training. Warmth and attention spring to mind but, again, the cat does not always want attention. It is difficult to 'bribe' a cat! What we have to do is try to catch the cat at times when it is ready to interact and encourage it as much as possible by playing on its particular 'weaknesses' for stroking, for particular tidbits or even access to a secure warm spot – this needs a little more thought than we use when we reward the dog merely by giving it a treat.

Cats can be trained to perform many of the tricks we teach dogs, such as giving a paw or sitting, but they require time and patience – two attributes most of us are short of! It is always easier to start the training when the animal is young, when it is open to suggestion and interested in new happenings. You can teach an old dog new tricks, but it takes a bit longer. An older cat probably perceives the value of what we offer as a 'reward' (affection or a food treat) to be a lot less than that of sitting by the fire, taking a nap or going for a saunter. Deciding on and doing just what it wants is often more rewarding. Some cats may be naturals at learning and interacting, while others may be too lazy or unresponsive to become involved.

Ann Head, who trained Arthur, the white cat that ate using its paw to scoop the food out of the Kattomeat tin, chose him because of his sweet temperament and desire to interact with her. She tried to see everything she got him to do from his point of view. 'The gift of patience is essential; it is all done with kindness,' she explained, adding, 'You can't force a cat to work!' It's all about good relationships and enjoying the work.

PUNISHMENT?

Dogs are easy to train. Consider the basic principles of training and you'll realise that we 'get away with murder' with our canine pets in our use of threat and punishment. Dogs learn despite our techniques, or lack of them. What could be less conducive to learning than a hall full of distractions such as other dogs, and a strange person standing in the middle giving orders, as happens in so many of our dog 'training classes'. The dog may do as it's told there, but not associate the learning with its everyday environment and continue with its old behaviour as before. So the 'training' of our dogs has not equipped us even to attempt to coax our cats to 'obey' – a cat would just up and leave rather than take such treatment.

Indeed, punishment is not even the opposite of reward. While rewarding increases the strength of an animal's response, punishment does not produce a decrease and the consequences of punishment may be unpredictable, especially in cats. The cat may not even associate the punishment with the misdeed – perhaps you have shaken it for bringing in a mouse or stealing the chicken off the table – but it may see your attack as coming out of the blue and entirely without reason. The more you do it, the more likely the cat is to try to avoid you in all situations, just in case you turn into that angry lunatic again.

'ACTS OF GOD'

There are times, however, when we want to prevent our cats from doing something, such as jumping on to the china shelf or the dinner table or, as my cat has just done, trying to open a newly painted window (which now has a fluffy finish!). In the case of one-off actions – such as with the window, which is normally 'on limits' – a sharp noise or hiss will stop the cat in its tracks and enable you to put it off jumping up. The 'sss' noise is most effective because cats use it themselves as a dramatic hiss, part of their repertoire to surprise or put off an opponent. Cats soon learn to abandon whatever action they have in mind if you use the 'sss' selectively and time it carefully so as to catch them just as they are intent on the act. The use of physical punishment or a lot of shouting and screaming will only make the cat fearful of you.

If you want to put a stop to a more long-term problem such as jumping on the cooker hob, a preventive measure in case it is hot on one occasion, then the 'act of God' approach can be used. The principle behind this is the association of an unpleasant (but not painful or dangerous) 'result' with the jump on to the hob. The knack is not to let the cat see it is you who is masterminding the 'happening', so it will associate it only with jumping on the hob. Thus, if each time it jumps up a fine spray of water falls from the heavens, or a sharp noise makes it jump, it associates the unwelcome 'result' with the hob. A pile of empty cans carefully balanced so that they collapse when the cat jumps up on the kitchen work surface will have the same effect. With any luck, the cat will then avoid the area in order to avoid the unpleasant event. The 'punishment' is actually an aversion and not associated at all with the loving owner, who is there to reassure and give back-up after such a nasty shock from that awful hob!

The learning process involved is the same as in the wild, where the cat must learn by experience to avoid danger in order to survive. Once a cat discovers that if it passes a certain gate the resident terrier will rush out, whereupon it has to go into overdrive to get away, it will never again saunter past concentrating on other matters. The one experience is usually enough to make it avoid the area altogether or at the very least to check carefully to see whether the little dog with the large teeth is out in the garden. Kittens have many such encounters every day and those that have to grow up in the wild must learn both to avoid and to cope with everyday dangers to survive.

WHO TRAINS WHOM?

We are probably not aware of how much our cats have actually 'trained' us. They are not prompted by notions of dominance or punishment, but are patient enough to keep on until we learn what they want. For example, a cat that wakes its owner at six o'clock every morning by scratching on the bedroom door wants attention. Although the owner may curse and shout, he or she will eventually get up and let the cat in. The cat's 'reward' is a warm bed and attention – even if the owner is a little bad-tempered. The cat has 'trained' the owner and rewards him or her with a warm friendly purring body and a little miaow. The same applies to asking for food, rattling the window to go out or scratching to get back in – it's the cat who trains us!

Although our cats can make their feelings extremely clear by using body language, we humans communicate mainly through the spoken word and often fail to read the body language of our own species. However, most pet owners would also like to be Dr Dolittles and talk to their animals. We can encourage or train our cat to 'talk' to us by using food and attention as rewards. By speaking in that special voice when you talk to your cat (let's face it, we all use a different tone or speak in a higher voice when we talk to our pets), you let it know you want to interact. To encourage it to reply, make friendly sounds as you prepare its meal, but only let the cat have its dish of food when it has 'spoken'. Make sure that your reaction is immediate and that the food is prepared and the bowl is in your hand ready to put in front of the cat as soon as it has spoken. The cat will learn to associate 'asking' with the reward of food or, if you stroke it only when it speaks, the reward of attention. This interaction is actually a two-way learning/training process because the cat soon becomes a double agent – taking what we have taught and using it for its own ends so that each time it wants something it only has to ask. Cats are not daft, that's for sure.

FETCH!

An interesting survey in *Cat World* magazine reported on cats who retrieved items their owners threw, not just occasionally, but many times, enjoying the game in the same way as dogs do. We train dogs, especially gundogs and those with a natural tendency to retrieve, to pick up things and bring them back to us – so we can throw them again. Cats do bring in prey, so the carrying back is a natural part of their repertoire, but their becoming involved in a throw-and-retrieve game is quite unusual. In many of the cases reported, it does not seem to have been the owner who taught the cat to play, but the cat who encouraged his human to keep throwing the item. One lady wrote, 'From an early age, he decided he wanted to retrieve. He found a piece of screwed-up paper, about the size of a cigarette bent in the middle, and brought it to me. I could tell from his excitement that he wanted to play, so I threw it for him. He brought it back and that was the start of a lovely game. His piece of paper lives in the fruit bowl and when he feels like a game he will go and bring it to me. It is his party piece and he will return it to whoever throws it.'

The cats in the survey often seemed to be obsessed with the game, retrieving for hours at a time, but quite why they do it, how they learned and what they get from it remains unexplained. From the sample of letters, it appeared that some kittens learned to retrieve by watching older 'role-model' cats in the house, although in some cases only one cat retrieved while others ignored the goings-on with the contempt only aloof cats can display. The owners thoroughly enjoyed this co-operative interactive game with their cats, although often it went on a little too long for their liking. One tired owner explained, 'From the moment I come home and settle down on the settee for the evening, he is dropping toys in my lap and anxiously awaits my tossing them across the room, whereupon he leaps after them with remarkable enthusiasm, as though his life depended on the capture and retrieval of the toy. Admittedly, this exercise can be quite tedious after about an hour, but I find it hard to deny him this ever so important game.'

Other owners had trained their cats in the same way as the dog (in one case it was because she was a frustrated dog-owner who treated her Siamese cat more like a dog) and in some cases the cat had grown up with dogs. One cat had been reared by a frustrated collie, which was recovering from a false pregnancy and from whom the kitten had also learned to growl!

Items retrieved included balls, pieces of crumpled-up paper or foil, toys, dressing-gown cords, string and laces. The sound of his favourite toy, a foam-covered hair curler, being scratched would drive one cat called Bono into a frenzy. His owners would sit at opposite ends of the room and throw it to one another while the cat, having taken up a strategic position between them, would leap into the air to catch it. Bono's attraction to curlers ended when he discovered slow-worms, which he then proceeded to carry around the house! One cat moved on quickly from pieces of paper and material to retrieving pieces of a board game while the game was in progress – a very successful, attention-gaining ploy, which is perhaps one of the reasons why cats take to such games and enjoy them so much. By learning how to initiate and then maintain contact, they can act out many of their play and hunt behaviours within the safety of their owner's presence and with his or her complete attention. These cats will initiate and finish the game and have their owners under complete control. Who said the cat is aloof, unintelligent or doesn't do as it's told? But then it's usually the cat who does the telling.

9

What cats want

WE HAVE LOOKED at the natural cat, its behaviours and how it interacts with us, but do we really know what our cats want? It is a simple enough question but, because they cannot tell us directly, we have to guess at the answer by analysing our cats' behaviour, both as a species and individually within our homes. As we have seen, cats have strongly individual characters and their personalities can range from quiet and nervous to bold and demanding due to a variety of factors, including genetics, experience and environment.

What exactly do we mean by 'want'? We can look at this question on several levels. First, 'want' can be as fundamental as the basic needs of everyday life, such as food and sleep. It can also be considered under a rather more 'frilly' definition, in the same sense as when we ask our children what they want to eat. The answer is not likely to be 'a plate of broccoli' – more likely 'several bars of chocolate' – the want takes priority over the need and is not necessarily what is best for the children themselves. Cats too will need food but may want smoked salmon if they feel they have a choice; they may need shelter but may want the best seat in the house next to the fire. And, while there is science available for the 'needs', we do have to make some assumptions for the 'wants'. There are some things, however, that we can feel quite confident about putting in the cat's 'want' shopping basket.

Welfarists looking at what animals need on a very basic level have come up with what are called the 'five freedoms'. These were initially put together when looking at farm animals that rely completely upon man for their care and have no independence of lifestyle or choice. They are, however, pertinent to how we keep our pets too. The five freedoms are:

i) freedom from hunger and thirst by provision of ready access to fresh water and a diet to maintain good health;

ii) freedom from discomfort by provision of a suitable environment that includes shelter and a resting area;

iii) freedom from pain, injury and disease by prevention or diagnosis with treatment;

iv) freedom from pain, injury and disease by provision of space and stimulation; and

v) freedom from fear and distress by provision of care and conditions that avoid mental suffering.

These five factors can be interpreted at the 'need' end of the scale, but also at the 'want' end of the scale. They provide an excellent framework by which to consider what cats do want, and then to let us add some frilly bits too!

FOOD AND DRINK

Our cats don't want to go hungry or thirsty, but some of them can be very particular about what they do eat!

As discussed earlier, cats have special requirements nutritionally in that they must have meat in their diet in order to obtain certain nutrients. Dogs are omnivores and can use vegetable matter to make certain nutrients that they require. Cats, however, need a high-protein diet (kittens need a diet containing 18 per cent protein and adult cats 12 per cent) compared to dogs, which need about 4 per cent protein as adults. They require lots of sulphur containing amino acids, especially taurine, arachidonic acid – a precursor for prostaglandins – and vitamin A, which they cannot synthesise from carotene. They also have high requirements for thiamine and niacin. Cats have lost the ability to synthesise certain of these key nutrients and can only get them from meat – perhaps their success as predators has meant that these chemical pathways became redundant as their hunting ensured a plentiful supply of meat and they were not forced to resort to vegetable matter. Structurally the cat's gut is typical of a carnivore and is short, reflecting the high digestibility of the cat's food.

For most pet cats that have access to the outdoors, their home diet can be supplemented with caught prey or food stolen from somebody else's house. There is an argument that cats have maintained the ability to hunt successfully because their association with humans may not have provided the quality of food they required. While cats were not highly valued as pets but lived alongside man with a quasi-pest-killing role, they may have been given some scraps but it is unlikely that they would have been given a diet that was nutritionally adequate for their high-quality needs. Thus, they maintained the ability to hunt rather than give up and live alongside us and rely on what was put in the food bowl. Indeed, cats kept completely indoors, or with limited access to a pen outside, are totally reliant on owner-supplied nutrients. Cats today can do this because the food we can now provide is nutritionally complete. However, many cats still exercise their hunting abilities and these hold them in good stead should they become lost or have to survive on their own for some reason.

If cats need meat, then their senses too will be adapted to meat intake – their senses of smell and taste will be sensitive to the nutrients that are in meat rather than those for other foods. Has the cat discarded the ability to discern other tastes because they are of little importance to its survival? Can cats tell the difference between mouse and vole, pigeon or sparrow? As in other mammals, taste buds on certain areas of a cat's tongue are sensitive to particular chemicals and the combination of signals from all of the areas on the tongue will help the cat to recognise a taste. It is thought that cats are sensitive to tastes that we would categorise as sour, bitter and salty. They do not seem to be sensitive to sweet tastes. Some owners report that their cats like sweet foods such as ice cream, but it may be other factors, such as the fat content or the texture, which are also attractive rather than the sweetness. We get a pleasurable sensation that we associate with 'sweetness' – cats may get the same sensation from a combination of amino acids available in certain meats which they find attractive.

Given the choice, cats will usually choose a food that has a high meat and fat content, a strong smell, a mixture of soft and crispy textures and a temperature of about 35°C. They enjoy variety in their diet and will often try a new food or flavour in preference to one they are more used to.

Cats perceive flavours based not just on the taste of the food, but also on its texture and temperature, factors that in turn also affect its smell. We already know that the cat's sense of smell is far superior to that of humans and the smell of food is particularly important to a cat in order to get it to start eating. The perception of taste and smell will affect whether a cat finds a particular food palatable. The texture of food also affects how much the cat will want to eat it. Cats do not have chewing teeth the way we do – they make the food smaller by tearing at it or shearing it with front teeth until it is small enough to be swallowed. Cats will usually eat tinned food or semi-moist food faster than dried food and will usually eat small meals now and again. This portion approach may mimic the pattern of catching small rodents throughout the day if they had to hunt for themselves. Typically, if food is available that does not go stale (e.g. dry food), cats will eat between seven and twenty small meals during the day and night. The temperature they prefer is that of freshly killed prey – if it gets too high they will be put off and if it is fridge-cold this may also have an off-putting effect, both because of the cold and the fact that it is likely to be less odorous at this lower temperature. These are basic but quite important aspects of feeding cats and, although many cats are not 'fussy', it may be useful to be able to tempt cats if they are not eating properly because of illness or injury.

Within our own homes, we probably have two or three cats, all of which have different preferences for the type or presentation of food that we give them. Some may be very fussy; others take anything available and break all the feline laws by stealing sweetcorn or some other vegetable the experts say they won't be interested in. Apparently, what a cat likes or dislikes is determined by a culmination of the types of food it has experienced throughout its life. Cats may not take to a diet which is low in certain minerals or vitamins such as thiamine, perhaps because on eating something of this flavour previously they did not feel well.

These are the cat's basic nutritional needs but, as all owners know, it can be a little more complicated than even this. Indeed, sometimes what the cat wants, again, rather like the food choices a child makes, may not be the best thing for it. Some cats become fixated on a certain food and are not willing to try anything else – it is fish or nothing, a certain type of dry food or a certain flavour of tinned food. While sticking to one type or flavour of a balanced diet is fine, just eating fish or liver is not, and could result in the cat becoming ill. Liver, for example, is rich in vitamin A and cats fed diets containing raw liver can develop hypervitaminosis A and may experience stiffness, lack of energy and skeletal problems – there is enough vitamin A for one day in just 5g of liver! These cats tend to be very stubborn and will stop eating rather than go on to something else. If you want to change a cat's diet, mix in the new food with the old and keep trying with small portions so that the food is always fresh and the smell is more appealing. Cats can very easily be put off stale food or food that does not smell.

The personality of a cat can also affect what foods it will accept. Nervous cats may not be happy with change; more confident cats will probably prefer something new.

Meat has a high water content and a cat eating a meat or tinned-meat diet may not seem to drink much water – this is because most of its requirement for water will come from the food. The cat has descended from a desert animal that can concentrate its urine very efficiently, and so will not need to drink a huge amount. Cats on a dry diet will need to drink more. Many cats also have their own little foibles about drinking water – some love it straight from the tap as it drips; others won't touch it unless it has sat for some time; some prefer water from the flower vase or from puddles outside. Indeed, most will drink it from anywhere except the water bowl!

Many cats cannot tolerate milk, although they do seem to enjoy it (probably because it contains plenty of protein, fat and carbohydrate). Often cats cannot tolerate the mild sugar lactose.

Cats are usually very good at maintaining their body weight at optimum level – the preference for numerous small meals allows them to balance their intake of calories carefully. A fat hunter will soon become a thin one again if it cannot catch its meals. Recently, cats have become much more prone to obesity, a problem we owners need to take seriously.

COMFORT AND SHELTER

A cat's environment needs to include shelter and a resting place. In earlier chapters, it became clear how important this part of its territory is.

An Englishman's home is said to be his castle; a cat's home is definitely valued as highly in feline terms. Indeed, a cat may prefer to stay with the territory rather than its inhabitants. When cats are kittens they are attached to their mother, but as they grow this attachment is often severed by the mother and the kittens are detached from her to fend for themselves. This attachment to their mother may be replaced by an attachment to their territory, something that can become very apparent when owners move to a new house just a few streets away or even a couple of miles from their original home. Despite all the care and love the owners can provide, some cats are compelled to return to the old hunting grounds, despite the fact that the new owners of the house do not feed it and may even actively discourage the cat from coming around.

Why this attachment to territory? What is so important to the cat? When we look at cats living without humans, we find that they have territories that they defend – whether they let other cats into their space depends on the food availability and, for female cats, the provision of a safe spot for the rearing of kittens. They need to feel secure in the area and be sure that their 'space' will be able to support them and their kittens. If there is a bountiful supply of food around, then other cats may be allowed in the area. Provision of a secure kittening spot is very important, and well worth defending

SPRAYING AND SCRATCHING

When spraying, cats take up a very characteristic position with their tail held high and quivering. They tread up and down with their back feet and squirt a small volume of urine on to a vertical surface behind. Scratching may not just be a claw-sharpening exercise – glands between the pads ensure that the cat's scent is also smeared over the scratched area.

too. Within the cat's territory may be areas that it will share with other cats and areas that are restricted to just that cat. The cat will organise its time and activities within these areas as it hunts, rests, etc. It may even time-share some areas with other cats, leaving scent signals in the form of sprayed urine or scratch marks to ensure they do not meet.

Just because cats live in our homes and we feel they are safe, it doesn't mean that their instincts for safety and a refuge are removed. Thus, in our homes cats are still looking for a secure territory with plentiful food but also a safe area. They may see our gardens as the area where they will meet other cats. They will spray and mark outside to ensure that other cats keep their distance at certain times of the day. Similarly, just because we neuter our animals does not mean that we remove the need for a secure spot for kittening. It is interesting to note that female cats seem much more determined to guard their spot in our homes – it seems more difficult to add a new cat to a home that already has a female cat in residence. Neutered males seem much more open to accepting a new resident, perhaps because they do not feel the basic need for a safe kittening area.

Whether the inside of our houses equate to that safe nest box we cannot be sure, but it can help us to understand the upset which the addition of a new cat, either deliberately or accidentally, to a cat's home can cause it.

The sanctity of that indoor area is illustrated by the common scenario of a resident cat suddenly beginning to spray around the home. A little detective work reveals that the tom from around the corner is coming in through the cat-flap when everyone is at work and eating the resident cat's food. It might even have a wander around, hiss at the resident or spray inside too! No wonder the cat that lives there is disturbed – indoors is no longer its sanctuary. Intruders have penetrated the castle and are threatening it inside, either visually or by leaving scents. It cannot relax any more. In many cases, such problems can be easily sorted out by closing the cat-flap or giving the resident a magnetic or electronic key on its collar so that once more only it can get inside. It can then relax again.

We can all understand the need to feel secure – if yobs could walk in off the street, eat our food and sit in our armchair while giving us some rather offensive language, we would not be able to relax. Even after they leave, we would be continually checking to ensure they were not hanging around outside ready to come in. Often the continual worry is almost worse than the reality, which may not be physically damaging but shatters any feeling of security or relaxation.

Once we realise how strongly this can affect cats, we can work to ensure that they feel safe in our homes; and, if we want to introduce another cat, we can try and follow some cat rules and begin to understand that the threat may not just be physical but also may be left with signals, which we, as creatures with a poor sense of smell, will miss altogether. To a cat, the smell left by another cat could be the equivalent of us finding a very threatening and abusive note inside our homes.

While the scent of another cat entering the inner sanctum of the cat's territory may be the ultimate threat, we have to understand the importance of familiarity of smell to the cat within its own home. As a scent-orientated animal, the cat is as familiar with the smell of its home as we are with the visual representation of ours. If someone was to come in and move all of our furniture around or change our colour scheme, we might be very upset. Likewise, bringing in a new piece of furniture or carpet will not only change how the house looks to the cat, but also will change the smell profile with which it has become familiar, comfortable and secure.

This is not to say that we cannot change our homes; it just means that we should be aware of the effect such change can have. Most confident cats will adjust easily and soon come to terms with the new smell; other more nervous individuals may take rather longer and be rather more traumatised. We must also realise that the totally indoor cat may be more affected by changes because it is not used to any upset in its home – no other cats come in and it does not have a garden life, during the course of which it would live a little dangerously and would be able to get used to the scent of other felines. Its life will be very secure and probably very unchanging – any small alterations can be seen as a massive change to its lifestyle.

Changes to the cat's environment come not only in the form of other cats or new furniture – new people, including very small people who cry a lot and smell of milk and other not-so-pleasant things, can provide change that can be seen as a threat to a cat's security. Again, most cats will take all of this in their stride, will get used to the smell of a new baby – or a new boyfriend for that matter – and will adapt accordingly. As time goes by, the baby will smell of the household and the household of the baby – they will all acquire a group smell that is familiar and reassuring. With a new person can also come a change in routine and the adaptable cats will usually cope very well and take advantage of more people being around or having waking times around the time everyone is in.

Finding secure places with a busy home can be quite difficult for a cat. If there are young children, dogs or other cats that may upset it, a cat will go upwards to find a safe place to rest. While most domestic cats will not go to such lengths as the leopard, which takes its meal up a tree to keep it safe from hyenas and lions, all cats will go skyward to find a safe spot to snooze. The more nervous the cat, the more likely it is to enjoy its vertical space. Tops of cupboards are often a favourite and high spots can make the difference between a cat being always wary and being able to relax sometimes – this can make the difference between a cat that sprays indoors and one that manages to maintain its composure in the face of threats or interruptions from below.

We want more than secure cats in our homes – we want cats that are confident enough to drop any defensive behaviour, to accept handling and to be relaxed enough to behave like kittens with us. Feeling threatened may make a cat behave very differently in two very similar situations. For example, I have a cat that visits our household to eat. Our cats do not like it and will chase it away if they see it. This particular cat is very determined and rather stubborn and is not chased away easily. If the human inhabitants of the house meet this cat outside its own house, about 100m down the lane, it will be friendly and interactive, even throwing itself on the ground and presenting its tummy for a rub. Try and approach the same cat in our house and it will begin to hiss and growl when humans get within a distance of about two metres. It is not safe to touch it at all. This is an example of what is termed the cat's 'aggressive field', or 'field of aggression'. When cats are relaxed and not feeling threatened or stressed, this aggressive field is smaller than the cat – we can touch and stroke it without a problem. When the cat is feeling under pressure – as in this case, when it visits our house, which is the core territory of other cats – it is very guarded and the field widens to about two metres all around it. Any intrusion into this area risks attack and will certainly elicit growling and threatening behaviour. The size of the field can change in an instant and could explain why cats can suddenly become aggressive.

Some of the items in this chapter outline what cats need, as well as what they want. Comfort could perhaps be termed a 'want'. Cats are excellent at finding the warmest spot or the softest chair. We must remember that our cats' ancestors were African wildcats and as desert animals would have lived in a very hot climate. Cats can tolerate heat better than we can – humans cannot tolerate anything over 111°F (44°C), but cats do not mind a skin temperature of up to 126°F (52°C). Some cats will sit so close to the fire that their fur becomes singed; they may walk over a hob which has not cooled completely without seeming to be very worried by the heat. Perhaps this is a throwback to an adaptation to the hot climate and the hot sands of North Africa. Interestingly, the skin on a cat's nose and upper lip is very sensitive to touch and temperature. When kittens are born, they use their noses as heat detectors, following the temperature gradient to find their mother and the warmest spot snuggled up next to her – food is also available here, of course.

We can use heat and comfort to encourage shy or nervous cats to share space with us. Even the most reluctant feline may creep into a room and find a spot near the fire on a cold winter day. If it realises that the spot on our lap is soft as well as warm, it may just pluck up the courage to sit on us, or at least next to us.

AVOIDING PAIN OR INJURY

Of course, our cats don't want pain, injury or disease. Body language among cats, while not complex enough to allow them to co-operate as a group as in the canine world, does give them a repertoire to avoid conflicts if necessary. Avoiding conflict prevents danger to life and limb through injury. Cats, like most of us, want a quiet life – they may fight if they have to, but would rather avoid conflict if possible. Most owners would not want to see their cat injured, but may sometimes inadvertently put cats into a position of conflict by keeping individuals together that just do not get along, or by keeping un-neutered cats in areas of high cat density, which almost inevitably means fighting and injury.

And, while cats would not volunteer to go to the vet, they certainly want to feel better if they become ill or injured. In this, what owners want for cats and what cats want for themselves differs very little.

SPACE AND STIMULATION

Most cats have free access to our homes and gardens and further afield if they want, so provision of space is not really a problem. However, it can become a consideration when cats are kept indoors permanently. They need space to exercise and to be able to get away from other cats, people or other pets if they want to. Stimulation may be an issue here too. Cats have a sophisticated sensory and motor nervous system – the means by which they see, feel, hear, taste and smell the world and the way in which they use these senses in a highly sophisticated manner to hunt and to communicate to reproduce and stay safe. It would be strange if they could just switch off all of this and live without much stimulation without some degree of frustration. Owners with indoor cats often apply the approach 'what you don't know you won't miss'. However, the situation may not be quite as simple as this. Perhaps if you have never tasted chocolate, you would be spared those urges to eat a giant bar of Fruit and Nut. However, a top predator may have instincts which drive it and which it needs to enact even though it has never been outside to hunt. Owners of indoor cats must be aware of this – every cat is different and must be monitored to ascertain its particular needs in this area. Some of these may be overcome by providing an area of fenced-in garden where the cats can enjoy the smells, sounds and sights of outdoors in safety.

Cats also need space to escape and this can be provided vertically rather than horizontally. Cats that share a home, whether they can go out or not, may need to be able to get away from each other if they do not get on exceptionally well. Provision of high places can be quite a simple way to ensure a less confident cat feels secure, and may avoid problems such as spraying.

ABILITY TO CARRY OUT NATURAL BEHAVIOURS

The last of the five freedoms incorporates care and conditions that avoid mental suffering and this must include allowing the cat to carry out its natural behaviours. What behaviours would be listed as 'natural' for a cat? These must surely include grooming, normal toileting behaviours, claw sharpening, hunting, sleeping and being sociable if they wish.

i) Grooming

Cats and grooming go together. Many beautiful pictures of cats depict them carrying out their methodical grooming routines. They may spend up to a third of their waking time grooming and are fastidiously clean animals – they hate it if their fur is coated with anything and will groom it off immediately. Indeed, being fastidious about their coats can actually be dangerous for cats, for it may cause them to ingest substances they would not normally eat. They are usually very careful about what they consume and most cats will not touch something that will be harmful to them. If a cat brushes past a fence that has just had creosote applied and then grooms it off, it could be affected by the chemicals, which are poisonous to cats. Likewise, licking tar or other chemicals off feet can have the same effect.

Why cats should be so fastidious while their canine cousins do not groom is probably to do with the sensitivity of the feline machine. Certain hairs on the cat's coat, including its whiskers, are very sensitive to movement and touch – these enable the cat to be highly aware of its environment as it moves through undergrowth or in the dark. If some of the hairs are stuck together or pulling as the cat walks it may be getting false information or missing information from its environment. Grooming will also remove odours so that the cat will not be so easy to smell as it creeps up on its prey. A carefully groomed coat will enable the cat to move easily, will keep it dry, waterproofed and free moving.

A cat that cannot keep itself clean will not be a happy cat – it will probably feel very uncomfortable. We need to consider this when we have the unhappy situation of an old or very ill cat that cannot get to its litter tray and may be lying in urine or faeces. If the cat is not likely to improve, we need to consider its quality of life very carefully. The cat may want to clean itself up but be unable to and this will probably cause it considerable stress.

Grooming also seems to have a secondary use of calming the cat. Cats often groom after they have been startled or have been confused momentarily. We see it sometimes in cats that tend to get overexcited when we stroke them – they grab our hands, bite or scratch them and then jump down on to the floor, at which time they often start to groom rather industriously. This seems to calm them down, relieving tension and allowing them to collect themselves again. However, grooming can be taken too far sometimes – some cats will start to over-groom and actually break off the hair and even lick the skin until it is sore. This behaviour can be brought on by some sort of stress in the cat's environment that it cannot change or get away from. It begins to groom in an attempt to feel better and may indeed get something from the activity but, if this grooming goes beyond normal grooming, it can actually injure the cat. It seems to be a way of trying to deal with problems when there is no other way out (see chapters twelve and thirteen for more on this).

ii) Normal toileting habits

Cats are also fastidious about their toileting habits. Mother cats have to lick the ano-genital area of their new kittens to make them defecate and this is then eaten so that it does not soil the nest and cause conditions that are likely to provide the right environment for infections, etc. to take hold. As kittens grow, they will leave the nest in order to urinate and defecate and will watch their mother and copy what she does. Thus, from day one they are being taught not to soil the den. They will learn to dig a hole, deposit urine or faeces and cover it up again. The reason for this is probably to keep the smells covered under the ground so as not to attract predators or give information to other cats in the area. When we transfer this digging and covering behaviour to our homes by providing litter trays, we must remember that cats will not want to use a dirty litter tray. Some cats may only use a tray once before they want a clean one. Others will use it a couple of times but will look elsewhere if it is very dirty. If we try to disguise the smell with deodorants or scents, this may put the cat off even more.

iii) Claw sharpening

As mentioned earlier, stropping or sharpening claws has two functions. The first is to pull the blunt layer of the old nail off to reveal a new pointed claw – a vital weapon for the hunting cat. The action of scratching also leaves a scent mark – whether the two can actually be separated or whether the cat means to do both at once, we do not know. But it is a behaviour cats need to express and they need somewhere to do it. Their choice of scratch post will depend not only on the texture of the post but also on its position. Wood is a favourite because the cat can get its claws into the surface to the right depth and pull downwards, but carpets are also appreciated! We think that cats may scratch in front of other cats as a way of asserting themselves and they may choose places that are strategically useful as marking spots. This is usually outside but can also take place within the house. Favourites are arms of chairs or settees, stairs and carpets in general. It is probably a very satisfying feeling to get it just right! They will also use scratch posts provided by us – sometimes they need a little encouragement to use them, for example by adding some of the marker scents, which will then degrade and tempt the cat back to top them up. This is easily done by gently taking the cat's paws and pulling them down in a mock scratch down the post. Doing this over a period of a couple of days should scent-mark the post and give the cat the idea of what it is for. Whether or not you provide a specific scratch post, cats will often scratch in the house. It can be very annoying but as it is one of the cat's natural behaviours we have to accept it and direct it if we can.

iv) Hunting

Cats are designed and made to hunt. (Chapter five outlines how they go about it.) Mother cats start to teach their kittens what hunting is all about very early on, bringing home injured prey when the kittens are about four weeks old so they can practise this skill. Good hunters usually have mothers that are hunting experts. Cats will hunt whether they are hungry or not – the areas of the brain that control hunger and hunting are different and are stimulated by different things. Whether cats stay in or go out, they will need to exhibit their hunting behaviours – some cats more than others. Owners must be aware of this and if the cat is not doing it for itself outside then they must play and provide mock hunts for the cat. Cats are only usually successful in about 10 per cent of hunts – they need to eat about ten rodents a day, which means a lot of hunting. Owners of indoor cats take note – physical and mental stimulation will be part of the job of looking after an indoor cat.

v) Sleeping

Cats are one of nature's best sleepers – they rest for about half of the day in a mixture of catnaps and deeper sleeps. If there is one thing cats have an instinct to find, it's a warm spot; indeed, it is pretty difficult to keep a cat off a hot spot. Cats love snuggling under duvets, curling up on the washing, lazing in those hammocks that hang off radiators or just following the sun around the house as it warms different windowsills.

We humans follow a 24-hour rhythm in which we sleep and wake at fairly regular times. Cats follow a more fragmented pattern. Instead of one large period of sleep and wakefulness during the rest of the time, they drift in and out of sleeping and waking cycles throughout the day and night. The periods of wakefulness may depend on different things – hunting patterns, patterns of its owner or other elements in its environment. A confident cat doesn't usually worry too much about where it sleeps – somewhere in the sun or near a source of heat is preferable. The more nervous cat may need to seek out somewhere it feels safe before it will make the transition from a nap to a deeper sleep. Newborn kittens spend 60 to 70 per cent of their time asleep. This starts to decrease when they are about three weeks old to levels of about 40 to 50 per cent of the day as adults. Of course, if the cat is surviving completely on its own in the wild, then it may have to spend a great deal of its time hunting down enough prey to survive on. Older cats may sleep at least 50 to 75 per cent of the time; like old people, they need to sleep more.

vi) Being sociable – or not

When writing about cats in general and when trying to pinpoint what they want, the wide range of individual characters of cats always ensures that it is difficult to make sweeping statements! This is very much the case when it comes to what cats want in terms of feline companionship. Just consider the cats you have owned and the differences between their preferences – some very obviously do not want another cat of any sort around and want to be the only cat in the household; others seem to need another feline for company. The important thing is to try to read our cats' preferences. The difficulty is that this only usually becomes apparent when we bring in another cat!

BEYOND THE FREEDOMS – ATTENTION AND INTERACTION

Our cats enjoy attention. The degree to which they interact with us depends very much on their personality and all the factors that affect this, from genetics to early environment. Most cats are highly adaptable and can live very happily alongside us with little attention or in a close relationship if that is what both sides want. When cats want attention they will seek it out and solicit it by rubbing themselves along us, making miaowing sounds or little chirpy noises, running towards us with their tail held up straight or by simply plonking themselves on our laps and purring loudly! How the interaction proceeds usually depends on both sides – how we react and how rewarding this is for the cat (and vice versa). Some cats have a large need for attention and interaction and are very owner-orientated – examples of this would be some Burmese and Siamese cats. Others only need attention occasionally and when they choose.

A cat's natural diurnal rhythm is quite flexible. It is quite happy to be awake mostly in the day, but equally it can become almost nocturnal. We think of the cat as a crepuscular hunter – using the half-light of dawn and dusk to hunt the small creatures that are active at this time. Cats are often at their most active at this time – as the descendants of desert animals which may have hunted when it was a bit cooler rather than in the heat of the midday sun, this would also be understandable. This can also mean that some cats, especially young and enthusiastic hunters, are up and ready for action rather early in the morning during the spring and summer. If they have access outdoors, they are usually up and gone before we surface and this offers no problems. However, cats that are kept in at night or those which target their people with their activity can try and chivvy sleepy owners into getting up and feeding them or letting them go outside at the first hint of the dawn chorus in the summer!

GIVE THEM WHAT THEY WANT?

This chapter has looked at a broad range of feline 'wants', from basic needs such as food to inherent behaviours such as claw sharpening. Some of these 'wants', then, go further than basic requirements and could be said to be the 'icing on the cake'. Like the children choosing chocolate over broccoli, some cats have the option to have more than is simply needed for survival, or even more than is best for them. When it comes to food, we have seen that our cats are pretty good regulators of what they eat in terms of calories (although this has been changing in the past ten years or so). However, as facilitators of these 'extras', we are in a position to give our cats what they want, or to refuse them. Is there any good reason not to give them what they want?

We often compare dogs and cats because they are the primary pets mankind has chosen to live with and they live alongside us in our homes rather than in cages or outside in pens. We fit in with their way of life and they fit in with ours. With dogs, we need to walk them and control their outdoor activities so they do not become social nuisances. With cats, it is more flexible and there are few behaviours that cause problems to other people.

Our experience with dogs has taught us that it is not always wise to let our canine companions choose what they want or to dictate the interactions we have with them. Some dogs, given the chance, will begin to take the upper hand with the human family if they are allowed to or are given the wrong signals. They can become aggressive if we then try to take back control. This happens because the dog is a pack animal – its behavioural repertoire allows it to fit into a group that works together for hunting and social interaction, such as breeding. Within this group, there is a hierarchy and a dog's behaviour will depend on how it fits into this hierarchy or organisation of individuals. This structure is necessary to ensure that the members of the group are not constantly at each other's throats (literally!) and trying to rearrange who is in charge or who does what within the group. Our human family replaces other canines as the 'pack' and how the people act gives the dog clues as to where it fits within this pack and thus what it is allowed to do or to challenge. A 'nice' family trying to treat a dog as an equal may have real problems if they happen to have a dog that takes advantage of their lack of command or inability to give direction in doggy terms. Such dogs, which may have been top-of-the-pack characters in the wild or opportunistic dogs that make the best of the situation to increase their status, then become rather uncompromising when the family asks them to do something they do not wish to do or when they do something the family does not wish them to do. This may be as simple as asking the dog to get off the settee or getting it to move because it is lying in the way – the dog may react with aggression because it feels that its owners do not have the 'right' to ask, due to the fact that they have inadvertently given it a higher status than them in the home.

This lack of understanding, or breakdown in communication, between people and dogs is typical of why some behaviour problems, such as aggression, can occur. Thus, what dogs want is not always good for the dog or the humans caring for it.

However, with cats we do not have this problem. They are not obligate social animals – they seem to have the ability to be sociable if they want to and if environmental factors are right. This sociability extends to people but again there are not built-in rules – because we have no overlap in social rules, it is hard to get the wrong message. Thus, there are very few behavioural problems caused by communication problems between people and cats – most occur because of environmental factors. And, because of this, there are no reasons for not doing as our cats want! They will not decide to take the upper hand or take over the household. Thankfully, cat owners can 'spoil' their cats as much as they like without a problem. Of course, providing too much food or giving in to feline demands for just one type of food can have consequences for the cat's health, and for this reason we must exert some control.

However, cats, being very clever animals, can sometimes manipulate a situation to be more rewarding for them. Being independent and not group-orientated creatures, the benefits will be entirely for them! These consequences are often a little tiring for the humans involved or happen at 'in-humane' hours. For example, a cat may want to go outside at 5 a.m. because it feels active and ready to start the day – the birds are singing and it sounds as if there is lots to investigate outdoors. The owner, at first amused by the gentle tap of a paw on the face and a nuzzle and purr, gets up in case the cat is hungry. Reacting to a sign to let the cat out, the person goes back to bed and thinks nothing more of it. Training Day One has been a great success – the cat has early attention, food and can go out in the sun – its owner is a very good pupil. The cat will now repeat the performance daily and, if its owner seems a little unwilling to leap out of bed at the first prod, will continue with renewed vigour until this happens. Cats can be very persistent and you only have to give in once in a while to provide enough reward for the cat to keep trying! Humans are bright enough to make great pets!

However annoying these training sessions, there are few if any consequences other than tiredness or annoyance. In general, giving in to our cats' wants gives us a feel-good factor and our cats reward us with attention and affection.

Interestingly, the comparison with children does have parallels in the cat world in one particular instance. Most people would agree that children who are given everything they want and who do not have parameters they can understand are not usually the nicest of human beings. They have to learn how to fit in with others and with the rules of our society. Our human childhood is long and children do have quite a few years to learn the rules.

Cats teach their kittens the rules too – these are not as complex as those for dogs, for example, because cats do not have to learn how to fit into a social group. Learning to hunt is much more important. How cats get on with other cats or different species is often decided within the first eight weeks of life, when the cat can form attachments to beings other than its mother. During its first few weeks, the kitten must learn to do as its mother tells it but then to distance itself from her as she prepares to have another litter.

Sometimes humans take over the role of feline mother when kittens are abandoned or something happens to their natural mother. This involves hand feeding every couple of hours until the kitten is large enough to be weaned. One would imagine that these kittens would be very attached to their human carers and would have a very loving relationship with them. Interestingly, many such kittens actually turn into rather nasty cats and react with aggression should their human 'mothers' try to stop what they want to do – rather like a spoiled child. We believe that this happens because humans can wean the kittens nutritionally but do not have the expertise to wean them behaviourally. Kittens, like children, have to learn to deal with frustration and be able to cope in an acceptable manner when they do not get what they want – part of good parenting is to ensure this happens. Humans rearing kittens probably feed them at every visit and give them what they want, enjoying the relationship and the interaction with such beautiful little creatures. However, they fail to teach them the lessons a mother cat would do naturally, and so perhaps giving them everything they want at this stage can have consequences for the relationship. Luckily for us, most cats are raised by feline mothers and have learned their lessons before entering our homes.

10

The intensity of the cat-human relationship

MANY OWNERS NOW want a closer relationship with their pets. This may be because the owners live alone and the cat is their sole companion at home, or simply because they are trying to cram a lot into their lives, which inevitably means that everything must be kept under more control.

WHAT MAKES US CLOSE TO OUR CATS?

This, of course, is not a simple question and any answer we attempt is bound to be multifaceted. The relationship will depend on the person's desire to interact with the cat; likewise on the part of the cat, as well as on its ability to interact. Before we can look at the relationship as a whole, we need to look at the factors that affect how cats interact with people. These include genetics, early exposure, experience and the way in which people interact with the cats themselves.

GENETICS

Like people, the way cats react to the world around them depends on a combination of genetics and experience. Also like people, there are cats that seem to be born bold and confident and others that are always nervous about tackling anything. Researchers who have attempted to characterise cat personalities have found that they can place them in broad categories: cats that are friendly and interact with people; cats that are friendly but rather reserved; and cats that do not want any contact at all (these were termed 'unfriendly'). In a separate study, research revealed that kittens from fathers that were in the friendly category were also friendly. Other researchers found that kittens from friendly fathers were also more likely to go up to novel objects and investigate them – they were more confident and bolder in general, so perhaps this also gave them a confidence with their interactions with people and their willingness to interact was interpreted as friendliness. Researchers who study people have found they can establish whether a baby is bold in nature or not by about the age of nine months, through studying the ways they react in certain circumstances. A nine-month-old baby would be the equivalent of a kitten of about three to four weeks in age – already trying solids and trying to explore around the nest – so the comparison actually fits very well.

We often tend to split our pet cats into pedigree cats and moggies. Pedigrees could be defined as cats that come from a pre-defined group; the genes available for them to use come from animals that look similar in many of their physical characteristics – be it coat colour or length or shape of body, size of ears or colour of eyes. Individuals are selected to comply with a set of characteristics that are defined for that breed. However, if we are selecting cats on looks, are we also selecting for certain behavioural characteristics that are within that group already? When we look at some of the breeds, it is obvious that they do have trends of behaviour within them. For example, Siamese cats are often very interactive with their owners and demanding of attention and tend to be quite vocal in their interactions. Persians, on the other hand, are less likely to be as active and are much quieter. However, within all cats, be they pedigree or moggie, there is a wide range of characteristics and it is said that individual personalities of cats in general, breed or no breed (moggies), span the complete range – you might have a quiet Siamese or a very active Persian. These may be the exceptions within the breed, but individual behaviours still arise that do not comply with the norm. We can guess what is likely to happen in some breeds, but certainly not all – many behave in as wide a range of ways as is possible within the cat kingdom.

DOES COAT COLOUR HAVE AN EFFECT ON BEHAVIOUR?

There has been some research into coat colour and temperament and there are many anecdotal stories about certain types and colours, such as tabbies or tortoiseshells. Some researchers have reported that black cats may be more tolerant of high densities of numbers than cats with the agouti gene (this gene produces a wild-type coat that resembles that of a rabbit). Others suggest that cats with the red or tortoiseshell gene are quicker to react if they feel uneasy. Certainly, many people report that tortoiseshell females (in fact, tortoiseshells are almost always female) are demonstrably intolerant of handling when they do not want to be touched, and that they react strongly to other cats being introduced into the household. That said, no definitive studies have been done in this area and we cannot make firm conclusions on this point. There are several speculative reasons for linking coat colour and behaviour – if some of the genes that control coat colour are placed close to genes which control behaviours or senses, then certain behaviour traits or input of sensory information may accompany certain colours. Moreover, the chemicals available for and used in coat pigmentation may also be associated with brain function and the availability for one may have some effect on the other. Lastly, pigment may directly affect the senses – white cats may be deaf because of a defect in the gene that controls hearing which is associated with the gene for white coats. This is a topic that will no doubt run and run – are redheads more reactive than blonds? – and we may have all sorts of personal reasons for agreeing or disagreeing. And, while the science may not as yet be up to speed on this issue, it continues to be a fascinating subject for speculation and conviction, based on personal experience!

TIMING OF EXPOSURE TO PEOPLE

There is a period of a young kitten's life when it is very receptive to forming attachments to other animals. Known as the 'sensitive period', it lasts from the age of about three to eight weeks. During this time, attachments are formed easily and quickly. If kittens experience people and handling during this period, they are likely to be able to form relationships with them in later life and to be friendly pets. If they do not, then it can be difficult for them to become confident pet cats. This is the reason why feral cats seldom make good pets: they can form attachments but if they have missed this sensitive period it takes a great deal longer and much more effort to acclimatise them to domestic living – in many cases, this will not happen other than from a distance. This highlights the thin line between the pet and the wild or feral cat – one is 'domesticated' and the other is not. The question is not simply one of genetics, therefore; early experience is also vital. It is thought that the stimuli that kittens receive during this period act to promote fast growth and development of nerve connections in the areas of the brain that control social behaviour and the forming of attachments. This social behaviour can be directed at people if they are in the kitten's sphere of exposure at this time. Researchers have found that the more often kittens are handled regularly during the first 45 days of life (up to a plateau of about one hour a day), the friendlier they will be to humans; indeed, it will affect their attitude to people quite dramatically. They will be much more confident in the way they approach new objects or situations than kittens which have not had this handling.

MATERNAL INFLUENCE

As discussed above, fathers can contribute genes for confidence that may result in friendly kittens. Of course, mothers too contribute genetically to their offspring. However, they also have an influence because of their attitude and behaviour to people. Father cats have no input into kitten upbringing, so they can have no influence in this way. Kittens learn a great deal by observation and a friendly mother that is happy to have her kittens handled and will let them interact with humans will encourage the kittens themselves to behave in a friendly manner towards humans. By the same token, a nervous mother reacting with fear to humans will convey danger to her kittens.

EXPERIENCES OF PEOPLE

Even though the sensitive period is a time when experience of people will bring about a dramatic difference in a cat's attitude to people, subsequent experiences will also have a great effect. Cats learn quickly and if they have been frightened or hurt they will take avoiding action to ensure their safety is not threatened in a similar way. Thus, they will take avoiding action at the first sign of danger.

This may simply be the appearance of a person, or even certain ages or sexes of people. Many cats have a fear of men, probably because they tend to talk and act rather more loudly than women – they are often less predictable in their behaviour, from a cat's point of view, and can appear to be more threatening.

HOW PEOPLE APPROACH CATS

Women have traditionally been more involved with the care of cats than men. One very interesting study examined the way cats and people who were not familiar with each other reacted together. The researchers looked at a sample of men, women, boys and girls. When they let the cats initiate the investigation of the people, they found that the cats approached everyone in a similar way and a similar number of times. However, when the people were allowed to interact with them, differences became apparent. In general, the men interacted with the cats from a sitting position, and the women, boys and girls got down to the cat's level. The children tended to approach the cats, whereas the adults waited for the cats to approach them. The boys tended to approach the cats more often than the girls did, and even followed withdrawing cats (which the researchers felt the cats did not like). The women interacted with the cats from further away and talked to them as they were approached; they also stroked them more when they came close enough. The cats reacted to the encouragement and were happy to interact and to comply with such treatment.

Another study showed that, if a person responds to their cat when it wants to interact with them, then the cat in turn will comply with the person when they want to make contact – the more the owner does, the more the cat responds, and vice versa; it is a mutually responsive and positive relationship. Presumably, the initial requirement is a cat that is happy to interact – one researchers would put in the 'friendly' box in the first place.

BRIBERY

We can use certain things cats like to cement their relationships with us. Food can be a motivator for interaction, as can attention. The warmth of a fire or a cosy room can be used to coax a shy cat to share space with people, or even get on to a lap. Different cats are motivated by different things – prawns may be irresistible to one cat, whereas another will not be in the least interested in doing anything for food. This can be one of the major difficulties in training cats – finding something that they find more rewarding than doing what they want to do!

COMPETITION

If only one cat and one person live together, then the opportunities for a one-to-one relationship are high, if both are willing. It may seem obvious, but researchers report that the smaller the family, the more attention the cat gives to each person. Single cats spend more time interacting with owners than cats in homes with lots of other felines. Interestingly, owners of single cats were less bothered about the cat being fussy and more tolerant of its curiosity than owners of lots of cats were. However, this is hardly surprising – parents with a single child may be much more tolerant of it demanding attention, making a mess or misbehaving. Multiply this up several times (and more) with more children and the situation can become intolerable, no matter how much you love them. Not only will more cats interact with owners in total, but they will also interact with each other. Often this will not be friendly interaction (just like children!) and there will be situations to try to sort out. In this way, caring for more cats becomes harder work and owners may feel guilty that they haven't been fair to all the cats or that not every cat has got the attention it deserves or needs.

These are some of the factors that influence how and why cats react with people and they suggest something about the extent to which they might approach interaction. But this chapter is about what people want from their cats.

People live with cats in a wide range of situations, from feeding feral cats on the farm or in the garden to keeping a single cat totally indoors in a very close relationship. We can manipulate the intensity and closeness of the relationship to some extent by first of all choosing which cats we interact with and then how we actually keep them.

Many people find great satisfaction in taking the wildest version of our domesticated cat, the feral, and becoming responsible for its care at arm's length. The cat will usually have been neutered, but, aside from this handling (which usually requires a cat trap to catch the cat and careful handling at the vet's surgery to ensure nobody is injured until the cat is anaesthetised), it is then allowed to go back on to its site and its health is monitored from a distance by its feeders. Re-catching ferals is very difficult – they learn what a trap is after being caught once and are unlikely to enter it again. Thus, they have to stay fairly healthy on their own, but their food is provided by carers. Some of these cats can become quite friendly – they will certainly sit and wait until their feeders come and will greet them as they bring the food. Some may tolerate a stroke or pat but many will simply stay at flight distance – the distance at which they can safely dash away should danger arise. While this may not make for a close relationship, it is a nurturing one and can be very satisfying for both sides.

The opposite end of the spectrum is the totally indoor cat, which centres its life and waking hours around the presence of its owner. Many such cats are pedigree and some are breeds that form strong bonds with their owners anyway, such as Burmese or Siamese. These breeds are more interactive than some others and can be quite dog-like in their devotion. They are also quite bright animals that need to be kept interested and prevented from becoming bored. Thus, their interest and their activity has no external component and can become very focused upon their owners; the interactions can be very close. This is the kind of relationship that some cat owners want too, but it puts a great deal more responsibility on them in terms of keeping the cat amused and not frustrated, especially when owners are at work or even when they just go out. Such cats can become overattached or bored – with behavioural consequences.

Of course, most cat owners fall between these two extremes: they have one or two pet cats that may have access outside some or all of the time and the cats fit their lives in around that of the family or person in a way that is mutually convenient to both. When we look at what we want from our cats, it is necessary to cover all these relationship choices as well as the conventional one, because it is in the extremes that we see the cat pushed to its limits.

DO WE WANT INDEPENDENT CATS?

One of the most obvious benefits of owning a cat as a pet rather than a dog is that it is a much less onerous task in terms of being responsible for its behaviour and its activities, both within the home and out with the public at large. Cats' popularity as pets has grown for both of these reasons. On the whole, cats are very happy to live with us but retain their independence as well.

Most cats that go outdoors happily live a Jekyll-and-Hyde type of existence, becoming kitten-like indoors and enjoying us feeding them and touching them; they relax and lap up the attention. Outdoors, they patrol like tigers, hunt a little if they feel like it and have the odd set-to with next-door's cat if it happens to be around. Their adrenaline-rush requirement satisfied for the day, they then return inside to become couch potatoes again. For most owners, this is absolutely fine – the cat comes and goes as it wishes. Some people close the cat-flap at night to try to protect the cat from cars and creatures of the night and to protect small mammals from the cat at dawn and dusk. Most cats are still free to do as they wish in the day, indoors or out.

Other people neither expect nor want independence from their cat. As usual, we need some science to try to find out what different people want from their cats – one such survey found that owners of cats that had a very free type of lifestyle and came and went as they wished rated their cat's independence highly and felt that this is how cats should be. Conversely, owners of cats that did not go outdoors at all didn't value independence highly in their pets but wanted them to stay in and be close to them. Presumably, those who rated independence highly would rather not have a cat than keep one indoors all the time because of the risk posed by a busy road near by or a dangerous neighbourhood.

CLEANLINESS

Part of the reason for the phenomenal success of cats as pets is their cleanliness. Their toilet habits can be left to occur naturally in the great outdoors (usually in the neighbour's finely tilled vegetable patch!), or can be controlled and managed by the use of a litter tray. And unless you count irate neighbouring gardeners, most cats' toilet habits do not cause social problems in the way that toileting in the street has for dogs.

Cats are also physically clean. In general, shorthaired cats seldom bring mud or dirt into our homes. Longhaired cats with access outdoors do tend to lend themselves to carrying in bits of stick and leaves (and even the odd slug) into our houses. We once had a semi-longhaired cat named Smokie who was rechristened Debris because of the ring of bits and pieces that were left on the cushion or bed after it has had a grooming session. Mud, which seems to fall off the delicate paws of the shorthaired cat, hung on as Debris moved through the house before finally deciding to snuggle down on the newly changed cream duvet or in the ironing basket recently filled with clean shirts for the week ahead. However, in general, cats are clean in all their habits and do not make our homes grubby in the same way dogs do. They certainly don't smell (not to the human nose, anyway) and don't slobber, so our homes don't have that 'eau de damp dog' that is so endearing of their canine cousins. House-proud people are thus generally happy to have cats around – we expect our cats to be clean and to use a tray if provided, and most cats happily comply.

NON-DESTRUCTIVE

When we talk about destructive behaviour in pets, we immediately think about dogs, which often tend to chew up their owners' homes if they are left alone. We have all heard of separation anxiety and how dogs, because they are of necessity pack animals, become distressed if they are separated from their pack. They have to learn how to cope with being alone and owners have to help them to do this if they want to have normal lives (such as being able to come and go without the dog eating the carpet or settee in their absence). We don't really think of our cats as destructive, although they can cause damage with their scratching habits. Some cats don't scratch furniture, carpets or walls at all in their human homes. Others have a favourite armchair or stair-rise that they just cannot resist ripping to shreds! Cats can be destructive, but the difference is that most cat owners seem to have a different attitude to cats doing this to the owners of dogs.

When Fido chews up the new beanbag, it is seen as a deliberately destructive action (even though it may be in response to the emotional stress of isolation). In cats, such an act is not seen as a premeditated action or destruction for the sake of it; it is seen as a claw-sharpening act carried out in the wrong place. Owners often try to introduce a scratch-post, with which they attempt to coax the cat into redirecting the behaviour on to an acceptable area. They accept that it is a natural behaviour in their cat. Having said that, in the USA the front claws of cats are routinely removed to prevent destruction in homes – perhaps a sign of a fundamental difference in the attitude to cats (or furniture) between the two sides of the Atlantic. In the UK, we do not agree with de-clawing. We have more outdoor cats and worry that by removing claws they will not be able to climb or to get themselves out of trouble or will come off worst in a cat fight because they cannot defend themselves. Indeed, the Royal College of Veterinary Surgeons terms the operation an unnecessary mutilation; it must also be a very painful operation for a cat to recover from.

Cats scratch for a variety of reasons. One is claw sharpening; another is to mark an area, both physically and via scent deposition from glands on the bottom of the feet. And, like the anxious dog that may chew objects, a cat may also be motivated to mark more if it feels the need – perhaps because it does not feel secure, because it feels threatened by other cats or because of changes to its environment.

In the UK, we often talk about the north/south divide – the differences between attitudes and lifestyles in the north and south of the country. One such minor difference seems to be expressed in the way we decorate our homes. Trendsetters say that using wallpaper to decorate our homes is coming back; in the north of the country, it does seem to be used a great deal more than in homes in the south. This observation brings to mind conversations that I had with cat owners at a series of pet roadshows in the UK. On answering questions from pet owners, I inevitably receive a lot of queries about behaviours – why the cat behaves as it does, how to understand what is happening and, if the behaviour is a problem, how to try and solve it. During the northern roadshows, it became very evident from a number of questions on this subject that scratching off wallpaper was high among feline behavioural problems. People simply did not expect their cat to be so destructive in the house. This query had not been evident at other roadshows elsewhere in the country, and on enquiry we found that not only was wallpaper commonly used to decorate homes in the north, but also that it often had raised contours or the effect of expensive fabric. These more elaborate – and of course more expensive – wallpapers were the cats' favourites!

On further enquiry, it appeared that the cats often scratched wallpaper in the vicinity of the front door or entrance into a room (which makes sense in marking terms). It also became apparent that the cats played with the flakes of paper that were shredded off. Do cats enjoy the sensation of pulling their claws through wood or carpets? Is the motivation to sharpen them rewarded by a feeling of enjoyment? Does embossed wallpaper provide a little too much pleasure? I have a feeling that the cats' initial marking and claw-sharpening experiments on the walls resulted in rather a lot of fun – not only in the sense of dragging claws through the paper and marking it, but in pulling off the bits of paper afterwards and playing with them. Suggestions that owners might use paint instead of wallpaper found little favour, and I suspect those cats are still enjoying the thrills of wallpaper removal while their owners grit their teeth at the wanton destruction!

COMPANIONSHIP

Cats do make excellent companions and are often very sensitive to our moods and needs. They provide a very personal companionship. People who own dogs often make new acquaintances, or at least nodding acquaintances, through walking their pets – people will be far more ready to have a chat or interact first by asking about the dog and then chatting more generally once there is a focus and an ice-breaker for the conversation. Aside from the very friendly cat that sits on the wall and enjoys a stroke from every passer-by, it will not be evident to strangers whether people own cats or not. The cat/human relationship is very one-to-one and interaction with others will not be a motivation for getting a cat.

Researchers examined the way in which we perceive the

response and support we get from our cats and have found that we do not regard them as replacing humans in our need for social interaction, but as a genuine source of support, especially when attachment to the cat is strong. Our cats can provide this strong help when we need them and are very important to us. Research has also revealed that cats can help to improve the mood of depressed owners.

TO BE LOVED

We want our cats to like us. We don't expect them to heel like dogs or to be obedient; we don't expect them to rescue us in a fire or attack the burglar trying to get away with our savings. In fact, we don't want many of the characteristics attributed to their canine cousins, including protection – having a cat will never make you feel safe. However, we do want to be recognised, to be greeted and perhaps treated a little differently to the way a stranger would be. Cats can do this, even in circumstances where it would seem that they are not really attached to anyone – feeders of feral cats will be delighted that the cats they feed recognise them as they come, do not run from them and may even allow themselves to be touched on occasion. This is akin to the enjoyment we get from interacting with some of our wild native animals – feeding or watching badgers or wild birds, for example.

For others, the relationship with a cat must be very intense: they do love their cats fiercely and they do want some sort of feedback. We have to remember that the cat is not a pack animal. The dog is an obligate pack animal – it wants and needs to be part of a group and has developed ways of keeping the group together through problems generated both externally and internally to the pack through threats and misunderstandings. Because of this, the dog will count man and his family as the pack and so will protect it accordingly – many of our breeds, such as Dobermans or Rottweilers, have been bred to have a more fully developed protecting instinct than others.

A survey of owners found that indoor cats were rated more highly as more active and interactive with their owners. The cats often initiated the interaction. Outdoor cats were rated as less curious than indoor cats. Did outdoor cats seem less curious because they were not always on hand to interact with their owners, because they used up their energies outdoors and perhaps slept more indoors? Indoor-only cats have less outlets for curiosity, for expending energy – both mental and physical – and are more likely to look to their owners for stimulation. Thus, while the contents of a handbag may not seem very exciting to a cat that has just seen off a couple of local moggies, stalked and caught a mouse and climbed a tree for the fun of it, they may represent something extremely exciting for the indoor cat without such external adventures in its life.

Interestingly, outdoor cats seem to rub against their owners more than indoor cats, especially when they come in from outside. Are they greeting or exchanging and checking scents to ensure that, scent-wise, their den and refuge has just the right balance of scents to ensure they can relax with the other members who share it?

Other research into this bond between cats and humans has revealed that people rate their own affection for their cat as high if they feel that the cat likes them too. The level of affection was also affected by the cleanliness of the cat, its curiosity and playfulness and its predictability. This is understandable – if a cat is soiling in the house, it can be very distressing for owners and, much as they like the cat, the feeling of frustration and annoyance may somewhat temper the owners' ability to say that, right at that

moment, they love their cat! If it is playful and curious, and if this manifests itself partly in interaction with owners, then the owners' enjoyment of the cat will increase, as will the quoted affection factor. Perhaps predictability was a measure of the closeness of the relationship – how much owners understood their cats and what they were trying to communicate, the need for a cuddle or to be fed, for example. If owners respond to their cats, then cats will respond in kind. This self-reinforcing, rewarding circle makes for a mutually enjoyable relationship – owners love their cats and their cats certainly seem to love them back.

PLAYFUL

Cats are expected to be playful – the first thing we do with kittens when we get them is to start dangling bits of string in front of them or give them wind-up toys or ping-pong balls to chase. The sight of cats playing is a joy – their grace and athletic prowess and the daft scrapes they get themselves into when they are overexcited are a great source of amusement and fascination. Owners of cats that don't play can become worried about their pets for this very reason.

Play is thought to prepare cats for hunting: it helps them to assess their senses and their physical abilities and test them out to see what is possible. It also gives them a chance to interact with each other and learn what is acceptable and what is not.

Some cats take play one step further than the others – they almost cross over into the canine camp of behaviour. It is not so often seen in moggies and is usually confined to one or two very interactive breeds – the Siamese and Burmese breeds. Some of these cats actively retrieve – they bring back objects that have been thrown and even put them in front of their owners to be thrown again. Just how this has come about we are not sure – it may be an extension of a natural behaviour of cats bringing back prey to the safety of the den. If these cats then get a reaction from their owners who take the object and throw it, the cat can retain and demand their attention for long periods of time. Both owners and cats enjoy the interaction and so the behaviour continues and is used when attention, or exercise, or interaction is required.

FRIENDLY

The cat is not an exhibitionist pet – cat owners don't seek to frighten people with them or to parade them up a crowded high street to get a reaction. Whereas we may meet and interact with lots of strangers with dogs, only friends or close associates are invited into our homes for long enough to find out about our cats. It still takes a little time for the cats to approach them and to make friends – if the friend can pat the cat and even elicit a purr, we are delighted. It can be very disappointing to own a cat that runs and hides as soon as anyone comes into the house – sharing our cats is a rather intimate affair but one that owners like to carry out with selected friends and relatives.

TO FIT IN WITH OUR LIVES

Cats live for about fourteen years on average, and often into their late teens or even their twenties. We may get our first cat while we are single. We may be out working all day but enjoy sharing the companionship they give us in the evening and at weekends when we are relaxing. The cat learns to centre its life around ours, waking when we are around and sleeping when we are out. The house is pretty quiet most of the time and the cat gets to know selected girlfriends or boyfriends who may visit at the weekend or evenings.

Almost inevitably, one of these friendships blossoms; a boyfriend or girlfriend moves in and adjustments have to be made. The cat may have to find an alternative night-time spot because it no longer has half the bed available to it, or because the new person does not appreciate having his or her toes pounced on midway through the night. Cuddling up on the sofa requires a bit more determination to get to the lap the cat wants – or may become easier, because there are now two laps available. On the whole, it does not change life too much and there are certain benefits.

If a third person suddenly joins the family – a small, helpless bundle that smells strange and is often very noisy – the situation becomes more demanding. Suddenly, the whole routine of the house is changed; the cat is not allowed in all of the rooms and is moved out of some very swiftly. There seems to be activity at strange times of the day and night. Again, there are benefits: mum and baby are around a great deal and the cat may even be able to get an extra cuddle while the mother sits and feeds for hours when the baby is very new. For most cats, this is not a problem and they soon adapt. For some very people-orientated cats, however, it can be distressing, simply because they cannot have their owners on tap as they have previously. The cat is not now the centre of attention and this, with the disturbing new smells and sounds, can make the cat very unsettled. With these cats, it is best to prepare them somewhat for the imminent arrival of the baby and the changes which will occur – owners need to distance themselves a little and limit access before the birth so that the cat does not find such a gulf of difference when the baby arrives.

A growing family often leads to a move of house. When this happens, the cat has to readjust to the new territory and get to grips with the gangs of other cats or dogs outside that must be negotiated when going out for a stroll.

Babies turn into toddlers (often rather dangerous for cats) and more babies come along and less time is available for the cat. The cat learns to avoid small grasping hands and keep its tail up and out of the way when it sits on the windowsill or other high spots, which it now values greatly.

In this time, it is quite likely too that owners will either positively choose to get another cat, or even a dog, or that a cat will turn up from somewhere (uninvited) and need a good home. Move over a bit more, original cat! Keep that puppy under control and learn to ask for more food, because it finished off the breakfast you only ate half of this morning, which you meant to return to later! Find somewhere higher to rest and feel safe. In fact, a dog does not really spell serious trouble. Another cat coming in causes much more upset and a large adjustment is required in almost everything the original cat has taken for granted, such as the security of the core part of the home, the ability to wander around the house without cause for concern and having to cope with strange feline smells. The house, which once was quiet and calm, is always active from the presence of a person or a pet and the cat has to adapt its lifestyle accordingly.

Growing children bringing their friends home mean more changes – some good, some bad – and the cat learns how to avoid the ones it doesn't like and enjoy the others. The same rule applies to other pets and cats in the neighbourhood.

Some cats will even live long enough to see the children leave home and peace return! Many will experience a change in the make-up of the mix of the adults in charge and with the change come more or less children, other pets and perhaps another change of home. Still the cat adapts.

These are lifetime adaptations, but there are also daily adaptations to our human rhythms – rather different to the feline rhythm. Although cats will hunt during the day and at night, the time when they are most active is dawn and dusk, when the small creatures they hunt will be active. When cats live with us, they adapt their time of sleeping and activity to suit us. While some of us do have cats that try to wake us as the dawn is breaking, most cats will learn to wait until owners are up and about before making their presence known.

TO HUNT OR NOT TO HUNT

There are now few situations in which pet cats are required to hunt to pay for their shelter and a little bit of extra food, although some farm cats will still be kept in this manner. And while there may be added (and usually unseen) benefits of cats keeping rodents at bay around the home, most owners would prefer it if their cats didn't hunt at all. Most people are now quite far removed from nature red in tooth and claw – the beautifully prepared meat we buy at the supermarket which has already been skinned or boned means that the nearest we have to get to basic food is a quick division to bite-size pieces with a sharp Sabatier knife – quick and clean and no messing. We are not used to seeing suffering or death and don't enjoy the presents from our cats we find on the kitchen floor in the morning. There is considerable pressure from conservationists to prevent cats from killing a small mammal and bird population which is already suffering from changes in farming practice that have removed a great deal of natural habitat.

NO SEXUAL BEHAVIOUR

Apparently, people don't have a preference for the sex of the cat they keep – they are just as happy with males or females. This is probably because most of us have neutered cats and both males and females that have been neutered behave in much the same fashion towards us – and, of course, don't display any sexual behaviour. Neutering has a very levelling effect on behaviour and irons out many gender differences. If we had to live with intact animals – males spraying, roaming and fighting and being probably more aggressive with us when we stroke them, or with females calling and having lots of kittens we have to rehome – we would probably have a preference, or simply not be so fond of cats as pets. For stress-free living in a high density of cats that behave in a predictable way (one of the values rated highly by owners as a factor in their affection for their cats), neutering is a necessity.

FITTING IN WITH OUR BELIEFS

After reading chapter five it will become very evident that the look and behaviour of the cat stems from its requirements to be an excellent hunter. The cat's very physiology relies on meat to stay healthy – it is about the most meat-centred animal you will find. Humans, on the other hand, are omnivores – we can survive with or without meat and can enjoy manipulating and changing our food as part of our relaxation, hobbies or culture. We also have the ability to consider the welfare of other animals and decide whether we actually want to eat them or not. Our physiology makes the choice possible.

However, we need to keep these personal beliefs and preferences in check – just because we can survive happily without meat doesn't mean that our cats want to take on this life philosophy. Not only do they not want the choice, they are obligate carnivores and cannot survive without meat. Why, then, do some owners insist on making their cats become vegetarian? They source a food that is plant-based and add the specific nutrients which cats need (most of which must come from the meat anyway).

Nutritionists have worked out what cats need in terms of the major nutrients so it is possible to put together a diet that is supplemented with these. However, we know much less about all the micronutrients and the interaction of different vitamins and minerals as well as amino acids and fats that keep cats in peak condition. And think about how the cat is taking to this new diet. Its body has very specific requirements and its senses have been developed to help it acquire them: its sense of smell tells it about the fats and amino acids in food; the tastes which give pleasure will no doubt come from meat-based compounds. The only vegetation cats usually eat is that which can be found in the stomachs of their prey or the bits and pieces of grass they consume, usually when they are feeling unwell or in need of a purge. How do they cope with this vegetable-based diet – do they enjoy it? Is it doing them good? It is rather like taking a Formula 1 car and trying to get it to run on two-stroke petrol and then wondering why it is not performing to its maximum.

I am afraid that vegetarian cats are one of my greatest bugbears – well, not the cats themselves, but the owners who do not realise that their feline Ferrari is not a lawn mower and it needs quality fuel. My advice to those who wish to have a vegetarian cat is to get a rabbit. An animal which has evolved to eat vegetation will certainly not look like or behave like the cat we know and love. So get a rabbit! Many are now kept inside – indeed, house rabbits are supposed to be our fastest-growing pet.

INDIVIDUALITY

The whole concept of cloning animals has made us think about what we would get if we could clone our pet – from all accounts it would not necessarily look like its parent (coat colour is not all controlled by genes as exemplified by 'CC' the kitten first cloned which did not look like her mum and, as we have seen already, character is influenced by many things as well as genetics – thus it may not behave in the same way either). But do we want one cat which is exactly the same as the one before? Most of us enjoy our cats for their individuality, the things they do or the way they do them that are unique to that cat and if recounted would allow us to identify that cat over others in the household or even generally. We want our cats to be individuals.

As we have seen, character is a lot more than the product of genes – early experience and the cat's environment can shape it dramatically. Thus, character cannot be guaranteed either – owners wanting an exact replica of their favourite cat may be disappointed. Indeed, while most of us may have had an older cat which was most loved and we never wanted to lose it, it would be very unfair to get another and expect it to be the same – comparison would inevitably be made on just about everything it did. Better to acknowledge that cat as a one-off, special, and move on to a new and different one, appreciating it for its own personality and individuality.

Scientists have tried to define individuality and to measure it, but this is actually very complicated because, if you are using different people to record characteristics, then the results could be influenced by the person too – for example, recording how cats were rated for friendliness or confidence could well be influenced not only by the personality of the recorder present, but on their experience of cats and their attitudes. You can make the research more objective and look at how long it might take a cat to investigate something new in the room and record this as a score of confidence or boldness. Of course, it is very difficult to define the subtleties of behaviour, let alone to try to find a way of measuring them that is reproducible – sometimes we can only look at very simple things and try to draw conclusions.

How do individual characters come about? Most people understand that the main influences on an individual's character are genetics and experience; experience gained from interacting with the world around them – the cat's environment and the people and animals within it (see the earlier part of the chapter, which looks at what affects our relationship with our cats).

Looking at the characters of young cats, what do we find that persists into adulthood? If we choose a kitten for its confidence and friendliness, will this change as it grows? Again, we have no definitive answers. Some people have found that kittens that are inquisitive and active at four months can still be categorised as such at one year old – perhaps, again, linked to this boldness or confidence. They suggest friendliness may change and that how predatory the cat is may also alter. The way in which you define how a cat behaves – for example, whether it is quiet and withdrawn or outgoing – may also depend on the situation in which it is being measured. A cat that is very easy-going in one situation may react very aggressively in a different situation. This sometimes happens when a new cat comes into the house – the resident cat may become jumpy or quick to react aggressively, even to its owners, and may not seem so affectionate. Perhaps this is because it is not feeling relaxed enough to go into kitten mode with owners because of the 'intruder' in the house.

BEAUTY

Most of us choose our cats because we like the colour or the pattern of their coat. It would not surprise readers to find that this too has been studied and the results show that our choice is often based on a cat we had as a child, or one we or a friend had owned previously – beauty is indeed in the eye of the beholder. However, when it comes to cats it is pretty hard to choose an ugly one. There are some rather battered old toms around, as well as those cats that have had a difficult start in life and bear the scars of their traumas, but in general most cats are very attractive. Thankfully, we are all different and many owners of pedigree cats with special coat characteristics often also keep moggies, enjoying the good old black-and-white mogs as much as the pedigrees with the spotted or striped coats.

WHAT WE DON'T WANT

As an owner of both dogs and cats, I feel reasonably qualified to compare the different way people keep their pets. One of the major differences is that very few cat owners want their felines as status symbols – they cannot really be shown off, except to friends in the home, and they certainly aren't used to threaten or frighten people in the macho way some owners display their dogs. Many dog owners tend to be interested in their own breed (about 80 per cent of UK dogs are pedigree) and not in canine kind in general. In my experience, cat owners like cats, be they pedigree or moggie, the same breed or different. In the USA about ten years ago, 'spangled cats' (cats with a beautifully patterned coat) were bred and sold almost as a fashion accessory – the price was high because they were supposed to be rare and beautiful. There are people who always want something different and will breed a wild species of cat to a domestic cat to try to recreate some of the fabulous wild coat patterns into our pets – the Bengal is an example of this. Others will take a mutation, such as hairlessness which arises occasionally in a kitten, and make it into a breed – the Sphynx, for instance – or we push our breeds to the limit with flat faces or pointed noses. There will always be a demand for something different, but within the cat-owning public the numbers of such fantasy felines are tiny and most people remain happy with the beauty of their moggie or what is available already in pedigree cats. We must hope that the breeders consider the welfare of the cat rather than the novelty value when they manipulate this animal which most of us feel is beautiful anyway, whatever its type. Some breed clubs are very forward thinking and have tried to ensure that extremes and difference are not valued more highly than health and functionality – always difficult when there is competition for looks.

On the face of it, most of us would say that we have few expectations of our cats. However, looking more closely at the relationship, it seems that perhaps we do. Can these expectations be merged successfully with what we want for our cats, and what they want from us?

11

How to make a cat happy

HAPPINESS' IS SOMETHING most of us would say we want for our cats, but we have no idea how to measure it. We could say that we know when they are content – they seem to be relaxed, are eating well, are physically at the right weight. They seem healthy and not in any pain, are confident in our home and interact confidently with those around them. However, what makes one cat happy may be torture for another. Not all cats are confident animals. Depending on their genes and their start in life, they may be very nervous animals and meeting someone new may be a terrifying rather than an enjoyable experience for them. As owners, there are things we can gauge – whether the cat looks happy and does not seem fearful or whether it chooses to do certain things with us. However, sometimes we take our own needs and expectations as those of the cat – what we want for it may not be what it wants for itself.

COMPANY

We humans are group-living animals – we enjoy social interaction and, depending on what motivates us individually, want to work with others, help each other, live within a family, socialise and generally be with people for a greater or lesser part of the day. Although we may want peace and solitude occasionally, too much can be isolating. It takes a certain special person to be a hermit, and solitary confinement is regarded socially as a serious punishment. We know how lonely we can feel if we are at home alone all day – at such times even a conversation with the window cleaner can become a very important way of making contact with others!

It is understandable, therefore, that, when we leave our cats at home while we work all day, we feel that they may be lonely. We don't want them to feel isolated or low and in need of company. This feeling can be reinforced by our cats on our return – they sit and wait for us to turn up, making us believe they have been expecting us for hours and have maintained a vigil in the window watching every car as it passes by. They then rub around our legs and miaow forlornly, running back and forward as we come in. Of course, we love them to miss us and lap up the welcome.

In reality, the cat has probably found a nice warm spot on a radiator or on a sunny windowsill and snoozed happily throughout the day, moving occasionally to follow the sun, have a snack from the ever-full food bowl or relieve itself in the tray or outside. It may even have made a patrol of the garden or a little hunting expedition before it feels the need for another rest. Around the time you are due home from work, the cat will stir itself and sit in the window to watch your return. Owners who don't leave dry food on tap for the cat will find their return exceptionally well cheered and will be accompanied into the kitchen with much noise and rubbing until dinner is served.

Remember, the cat's ancestor – the African wildcat – is a solitary living species, seldom meeting its own kind except for mating or raising kittens. Our own domestic cat can be solitary or sociable; however, it isn't an obligate pack animal like the dog, or even humans. And, while some females may raise kittens together, there are no other aspects of feline behaviour in which labour is shared or there is co-operation – it is every cat for itself.

Most cats will alter their periods of activity to fit in with their owners. This is especially true of cats that are not let outdoors – they can't do the equivalent of nipping next door for a cup of coffee or go out for a spot of amusement such as winding up the ginger tom around the corner. They are very reliant on their owners for activity and stimulation – very little happens unless owners are around.

For these cats, company may be a very good idea – however, it is harder to introduce a new cat to a resident cat where its territory is confined to a small indoor area and there is little room for escape from one another. The way introductions are made in this situation can be very important. Thus, if you intend to keep cats indoors, it would be wise to think ahead and get two kittens together – siblings usually get on better because they have spent that sensitive socialisation period together, a time when bonds can be formed easily.

There are some cats, usually of the more emotional, more reactive and interactive breeds such as the Siamese or Burmese, who do become very attached to their owners and can suffer when left alone. These may benefit from company – even from a dog, or perhaps from some behaviour therapy to help them 'get a life' away from their owners. While some owners may enjoy this level of dependence and encourage it initially, it can become very wearing and going out becomes an extremely guilt-ridden procedure. Most owners will want their cat to retain its independent nature and some sense of feline dignity.

Perhaps the message here is to 'know your cat' – don't assume it wants another feline around just because you do, or because you want to assuage your guilt at having to leave it alone for long periods of the day. Some cats are perfectly happy like this and would be very upset at the introduction of 'a friend'. Others will need someone or something to interact with, depending on their nature and what they may have been used to. However, again, don't assume that, just because two cats got on previously, the same will happen again if you replace one that has been lost – it is never that easy! I would not dream of suggesting that a lonely person needs just anyone to come and live with them to keep them company. Close-quarter living needs characters that like or at least can tolerate each other. The same is true of our cats. We are already aware that each cat has a very individual personality. It would be arrogant to think that we can force several together and expect them to become bosom buddies.

Sometimes, we use the excuse of the cat needing company because we want to get another cat. There is nothing wrong with wanting more felines in the house – cats are eminently desirable. However, acknowledging this motivation can make our approach a little more measured and make us less expectant that the resident cat should be grateful! The onus is back on us to try to make it work.

WE WANT OUR CATS TO BE SAFE

Any cat lover would say yes to the question 'do you want your cat to be safe?' However, with animals such as cats, which traditionally have come and gone from our homes as they please, safety can be a difficult issue. Owners who rate their cats' independence highly have to balance the risks of going outdoors with the value they place on their cats' right to free choice of lifestyle.

For some people, even the tiniest risk to their cat's safety is something that they cannot accept and for them a cat must be kept inside all the time. This will remove some, but not all, the risks of injury for cats. True, an indoor cat cannot end up in a fight with a cat that is infected with feline immunodeficiency virus (the cat version of HIV) but, cats being cats, it can get itself into mischief indoors too – see table below. When we look at the table of outdoor and indoor risks, it is interesting that the outdoor risks are all associated with safety and health; the indoor risks are more associated with behaviour.

INDOOR RISKS:	OUTDOOR RISKS:
Behaviour problems because of boredom or frustration	Injury from cats, other cats, dogs, people etc.
Fear of change – over-reaction to change eating or novelty	Poisoning – directly from prey that has been poisoned
Obesity through lack of exercise	Disease contracted from other cats
Overdependance – becoming too reliant on owner	Infestation with fleas or other parasites
Dangers within home – getting stuck in washing machines etc. Poisoning from house plants	Loss – shut in sheds/cars etc.
Escape – not streetwise if get out	

Take, for example, the question of poisonous plants. A cat with access outdoors, if it wanted, would be able to sample just about any and every poisonous plant it wanted, from those available inside to those in all the gardens in the area. However, such poisonings are rare in outdoor cats. The indoor cat is another matter and will often nibble on pot plants that normally it would not touch, such as the very poisonous Diffienbachia or dumb cane or a vase of lillies, which are very toxic to cats. The reason for this is probably that outdoor cats have access to a wide range of grasses that they do nibble, especially, it seems, if they have digestive upsets. Thus, if they feel the need, they can find and select suitable non-toxic plants that will do what they need in terms of digestion or being sick (we are not really sure exactly what happens in the cat's digestive system and why small amounts of vegetation are important). An indoor cat may not have the right vegetation available to it and may be driven to try to find a suitable substitute – sometimes with serious consequences. Thus, the owner of a cat with access outdoors will not have to worry about indoor plants; the owner of an indoor cat will have to be very careful about what the cat has access to. Likewise, the entry for behavioural problems on the indoor cat side of the table could be quite wide-ranging – indoor cats may become frustrated and bored and problems can arise. Thus, we must look at mental as well as physical dangers for our cats when we are choosing their lifestyle.

For some owners who live in very built-up or dangerous areas, or right on a road where it is highly likely that cats will get run over, having a cat that will survive outdoors is a long shot and they may choose to keep one indoors. Later on, we will discuss the question of whether a cat should stay in and, if it does, what more owners should be doing to keep it healthy.

Another aspect of safe cat-keeping is identification. If cats do go outside, owners often want to be able to identify them so that they can be returned if they become lost or injured on the road. There are various forms of identification that can be used, such as microchipping, tattoos or a collar with an address disc or phone contact.

Collars in themselves can pose a risk for cats – some years ago, it became apparent that a few cats were becoming caught up by the collar as they climbed or went through the undergrowth and were actually strangled by the collar. Feline welfare organisations suggested that elasticated collars would be the answer – the elastic would stretch and allow the cat to wriggle its way out of the collar. It has become evident now that perhaps this advice caused almost more trouble than the collars that did not stretch. A survey carried out by the Feline Advisory Bureau, as well as surveys done by other organisations, has found that collars that can stretch may indeed allow the cat to escape if it becomes hung up by the collar; however, they also allow the cat to get its front leg through and become stuck. There have been many very nasty injuries to an area equivalent to the human underarm where collars have cut into a cat's flesh. These injuries can be very difficult to heal because it is an area that is moving all the time. Even if the cat is not injured, its accident can be very frightening for both the cat and the owner who finds it; the cat will probably find that it cannot get home because it is unable to walk. Collars may also stretch so much that they get caught in the mouth or stuck on the teeth – again a very frightening experience that could produce serious injuries if the cat is not found and rescued. Some manufacturers have come up with a better design for collars – a snap-open variety that comes apart if the collar is pulled. These do seem a much better idea, even though the cat may get through a few more of this kind of collar because they open and get left at the scene of the tangle.

I certainly wouldn't advocate wearing a collar simply for

decoration or to keep away fleas. There are other ways of tacking fleas that are more effective and do not add the risks associated with collars.

The question of whether bells worn on cat collars are effective in helping to cut down the numbers of birds killed by cats has been investigated by the RSPB. The evidence seems to show that wearing a collar with a bell does coincide with the cat catching less prey. Once again, the benefits and the risks need to be measured. If wearing the safest possible collar with a noisy bell attached does stop cats catching birds, then perhaps the small risk of associated problems is worth it.

Microchipping is definitely a good idea. A rice-grain-sized chip can be inserted under the skin very easily and provides an individual code for the cat that is readable using a hand-held reader. Most larger rescue centres now have one. However, if the cat is killed on the road or it gets lost in a new neighbourhood, it is unlikely that it will be checked for a microchip, and the owner may never find out what happened to the cat. Cats that wear collars do look as though someone owns and loves them and are less likely to be 'rescued' for simply walking around – and, if they are found dead, the owner has much more chance of being told. So, as you can see, even the identification issue can be a difficult one with cats.

In summary, cats do not make things easy – their independent and very active lifestyle can be risk-laden and options for their safety are not straightforward.

HEALTH

On average, cats now live longer than they did, for example, thirty years ago. Advances in the quality of food and healthcare we provide can mean that cats live well past the average of about fourteen years old. What can we do to make sure they stay as healthy as possible?

i) Neutering

Neutering removes much of the motivation for fighting and roaming in male cats. In this way, it cuts down on the transfer of disease through biting and, if the cat is wandering less, reduces the chances of it crossing dangerous roads. An un-neutered male is unlikely to live for long – sometimes as little as two or three years, but probably more commonly five or six years – as it has a high-risk lifestyle. Similarly, neutered females do not have the risks and trials of pregnancy and kitten rearing. Neutered ferals can live into double figures and, as we have mentioned, neutered pets may now have a life expectancy of more than fourteen years.

ii) Vaccination

The subject of vaccination is in the media a great deal these days. Worries over the MMR jab for children and other related issues – such as vaccination and Gulf War syndrome – have made people wary. However, we are looking at the problem from a very privileged position – one in which most cats are not suffering or dying from cat flu or enteritis because of vaccination that has already taken place. Vaccination is vital to the health of our cats, both individually and as a population. Just which vaccines a particular cat has and how often it has them should be looked at for that individual cat and discussed with the vet. Some indoor cats are very unlikely to even come into contact with certain diseases; others which go out are at much higher risk. Providing protection is vital to the health of our cats.

iii) Preventive care – worming and flea treatment

Treating our cats for fleas and worms is becoming easier and easier. Manufacturers are now producing formulations that are simple to administer. Gone are the sprays loathed by all cats, and even tablets (not easy to get into many cats) are being replaced by spot-on treatments that are simply put on to the skin at the back of the neck. Keeping cats parasite-free will help their overall health and well-being.

iv) Feeding

The choice of cat foods available today can be quite overwhelming. However, there are many very good-quality foods around and they provide a balanced healthy diet for our cats. We need not fiddle around with homemade diets, which can often be deficient in nutrients the cat needs unless owners are very careful about what they are doing. For cats that go outside, there is the opportunity to top up with small prey such as mice, or to nip around the corner and eat the food left out for a neighbouring cat. However, for the totally indoor cat this is not possible and it is therefore even more important for the owner to get the cat's diet right.

v) Good veterinary care

Veterinary care for cats is improving all the time. There are now vets who specialise in cat medicine and veterinary practices that are feline-only. Good care is available for cats and it is up to owners to find a feline-friendly practice near them. Referrals to specialists for difficult cases are also a possibility. As with any problem, early investigation and diagnosis should improve the chances of successful treatment.

FITNESS

Cats seem to stay quite fit without trying very hard. Even well into their teens, they can sleep for five or six hours and then get up, stretch and jump on to the wardrobe from a standing start – no warm-ups required. They maintain their suppleness well and don't seem to suffer from the same arthritic problems as dogs, or at least not as early in their lives as their canine cousins seem to.

One of the most common problems threatening our cat population today is the same as that for the human population – obesity. Cats are getting fatter. Historically, cats have been very good at maintaining their bodyweight within normal range for a fit and healthy animal, and they don't get fat very often. The level of calories we provide for cats in our homes can be controlled very easily – we open the packets or get the tin opener out; cats are clever, but they can't yet put the shopping away and fill their own bowls. Of course, they can, if allowed outdoors, visit the neighbour for a snack or catch their own. However, a cat going out to catch some dinner will be an active one and therefore much less likely to be suffering from a surfeit of calories.

Obese cats are usually middle-aged – the youngsters keep up an active lifestyle and very old cats tend to become thin rather than overweight. Middle-age spread on a cat tends to build up under the tummy in the area between the back legs and can hang rather like an apron or skirt. Some breeds, such as Burmese and Siamese, can look quite slim but have rather a large store of fat around their middle.

Lifestyle is also a factor. Cats with access outdoors and which enjoy hunting and patrolling the neighbourhood will be using up energy and keeping fit. Indoor-only cats may be more sedentary. The warmth, food and perhaps lack of stimulation are all a good recipe for more sleep and less exercise.

To summarise, we all want our cats to be happy and healthy. Sometimes steps to ensure this can be put into action relatively easily. We can ensure that our cats are vaccinated and have preventive health care, good food and prompt treatment if they become ill. In other cases, such as the question of company, we may impose our needs, wants or interpretations on the cat. On the issue of safety, we may want to rule out every possible risk, no matter how minor, which may lead to a very safe but very boring existence for our cats. We need to get the balance right.

12

Stress and health

IN PREVIOUS CHAPTERS, we have looked at what makes cats into the fabulous creatures they are; what they need and they want out of the relationship with us, and what we want from and for our cats. It wouldn't be surprising to discover that sometimes these desires and emotions do not always slot together smoothly. It would be pretty miraculous if everything worked perfectly in a relationship between two different species, especially if one of those species is emotional and demanding, needy and often irrational – and I'm not referring to the cats! What is perhaps even more unbelievable is that it works so well – in the majority of homes, cats and people live together very easily. This chapter focuses on those times when it doesn't work, when the cat is feeling under pressure – sometimes because of something directly attributable to its owner, sometimes not. Owners need to be able to pick up the clues to an unhappy cat or one which is not feeling comfortable about some aspect of its life. Humans also have control, at least physically, over many of the factors in the cat's environment and this can cause stress and conflict, albeit unintentionally.

Stress is a word that is used in a multitude of ways and, these days, in almost any situation. Stress can be a good thing and a bad thing – we need some stress in our lives so that we can learn to deal with challenging situations. Kittens kept in a boring and unchallenging environment will not learn how to investigate things, how to overcome fear or how to tackle problems, because they do not meet anything new. We think that it is vital for kittens to meet new people, smells, sights and sounds and experiences very early in life. This is sometimes termed 'stress immunisation'. Kittens learn which strategies work to cope with problems or new situations just as the immune system learns how to deal with a disease if it has had a chance to meet it before in a weaker form and has already created the antibodies to fight it – vaccination, in medical terms. When kittens are only a few weeks old, their curiosity is stronger than their fear. Protected by their mum, they learn how to investigate things and find out what they genuinely need to be fearful about. As they grow, curiosity is then replaced by fear as a first reaction. The cat that has not had these early learning experiences may not be able to deal with novelty when it presents itself – this can manifest itself in a permanently anxious cat.

In the broad sense, we blame stress for the way we feel when we have to deal with situations that make us uncomfortable, unable to cope or feel scared, uneasy or bad-tempered. And often, the finger is pointed at stress not just for the one-off situation that resolves itself quickly but for any ongoing, unrelenting things that mount up and up, making each small item into an issue and the cumulative total much greater than its components. Thus, a small thing that in itself is of little significance can push us over the edge.

Stress can be a great blame-all for just about every problem we suffer. However, it does allow us to express the way we feel when external factors and situations have an effect upon us.

Do animals feel stress? And, if so, how does that stress manifest itself? If our cats seem relaxed around us and do not display behavioural problems, can we assume they are content? We would like to think so. If they are exhibiting behavioural problems can we conclude that they are not happy with something in their environment and are feeling stressed? Not always – a cat that defecates outside its litter tray may not be feeling that it cannot cope – it may simply be that the litter tray has not been changed and it does not want to use such a dirty toilet. Thus, not every behaviour that is out of context can necessarily be thought of as a product of 'stress'. In this case, there would probably have been a small conflict within the cat's mind – not wanting to soil its den but not wishing to use the tray. The stress it felt was probably limited and in this case resolved fairly easily by going elsewhere.

This is a different scenario to the cat which begins to urinate or defecate in the house while it has a perfectly clean and well-positioned tray that contains litter that it likes – something else is going on here too. Conversely, the quiet cat may not be a happy cat. One behaviourist comments that cat behaviours are usually dominated by inhibition – they tend to shut down when they feel under pressure rather than become stimulated, aggressive or shout about the problem! They tend to sit quietly or are subdued or depressed – they will remove themselves from the situation if possible. Most cats seen by behaviourists are either spraying or messing in the house, scratching the furniture or, occasionally, are aggressive. It is suggested that this is only a small proportion of cats with problems and that we are missing the ones that are anxious or depressed because they tend not to cause any trouble.

However, as we learn about behaviour changes in different situations and ascertain the motivation for these changes, we do find that, limited as our knowledge of normal feline behaviour and of being able to 'read' our cats is, many behaviour changes do seem to follow changes to the cat's life that it has not welcomed.

We do know that most factors which cause cats to feel stress are actually associated with the cat's environment rather than its relationship with its owner. This second scenario is much more common in dogs where the human is part of the pack and the motivation is to remain part of the pack and to try and fit in with it – misunderstandings in the relationship in this case can provide a great deal of conflict for the dog and it will exhibit certain behaviours as a result. This is not to say that the cat/human relationship is not important – it is just that environment is probably more important; the cat functions more as a part of the environment than as part of a pack. Thus, the most common causes of stress are threats to security from animate or inanimate factors – for example, other cats, household changes (such as renovation) or changes in routine. In chapter ten, we saw that the most important factor for cats was security of their environment. The most common causes of stress for cats are those that threaten their resources, mainly the sanctity of their homes and their core territory, which many cats would want to have to themselves and to remain unchanged.

As with people, what causes stress in one cat may have little effect on another. The individual may suffer from excessive stress and react in some way. However, the meaning of 'excessive' varies from individual to individual and depends on several factors, such as how and when the cat met and dealt with stress as a kitten, how it learned to cope with it at the time, and the type and duration of the stressing factor it is now experiencing.

IMPROVING SECURITY WITH SCENTS

Behaviourally, cats cannot show their stress or emotions by using facial expressions or by getting cross or crying, as humans do. What cats may do first is to increase types of behaviour or activities that usually make them feel safe or secure. For example, some may try to leave more scent around from glands on the head and face, which make them feel secure. They may try to remove themselves from the situation – if there is a new cat in the house, they may stay outdoors more. If there is a despotic cat terrorising the neighbourhood outside, they may stay indoors much more, only popping out briefly from time to time when they have to or when they feel it may be safe.

If the situation does not change and the stressful factor does not go away they may increase their marking behaviours, which may be stepped up quite considerably. Instead of just using facial markers to rub and mark items in the house, they will start to scratch the furniture more in order to leave more of their own scent as reassurance. If this fails to resolve the problem, they may begin to spray indoors, leaving scent signals even we humans can pick up.

OVERATTACHED CATS

Anyone who has owned several cats (not necessarily at the same time) will have recognised that different cats have different needs when it comes to attention and interaction. If cats can move freely between home and neighbours and friends, they may solicit attention from anyone they can find. If, however, a very interactive type of cat is left alone at home for a very long day, it may focus all of its needs on to its owner when he or she is there. Such cats can become very clingy or overattached and move away from the 'normal' to very abnormal behaviours. Such cats may become anxious and withdrawn when away from their owners and never begin to relax or explore without the presence of their owners. When their owners are there, they demand constant attention. These cats may have strange sleep patterns when their owners are away and may groom excessively, licking and chewing or sucking at the hair and skin or even biting their nails. These are examples of 'displacement activities' – behaviours that are performed out of context by animals in what is known as a 'conflict' situation. It is thought that the animal is feeling emotionally tense or stressed and this activity helps to relieve it, if only temporarily.

RESCUED CATS

We are much more aware of the way we keep cats in the rescue situation now. Thankfully, there are far fewer people who simply cram their houses full of cats in an attempt to rescue them from the street. Frankly, the cats would be better off on the street. Not only are these cats at very high risk of catching or passing on all sorts of diseases, they will feel very stressed by a situation of having to be in such close proximity to such a large number of cats from which they cannot get away. While some cats will seem to be quite happy, others will be sitting quietly under a bed or hunched in a corner, trying to go unnoticed. These cats are highly stressed and become passive and depressed and may lose interest in everything going on around them. Of course, such cats will not be causing any trouble and will probably go unnoticed and so may well remain there for a long time.

Some work has been done looking at how cats in rescue react when housed in groups of four to seven cats. For the first few days, new cats try to escape or stare at the other cats, hissing and growling. After a week or so, they calm down and are less vocal. Researchers looked at some other ways of measuring stress other than just looking at how the cats were reacting. They realised that even when the cats seemed more relaxed they were still suffering from stress, but in a more passive and hidden manner. Over the next couple of weeks, the cats hid less but still avoided other cats when feeding. This should give us an insight into how cats feel when we bring a new cat into the household – especially if they cannot get away. It should also help us deal with cats in the very stressful situation of rescue – a period when a cat may be changing its environment several times in quick succession – what we can do to minimise the stress and help cats to settle in to whichever home they are in. In chapter thirteen, we look at some of the ways we can minimise this.

NERVOUS CATS

Earlier, we looked at what factors contribute to the personality of a cat. Kittens that are kept in isolation from an early age are often unable to cope with the activities of the normal world – they remain fearful and will avoid any situation that is not comfortable for them. If cats are continually faced with a stressful situation from which they cannot escape, they may even develop phobias or depression and become very unreactive, not eating or sleeping in normal patterns. These are extreme cases, but, in general, life is hard for the anxious cat and treatment can be very difficult – in this case, prevention really is much better and easier than cure. See chapter twelve for more on this.

AGGRESSION

Just like other animals, cats exhibit different types of aggression. While it may not matter to the person or cat on the receiving end just what type of aggression caused the attack or reaction, understanding the motivation and cause can be vital in trying to prevent it in the first place. We are happy to accept some forms of aggression in our cats: we don't mind if they chase other cats out of our garden; we understand a mother being defensive of new kittens; and we even understand that we may have had a hand in the problem when our cats grab us while we are tickling their tummies!

We know ourselves that if we are stressed we may become much more reactive to small things – we can be very bad-tempered if we feel that we cannot cope. Earlier, we looked at the idea of cats having a field of aggression, or aggressive field, that surrounds them. This field can be smaller than the cat itself, in which case the cat can be approached and fussed and will be quite happy. Or it can grow considerably if the cat is feeling under threat or unhappy so that anyone or any animal that comes within that zone is likely to be hissed at or scratched. This is an excellent way of thinking about cats and how quickly they can react if they feel threatened. If a cat is feeling agitated, it may well strike out at anything that comes near it – for this reason, it is very unwise to try and lift one of a pair of sparring cats out of the way – it may simply react and scratch or bite. Better to distract them both with noise or water and try to put some space between them.

One of the most common 'aggression' problems behaviourists are asked about is known as 'petting and biting' syndrome. The name describes the problem. Owners start to stroke their cat and it turns and grabs their hand, often holding with its front feet while kicking with the back ones. Cats vary in the degree of stroking or tickling required to elicit this response. Very reactive cats may react after merely having their head stroked for a short period – others are very laidback and can be tickled all over before they even think about getting upset. Some of the answer lies again with that old chestnut security. The cat has to trust you as it sits on your lap and relaxes. Accepting stroking is a learned response rather than a natural behaviour and cats are literally putting themselves in our hands. Some may not have had much handling as kittens. Feelings of pleasure and relaxation suddenly conflict with feelings of vulnerability and the cat snaps back to attention and reacts with defensive aggression, grabbing the hand that is stroking it.

Occasionally, cats go beyond reactive or defensive aggressive into proactive aggression. In such cases, owners remark that their cats attack them without provocation or prevent them from going to various places in the house – they may try to stop them from going upstairs, for example. Often these cats are kept permanently indoors. They watch birds or other cats in the garden and become excited. However, there is no means of getting rid of the pent-up energy or adrenaline and they become 'wound up'. Seeing a movement (for example, the owner walking past) may well trigger a reaction and the cat attacks. While some cats are happy with a completely indoor existence, others become very stressed – some people say it is caused by a 'profound lack of visual stimuli' – i.e. the highly movement-motivated cat is suffering from a lack of stimulation. Such cats may have mad dashes around the house with very high levels of activity (such as kittens exhibit) and may become aggressive to owners.

EATING AND STRESS

The use of eating behaviour as a stress indicator is shared happily by behaviourists and vets – changes in eating behaviour can indicate a disease; they can also indicate that a cat is not happy in some way. Normally cats enjoy a change in diet and will even eat a less palatable food just because it is different – they often return to the original food after a couple of meals of the new one. However, change a cat's environment and you will find that it prefers to stay with the original food – it feels more secure with something it knows.

New surroundings such as a new house or a visit to a cattery can reduce the amount the cat wants to eat, as can new people or new animals in the home.

If the cat needs a special diet to help it deal with a particular disease, the best idea is to introduce the change gradually while the cat still has access to its original diet (unless it is vital to change the diet immediately). In this way, the cat becomes familiar with the new diet – if it is not feeling well, it may have an even greater need for security and so will be loath to try something new.

Similarly, if the cat has to go somewhere else, for example to a boarding cattery, ensure that it is given a diet it knows – the familiarity of the food will lessen the stress felt at the change.

As we saw in chapter eleven, poisoning is rare in cats. With free access outdoors they seldom, if ever, sample poisonous plants and we do not need to worry what we grow in our gardens from a feline point of view – especially as cats wander to other gardens anyway and we have no control over what other people grow. However, cats that are confined indoors or in a pen are much more likely to sample vegetation that they would not normally touch. This may be because they have a need for some plants in terms of self-medication but these are not available in this indoor situation or are limited in a run. Boredom may also be a factor that turns their attention to the plants they would normally ignore. Whatever the reason, it is another consideration that owners of indoor cats must consider – remove anything dangerous and ensure that cats have access to grass or herbs that they can chew safely.

Some cats exhibit what is called pica – the eating of non-nutritional items – for example, some have a strange need to eat woollen garments. This trait was first documented in the 1950s and seems to be found mostly in Siamese and Burmese cats. Research revealed that most cats began by eating wool but then progressed to other fabrics too – some even had a taste for electric cables. Some ate or chewed material regularly, others randomly. They selected jumpers, towels, woollen furniture (including tweed settees!) or underwear. Most did not come to any harm, but some needed surgery when the 'food' became an obstruction in their digestive system.

While it is always important to have the cat checked in case there is a medical cause for the problem, it is thought that eating unusual items such as wool or cotton can be a disorder of the cat's natural hunting behaviour, which is to stalk, pounce, tear off feathers, fur and skin, and eat the prey. Not only do skin and feathers pass through the cat's stomach, but also the cat has an instinct to do the tearing and plucking before swallowing.

Some pet cats become compulsive about this part of the predatory sequence – tearing off feathers and skin bit by bit and swallowing it all. Eating ordinary cat food gives these cats no opportunity to tear and rip, so the cat looks for this somewhere else. Cats will tear and rip and then eat the wool, fabric or whatever they have chosen as their 'prey'.

Wool eaters are often pedigree breeds kept indoors without access to prey, although not always. In the past, experts suggested feeding high-fibre food, gristly meat and making mealtimes more frequent in the hope that this would make the cats feel that their stomach was full. It would also give them lots of opportunity to chew. Now they suggest supplying something closer to nature – something for cats to tear and shred such as dead whole turkey chicks, day-old chicks or dead whole rats and mice sold frozen by pet shops for reptiles. Other food supplies can be given in the form of dry pellets contained within a toy – the cats have to move the toy around to release the food – again, this gives them something to do and simulates a kind of hunt for their food. More hunting play is also suggested, giving the cat a chance to play out all those hunting expeditions it would be undertaking if it was in the wild.

NIGHT CALLING

In the past ten years, an interesting phenomenon has come to light in older cats. Owners find that their cat (usually more than fourteen years old) starts to call out at night when the household is fast asleep. They leap out of bed to see if the cat is all right. The cat has a quick cuddle and is checked over and then happily goes back to sleep. At first, owners are fearful something is dreadfully wrong with their cats; however, after having them checked over by the vet and the cat seeming fine in the daytime, they begin to get a little less alarmed by what soon becomes regular night-time calling. We think that older cats are feeling less secure and more dependent on their owners for that security – in the night, when alone, they suddenly feel the need for some reassurance. Owners usually oblige when the call goes out. However, it can get very tiring! The cat feels less stressed about life but owners start to feel as if they have a baby in the house that needs regular feeding!

This is one of the ways in which our cats do actually come to us for help when they feel anxious – many times they do not, or cannot, and so we have to be able to spot the problems ourselves.

HEALTH AND STRESS

Until very recently how we looked at our animals was divided very crisply between physical health and illness, and acceptable and 'problem' behaviours. Illness was considered purely in veterinary terms and treated medically or surgically, while bad behaviour was countered by punishment. However, over the past twenty years, and especially during the last ten years, we have become aware of the motivations for 'problem' behaviours and at the same time have begun to notice the overlap between both the physical and psychological health of the animal.

Vets and behaviourists are moving closer together in their fields of work and realising that some medical problems should be interpreted in the light of the cat's interaction with its life and its lifestyle. Once ignored by the veterinary profession, it is now accepted that stress can have major effects on the health of our pets as well as on their behaviour. The effects of psychological stress are now the subject of great interest in both animals and people – often in relation to how it affects the immune system.

Stress can come in many forms – it can be sudden and short-lived or it can be a long-standing problem. How this impacts on the animals varies from individual to individual. It is a very complex subject, but one that has raised enough interest for people to start looking for answers.

We have been aware of the detrimental effects of stress on the immune function in animals we farm (especially those we keep in high densities) and how this can impact on production. The central nervous system and the immune system communicate with each other. It may be that stress factors cause immune cells to be redistributed in some organs (for example, the skin, the digestive tract or the bladder) and affect them in the same way. These changes start to explain some of the veterinary problems we feel may be stress related in our pets.

HIGH BLOOD PRESSURE

Some stress-related problems in cats closely resemble diseases in humans. For example, did you know that cats can suffer from high blood pressure? This hypertension, as it is known, can cause or exacerbate illness in cats as it does in people. It can result in heart problems and even blindness because of damage to the eye. One scientific paper written about blood pressure in cats was entitled 'Evaluation of white-coat effect in cats' (Belew and others, *Journal of Veterinary Internal Medicine*, 1999). White-coat effect is an accepted finding in people – in 1940, it was recognised that blood pressure and heart rate measured in a clinical setting were higher than if the readings were taken at home. This is thought to be a defence reaction in response to the stress associated with the clinical setting. Researchers measured the blood pressure of cats in a clinical environment (such as a veterinary surgery) and found that the same thing happened – the cats' blood pressure rose. Thus, for a veterinary surgeon who is trying to get a blood pressure reading from a cat it is advised that a quiet, undisturbed environment is the setting – the cat is given time to get used to its surroundings – and that several readings are taken.

To summarise, we now believe that cats probably experience the same feeling of fear and tension in a hospital or veterinary surgery that humans do, and that this can result in increased blood pressure in both species.

LOWER URINARY TRACT DISEASE

Current studies are examining a problem called feline lower urinary tract disease (FLUTD), some of which is what we would equate to cystitis in humans (more often women). FLUTD is seen quite commonly in veterinary practice – cats often strain to urinate, may urinate in strange places (for example, outside the litter tray) and may have blood in their urine. Occasionally, there is complete obstruction of urination and this can be a life-threatening condition.

Anyone who has suffered from cystitis knows what an uncomfortable problem it is – in people it causes pain during urination and a feeling of constantly needing to urinate. Cats often urinate outside the litter tray – perhaps the urge to pass urine was just too great to give the cat time to get to the tray. Perhaps cats are suffering from similar types of symptoms to people. Often no cause for the disease can be found in cats – in fact, in about two-thirds of cases there is no apparent cause. The same thing has been noted in some women, and is referred to as interstitial cystitis. It has been suggested that stress and psychological factors are among what is know as the 'flare factors' for the problem – i.e. they seem to make it worse or even cause it. One theory is that stress causes changes in the nervous system which releases neurotransmitters that can act to cause, or exacerbate, local pain and inflammation. The same may well happen in cats. A thick layer of mucus lines the bladder and protects it from bacteria and from damage from crystals in the urine. Cats with feline idiopathic cystitis (cystitis of unknown cause) have been found to have lower levels of this protective layer. While it is not known whether this defect caused the inflammation in the first place, its presence is thought to make it worse.

A recent study suggests that there are a number of factors that may be 'flare factors' in cats, the most significant of which is conflict with another cat in the house. Others have included abrupt changes in diet, environment, weather, overcrowding, owner stress or the addition to the household of new pets or people. Stress associated with urination is particularly important and may have a number of causes – for example, the cat may not like the type of litter or the position of the litter tray because it makes it feel vulnerable or exposed; it may face competition for the litter tray from other cats or experience aggressive behaviour from other cats while on the tray or urinating outside.

Another study, in New Zealand, looked at the elements that seem to influence the development of FLUTD. Being overweight and inactive were common factors. It is thought that such cats sit around more and do not empty their bladder as often as perhaps they should – the urine becomes very concentrated (a process cats are very good at anyway) and it can provide an excellent environment for the growth of crystals within the urine or for concentration of infection or other factors within the bladder that might affect its function. In addition, many cats with this problem came from multi-cat households – could this be the stressor (the problem causing the stress)? Moving house was another common factor – again, a stressor. Interestingly, winter and the weather was also found to have an effect – cats didn't want to go out in the cold or rainy days, and so urinated less.

GLUCOSE LEVELS

Cats also suffer from what is known as 'stress hyperglycaemia' – an increase in the glucose in the blood caused by stress. This can be a problem for veterinary surgeons trying to ascertain whether a cat has diabetes or not – simply taking one sample that shows elevated levels of glucose will not be enough to make a diagnosis – the cat may merely have been stressed by the procedure and by simply being in the veterinary surgery. Interestingly, vets have found that it is not easy to tell which these cats are by just looking at them. Some cats, which are very stressed and almost have to be taken off the ceiling, will have normal glucose levels in the blood; others, which appear calm, can develop severe hyperglycaemia. As usual, the cat makes it very difficult to judge its behaviour and there is wide variation between individuals.

SKIN PROBLEMS

Some cats suffer from skin problems such as overgrooming and an acute sensitivity of the skin. Cats with this hypersensitivity may bite or lick at themselves, the skin can twitch or even ripple and the cats may jump up and run as if stung and seem very agitated. Cats may also become aggressive, perhaps because they are constantly aggravated by their skin and may not be resting or sleeping properly. While there can be simple causes for itchiness or sensitivity, such as allergy to fleas or other types of skin problem, for some of these cats no cause can be found. Cats that overgroom can 'self-barber' (an excellent term noted in an American publication) by breaking off hairs or even pulling them out. They may have bald patches where they have removed all the hair and the pattern of the baldness may be symmetrical as the cat grooms each side excessively to the same extent. This can be very extensive and may affect the whole stomach, the cat's sides or flanks and its back, or may occur just along the outside of the thighs and the stomach. Researchers have suggested that there is a change in the nervous system in these cats and that the nerves in the skin may be stimulated and thus cause this very sensitive reaction – it is thought that this can be exacerbated by stress. Interestingly, a few cats also nail bite, splitting and breaking the nails.

Many researchers have examined 'psychogenic alopecia' (behaviourally induced hair loss) and investigated a large number of cases in great detail. In most cases, they found that there was a medical cause, such as allergy to fleas, for the hair problems. They concluded that it was actually quite a rare problem and should be kept in proportion and investigated fully before rating it as purely behavioural.

IMMUNE CHANGES

It may be that in many of these cases, the body reacts to stress by producing a change in the immune system – perhaps in anticipation of an injury so that the body is ready to react if a problem occurs. However, if the stressor does not go away and the cat is subjected to constant levels of stress, the body continues in this mode. A free-living or feral cat may be able to resolve this by removing itself from the situation – be it another cat, changes to its environment, lack of stimulation and boredom or another reason. Cats that live with us may not be able to do so quite so easily. Those cats that have access to the outdoors may remove themselves to the garden for quite long periods when a new cat is introduced and gradually get to know and (hopefully) accept it. For cats that cannot go out or have nowhere within a house to retreat to, the stress continues. Likewise a cat that is suffering from overattachment cannot resolve the problem if it has no access to company.

The study of how stress affects our pets is a relatively new area. We know it affects behaviour and now are beginning to be able to pinpoint some of its effects on health. The above examples may be joined by many more as our knowledge improves. Measuring stress is not straightforward – there are biochemical parameters we can measure but none gives a direct answer – we must combine all the methods we can to pick up the clues as to how our cats are feeling and to help them if they are suffering. This should become a joining of veterinary and behavioural studies, as both disciplines can feed into and learn from the accumulated knowledge, applying it to help cats recover physically as well as mentally. Pet owners too can pick up the signals if they know what to look for and what to avoid.

13

Getting the balance right

IN THE PREVIOUS chapter, we looked at some of the problems that cats have which we feel may be associated with stress or conflict. Conflict in this sense means conflict within the cat rather than between cats, although aggression between cats can indeed be one of the major causes of stress.

The aim of this chapter is to look at ways in which we can understand and minimise the stress some cats may be experiencing. As explained before, the majority of cats are probably very happy and relaxed in their households. However, some trends of ownership are pushing them into situations in which some cats will not be happy.

UNDERSTANDING AND RESPECT

The first thing we can do is to understand and respect the cat for the animal that it is, not what we want it to be. In chapters three, four and five, I have tried to explain how the natural cat behaves.

Of course, cats have lived closely with mankind for thousands of years and in some senses it is difficult to remove humans from the equation; however, given minimal human input, cats choose to behave in a certain way and we must be aware of this. The cat is a finely honed hunter and has many innate behaviours connected with this primary activity. We must not deny this aspect of our cats – the way they look and act is a function of this hunting ability.

The cat has already shown how adaptable it can be. It lives in regions that vary from sub-Antarctic islands to deserts, from desolate regions to dense cities. It can live alongside us with very little human input or in an intensely one-to-one relationship with its owner. There is no doubt our lifestyles have changed, and our cats' lives have changed along with our own. The reality of today's society is that we live much faster and have greater expectations of what we can do and how we can control our environment, including our pets. Pressure is on us to earn more money to pay bigger mortgages and to have possessions and services that go with a certain standard of living. This means all the adults in the household have to work and must have more control over their lives in order to keep abreast of everything that is going on. The ever-adaptable cat fits in well with this but we are in danger of forgetting it is an animal, with special needs that are not swayed by the pressures we have on us. Not only do we forget it is an animal, we do not even realise just what a fantastic animal it is.

Perhaps as recently as ten years ago, people would have been very amused to hear of a cat with 'behavioural problems' – cats simply weren't considered in this way. Now we accept that our pet felines do indeed sometimes exhibit behaviours that we do not find acceptable in our homes. We now have enough knowledge to try to tackle them and to ascertain just what it is that is causing our cats to behave in this uncharacteristic way.

The kinds of behaviours we are considering are spraying and marking in the household, aggression between cats and towards people, overgrooming, nervousness and depression. There may not be only one cause of the problem and for some cats a certain lifestyle just doesn't suit their personality. Whereas one cat may be happy jostling for position in a house full of other felines, another will spend its life hiding in the corner; while one cat may be happy to laze away its days in the comforts of a permanently indoor environment, another may go crazy trying to get outside. There are not hard and fast rules, just ideas on how to pick up that there is a problem and perhaps how to overcome it.

CHOOSING THE RIGHT CAT

One of the first areas to look at is how we choose our cats, how we socialise them and how we expect them to fit in with our lives.

As outlined earlier, most of us choose a cat or kitten because of its coat pattern, a preference that is often influenced by a cat we had as children or one which friends had. We may also be influenced by the media – currently both silver tabbies and Bengals, both of which have spectacularly beautifully marked coats, are used in a variety of advertisements and their popularity is growing rapidly. The rise of the popularity of the Persian may have had something to do with a certain carpet advertisement that featured a glamorous and elegant white fluffy feline lying gracefully on said carpet to suggest luxury and softness. Anyone who thinks they might like a cat will be tempted by these images of beauty. Not that there is anything wrong with wanting a beautiful cat (or perhaps we should say a *more* beautiful cat). However, this popularity brings with it an increasing demand on breeders to produce kittens and there will always be unscrupulous people ready to take advantage of a demand in order to make money. There are excellent breeders of cats, but there are also awful ones, and the average person who has never bought a pedigree kitten can easily be persuaded to take a kitten that may not be well or may not have been socialised properly because it was mass-produced and did not have the time and attention required to ensure its health both physically and psychologically. Both of these scenarios can produce cats that are not confident with life and for which living in a busy world can be very stressful.

Kittens need to meet novel situations, people and objects when they are very small – between three and seven weeks old. If they are mass-produced in a situation where they are kept in an unstimulating environment at this time, such as a garden shed or even purpose-built accommodation, they are unlikely to have met everyday situations during this period. If a breeder has several litters of kittens at a time kept outside and is also working, he or she may not have the time (or the knowledge or expertise) to understand the effort that is required to ensure that kittens are well-balanced and confident with life. Nervous kittens will not make good pets.

Most people want a cat that is friendly, confident and joins in with the family and other pets, if they have them. Here are some ways to avoid the pitfalls.

BUYING A PEDIGREE CAT

Do your homework. Find out about the breed you want and whether the general characteristic and behaviours it is said to have will suit your lifestyle.

If you do not have time to groom a cat every day, do not consider getting a Persian (categorised as a longhair); you may not even want to consider a semi-longhair (for example, a Birman or a Maine Coon), which will still need some grooming. A Persian will not be able to look after its coat on its own – it will need you to help. In order to do this, you will need to start grooming the kitten every day as soon as you get it – even if its coat is not yet very long. In this way, the cat gets used to it and accepts it as a normal way of life. You will have to learn how to do it and what equipment is necessary. A good breeder will help you and give you advice on what is appropriate – find out first.

If you want your cat to be independent and not live in your pocket, perhaps you should not be considering the more interactive breeds such as the Siamese or Burmese or the Rexes. These will demand attention, are likely to be quite noisy and may get bored if you do not provide stimulation for them – these are not low-maintenance cats either. However, if you do want something interactive and even quite dog-like then they may be for you. If you do not want an active outdoor cat, the breeds such as Maine Coons may be best avoided.

Ask the breeder about the breed, but try to do your own independent research too. Some breeders will be very honest about their breed and the particular characteristics of the cats they breed. They will not want to sell to you if they do not feel you and the cat will fit well together. Others may just want to sell a kitten, not minding to whom and to what circumstances it goes. On the other hand, some breeders are very prescriptive and may not sell a kitten to a home where it would be allowed outside or are very dogmatic about the diet the cat should have. If you have not found out anything for yourself, you will not know which of these scenarios you may be in! One way to do this is to go to a local or national cat show and talk to the breeders and other owners there – get a broad view from a number of people. It will probably become evident who is being sensible and who might be able to point you in the right direction. You can also see the cats in real life and find out the characteristics of the breed.

Anyone can become a 'breeder', you just need to be able to put two cats together at the appropriate time. The good ones know a great deal about the health and behaviour of cats and can pass good information on to you.

Likewise, be careful about health. Good breeders will ensure the kittens are healthy and have been vaccinated before you can take them home. They will be around thirteen weeks old by this time. Check for yourself too. Don't take on a kitten that has a runny nose or runny eyes or an upset stomach. Do not be taken in by stories of kittens scratching each other in the eye (hence the runny eye) or feel sorry for the kitten. If you are happy to take the risk that the kitten is not very healthy and accept the subsequent veterinary bills (and probably some heartache), then go in with your eyes open; some people just cannot resist taking a poorly kitten home to get it out of bad circumstances or because they feel sorry for it.

When you do go to visit the breeder, look at the health of all the cats there. If there are lots of cats and kittens everywhere and the place is not pleasant to be in or smells unpleasant, then there is a strong chance that the hygiene is not good and disease may be rife. It is best to keep cat numbers down to ensure that they can be managed and socialised properly and that disease risk is kept to a minimum. Be prepared to leave without a kitten before you go – most of us (and I am equally guilty on this, having done it once myself) want to go home with a kitten. We do not want to wait another day; however, we may take on one which is not healthy, will cost a lot to put right, will cause heartache, may never be a confident pet or may bring home disease to our other cats.

Sometimes it may just be that the cat stays nervous and never makes the kind of pet we want. This kind of cat is often the one which objects very strongly to us getting another feline and so we are left with one cat for the next fourteen years, which is not really what we wanted.

Another factor in getting a very attractive pedigree cat is that people worry that if it goes out it will be cat-napped or stolen. For this reason, they keep it in indoors. If they had chosen a moggie, this fear would not have been a factor and they would have let it go outside. In this case, it is time to think about the cat's feelings. Moggies are just as beautiful and graceful as pedigrees. Why not get a moggie that you are happy to allow have a rich and varied lifestyle and which you can enjoy without the worry?

TAKING ON A MOGGIE

Moggies come from various different backgrounds – often from 'accidental litters' produced because people have just not got around to neutering their kitten or from rescue centres. Again, there are some basic guidelines.

A cat from a rescue centre is indeed in great need of a home. But be careful about the type of environment you get it from. Like breeders, rescues. can vary dramatically in their quality. The good ones keep cats in separate pens with runs in a clean and friendly environment. They will be organised and the hygiene will be excellent. The bad ones will have rooms full of cats all lumped in together and will be disorganised and very unhygienic. Just because the people who run rescues have their hearts in the right place and like cats does not mean that they are doing a good job. As with anything, knowing how to do something well takes knowledge and experience. Managing a large number of animals successfully to keep them in a happy and healthy state actually takes great organisation and discipline – just liking cats and wanting to do good is not enough. Again, choosing the wrong source for your kitten could mean you end up with one that is not healthy.

Just as breeders need to spend time socialising their kittens and getting them used to 'real life', so do rescue facilities. It may be more difficult to let kittens learn about life in a rescue because they are confined to a pen – rescuers will have to work extra hard and spend plenty of time handling the kittens and introducing new toys and situations.

Sometimes the kitten from the 'accidental' litter is the best bet of all for getting a well-rounded and confident cat. Often the mother cat has the kittens in the house in the midst of various adults and children, dogs and other creatures. The kittens sample lots of different people and all the everyday goings on, such as vacuuming and cleaning, televisions and doorbells, noise and activity. They will go to their new homes thinking all of this is perfectly normal and will be able to cope with just about any situation that is thrown at them.

MATCH YOUR NEEDS

Whether you are going for a pedigree or a moggie kitten, it may be very useful to match your needs to that of the source of the kitten. If you have dogs or children, try to find a source where these are already part of the kitten's life. If you have a noisy and active household, try to find a kitten that is used to this already and will simply slot in without being scared to death by a lifestyle so completely different to the one it has so far experienced. Ask about handling and where the kittens are kept – do they see people? Ask about the mother and if you can see her for yourself – a confident mother who is happy with people will be passing similar messages on to her offspring.

PROVIDE SOME CONSISTENCY TO THE CHANGEOVER

Going to a new home is a huge change for a kitten – it leaves its mother and the only place it has known and enters a new world that smells, looks and sounds very strange. Within this context try to minimise the stress of all the 'newness' by (initially anyway) sticking to the same food and litter that the kitten has been used to. Bring a blanket or old T-shirt or piece of bedding from the original home so that the kitten has something that smells familiar. Put this in the kitten's bed for reassurance.

HOW CAN ALL OF THIS HELP?

In many cases of behavioural problems, prevention would have been a lot less painful than cure. Indeed, in some cases, it may prove impossible to overcome the inadequacies of the kitten's first two months of life. For example, a very nervous cat may never enjoy being in the company of more than its owner and even this confidence may take many years to build up. It must be very stressful to live a life frightened of every movement or sound going on around you. It is not very rewarding for most owners either.

If you can match your new kitten to your household needs then you stand a much better chance of getting a cat or kitten that will be happy there. If it is healthy from day one, that can only be good too. Don't underestimate how much hair is shed by a longhaired or semi-longhaired cat – if you are house-proud it will bring more work and perhaps some aggravation. If so, perhaps a shorthaired cat would be better for you.

Another scenario where some forward thinking will help is where the cat is going to be an indoor cat – it will not have access to the outdoors for various reasons that have been outlined earlier. In this case, owners often feel very guilty that their cat is getting bored or lonely if they go out. However, introducing a new cat to an indoor-only cat can be difficult and owners don't want to risk upsetting the cat too. The answer is to get two kittens to begin with. Litter mates usually get on well – they have formed attachments during their early sensitive period and are more likely to get on than kittens that are not related or adult cats brought together.

GETTING ANOTHER CAT

As I have been at pains to point out, the cat comes from a solitary-living ancestor but it can be sociable if it wants to and if the circumstances are right. Cats too are very individual characters – what suits one may not suit another.

Cat lovers enjoy their cats and they often want to have more than one. In terms of time, space or energy, having two cats makes very little difference to having one – the cost of food and veterinary treatment will be doubled but that may not be a problem. How will you know if your cat would like a friend? You may not. Your cat may have lived with another cat but that does not guarantee that it will get on with another cat you bring home. There is not really anything to do but try. The important thing to realise is that you are getting another cat for you and not necessarily for the good of your resident cat. It is very likely to be happy with the single cat arrangement as it is!

However, if you do want to go ahead, then again planning is important. What age or sex should you get? How should you introduce the two cats to each other? These factors will all have a part to play in the successful integration of the new cat.

When it comes to the age of the new cat you are getting, it is probably true to say it is easier to introduce a kitten than it is to introduce a new adult cat to a household. Kittens pose less of a threat and are much less reactive themselves, responding with play rather than by becoming aggressive in the presence of the resident cat – thus, they do not escalate the tension by adding to it. They are not mature and do not pose such a threat initially.

Which sex of kitten to choose is also an interesting question. Anecdotally, it seems that female cats are much more defensive of their territory than neutered males. This would be understandable in the context of wanting to have a safe core area for the bringing up of kittens. Just because cats are neutered does not mean that they lose this instinct – neutered females are in the same hormonal state as females that are not in season; they may thus still behave in a similar fashion. Neutered males seem to be more open to letting other cats into the household – they are in a different hormonal state to the entire male and perhaps do not feel the need to be so defensive about the area. That said, they are territorial animals and will not take kindly to a new cat in the area, initially anyway. If the resident cat is female, it may make sense to get a male kitten – remember the feral cat scenario in which female cats chased away other females pretty fiercely whereas they let males come and go. Neutered males may be happy (eventually) to accept either sex – individual characters excepted, of course!

MAKING INTRODUCTIONS

Just how you introduce a new cat to the household can also make a difference to the levels of stress. You can do quite a lot to ease the new cat in. This is where it is important to remember what is important to cats – security of their core territory from the presence and smells of other cats. Getting a new cat will violate this quite considerably!

First of all, choose a quiet time – not Christmas or when you have a houseful of guests or visiting children. Have everything ready for the new cat so you can work smoothly and quietly. Whether you are introducing an adult cat or a kitten, the principles are the same.

The first thing to try to sort out is the scent problem. It would be better if, when your resident cat first sees the newcomer, its scent is already familiar. Thus, while it might be tempting to just bring the new one in and 'let them sort themselves out', this can lead to chases and aggression and a situation that is very difficult indeed to resolve. Bring the new cat into the house and put it in a separate room. Settle it down with something that smells familiar to it, and give it a tray and food. If it seems to want cuddles and attention, then give some; if it needs a little time to explore and relax, leave it for a while. When you return to it, bring food or a tidbit so that your presence is associated with something good. Stroke the cat and then go and stroke the resident cat, beginning to mix their scents. Wipe the new cat with a soft cloth, especially around the head area where the glands that produce pheromones are situated. Dab this around the house – you will not be able to see or smell anything and may feel a little ridiculous – however, watch the resident cat take note of the smells and you will be reassured you are doing something useful. Stroke your resident cat and mix that scent by stroking the new one. In this way, you start to integrate the smell of the resident cat and the house on to the new cat and vice versa. You can swap the cats around so that they get to smell the parts of the house that the other one was in. However, don't let them meet for about a week. By this time, the new cat will feel a bit more 'at home' and the resident will have become familiar with the new smells; indeed, it will be smelling of the new cat itself.

However, it is still not time to 'let them sort themselves out'. The best approach to letting cats see each other while preventing any type of bust-up is by using a kittening pen or dog crate. Dog crates are often used in the back of cars to keep dogs where they are supposed to be. Kittening pens are about the same size and often used by breeders to house cats with kittens within the home. It provides a den and enables them to keep the cat and kittens safe. These pens are usually made out of metal or plastic-coated metal and are about 1m high by 0.75m deep by 1m wide. The door can be open or shut securely. It provides ample space to provide a bed (a cardboard box with a cosy blanket or an igloo type of bed will give the cat a feeling of safety rather than being exposed) as well as a litter tray. You can put a blanket over the top to increase the feeling of security if you need to – depending very much on the cat or kitten. Use this to provide the new cat or kitten with a den as soon as you get it. After a week or so, you can move the pen to the kitchen or another room more in the hub of the house. The new cat will be familiar with the pen and will then have to get used to the new position. This is when you can start to let the cats see each other. Within the pen, the new cat is protected and secure. There will probably be a certain amount of hissing and growling and the resident cat may simply run outside. However, it will return (especially if you tempt it with some favourite food). The cats can watch each other and can even sleep in the same room (one in the pen) and so get used to each other. Obviously, you can let the new cat out when the resident is outside or shut in a different room. When you think they are tolerating each other quite well, you can open the cage and let the new cat out. Leave the cage there as a refuge. In fact, if you have a new kitten, the cage is excellent for allowing you to go out and know that it is safely shut inside with food and a litter tray rather than getting itself in trouble in the house (kittens are notorious for finding some way of getting stuck on or in something). Most cats are very happy inside for periods of time.

The cage is also an excellent way to coax nervous cats to integrate into the household. The pen can be placed in a room where it is relatively quiet but where there is some activity and the cat has to watch proceedings while still feeling safe inside. Very nervous cats would have run off and hidden under the bed just in case there was life-threatening danger (if you are a nervous animal, everything is life threatening). From under there, they never learn that in fact there is no danger and it is actually quite nice being able to observe what is going on and get choice morsels of food from your owner for just sitting there! Once the cat seems more relaxed with this room, you can move it to a place of greater activity so that it can get used to that too. The pen can eventually be opened and the cat can go in and out as it pleases. The pen can be used to introduce dogs too – it ensures safety but allows meetings.

If you can't get hold of a pen or crate, then you can use a cat carrier or basket for initial introductions. Obviously, you can't use it as a den or base because it is too small – however, it does allow the cats to meet in safety. Place the new cat or kitten in the carrier and place it on a coffee table or a chair. In this way, the cats are not on the same eye-level and it is harder for them to make aggressive eye contact. Let the resident cat come in and praise both cats and reward them with food (they may not be interested initially) – you want them to associate each other with good things, not shouting or telling off or a chase or fight. You can feed the cats in the same room and move them gradually closer together, again getting them used to each other's calm company.

When you feel that it is time to let them out together, then withhold food so that both cats are hungry. Choose a room where there are plenty of hiding places and high shelves or furniture that the cats might use to get off the ground. Put the cat's food down and let the new cat out – don't try and get them too close initially. Keep a watchful eye – they are likely to try to hide from each other at first. You can then gradually let them into the rest of the house when you feel the time is right.

This all sounds very easy. However, few cats will simply then curl up with each other and become bosom buddies. Most will take weeks or months (and even sometimes years) to relax with each other. It is usually easier with kittens and they may become quite close; however, bringing in a new adult cat will probably be more difficult and the best you may be able to hope for is that they tolerate each other in the same room. Every cat is different and the way it reacts will depend on its personality and previous experiences of mixing with other cats – it will also, of course, depend on the new cat. If it is fairly quiet and lives alongside the original pet in a peaceful manner, then things will probably settle easily. If it is a bully or a cat that itself does not want to share a feline home, then it may be more difficult, both for the resident cat and for you!

TOO MANY CATS?

Adding cats to a household can be very easy – for people, that is. It may not be so straightforward from the cat's point of view. They all look great draped over the furniture; you love them all individually and you can cram quite a few into an average house. Collecting cats can become addictive. In chapter twelve, we saw how cats that are stressed will often internalise their problems – they will go quiet; they will huddle away; they will stay outside or remain hidden under the bed. You can get away with putting quite a lot of stress on some cats before you get any visible signs or reactions. Of course, some people seem to be able to keep about ten cats together without any of them seeming to be the least concerned. However, for the rest of us mere mortals, it is often a mistake to keep more than three cats. At this level, something almost inevitably grates on one of them and you may get behavioural problems. I am not basing this statement on research findings – it is borne of listening to problems and talking to owners over many years. Know when you have enough and don't upset the apple cart if the situation is happy already! Most behaviourists only keep one or two cats.

And it is not just in our homes that large densities of cats can cause a problem – some urban areas have huge numbers of cats living very close together. This too can cause problems for cats.

INDOOR-ONLY CATS

Throughout this book, I refer to indoor cats and by these I mean cats that are not allowed outside at all. Their owners may keep them inside because they live close to a road or in an area where it is dangerous for cats to go out. Sometimes owners just want to keep their cats safe from all danger and keep them in despite living in a relatively safe place. Safety is one of the things we want for our cats and it may be the cause of some problems because the cats themselves do not appreciate the limitations it places upon them. Of course, if you want to have an indoor cat, you cannot simply take one that is used to going out and keep it in. Most cats will be very upset by this and will spend a great deal of time trying to escape from the household; they may develop behavioural problems because they feel frustrated at being confined.

Living in the middle of nowhere in the countryside, I am in a privileged position to talk about how cats are kept. My own cats can roam with relative safety and there are few other cats in the vicinity. I realise I am lucky to be able to do this. I have lost cats because they have been run over or through unforeseen accidents, but I feel that the quality and richness of their outdoor lives is a match for the risks. As I watch my cats in the garden and going about their very independent lives, I have no regrets. I also have lots of open windows and children who would never remember to keep doors closed – to have to keep on telling the children to shut them would introduce another stress factor for the whole family!

Many people who keep cats indoors will say their pets are perfectly happy. They may be so – cats vary hugely in their personalities and some may not even want to go out. Nervous cats especially may choose to stay indoors rather than face the threats they perceive to be outdoors – they make excellent indoor cats. Other cats are just naturally going to want more and these are the ones to worry about. Owners can do a great deal to keep their indoor cats stimulated. Remember that cats typically eat between seven and twenty small snacks a day. If they were not fed by people they would have to catch all of these. Researchers say that only one in fifteen hunting episodes is successful, so to catch even ten small meals a cat will have to try 150 times – that means a lot of activity. Hunting behaviour can be driven by hunger but it can also be carried out independently: cats almost automatically react to movement or sound as their instincts drive them to keep hunting. This is a lot of activity to miss out on for the indoor cat, especially at the young stage of around one year old. Cats with access to the outdoors and which hunt will be pretty prolific at this age and up until about three years old, when hunting activities seem to tail off a little (although some cats keep going at a higher level throughout their lives). The young indoor cat may become bored or frustrated if its owners are not giving it a level of play or mock hunting to satisfy this outlet of energy. We all know that our dogs need to be walked in order to exercise them and let them enjoy running free and investigating smells. If we do not, we know that they will have lots of pent-up energy and may become destructive or even aggressive because they have not worked off the need to do something. Likewise, teachers know that, if young children have to be kept in the classroom over lunch or breaktime because it is raining, they may be more fidgety in the afternoon. Many of them need to go out and run about to move around and burn up some energy. We do not seem to think the same way about our cats. Because they tend to lie around and sleep when they are indoors, we think that they are happy doing this. They probably are if they have spent several hours patrolling the garden or hunting. Cats need stimulation and exercise too.

Owners of indoor cats (especially young ones) need to be playing with them a great deal (remember: 150 hunting trips!) and providing new things for them to climb into and on to and investigate. There is probably a case for environmental enrichment, as is provided for animals in zoos – letting the cats find their food hidden around the house, for example. In this way, their minds are kept active and they get to 'hunt' for their food. Indeed, some breeders have been providing large exercise wheels for their cats – along the lines of those used by hamsters.

Apparently, the cats love them – it certainly gives them a chance to burn off some energy.

Some very active and sociable cats such as Siamese can become very attached, indeed overattached, to their owners in these circumstances. They sleep when their owner is not around, and when they are present they become very demanding and very dependent upon them. Some people like this intensity of relationship and if the owner has nothing else to do then perhaps it is quite mutually rewarding. However, if the owner has other things to do, such as work or the enjoyment of a social life, the cat can become very upset when he or she is not there. When the owner is there, the cat is totally demanding – as one friend put it, 'The cat does not have an alternative life of its own, so it takes over the owner's.' These cats may start to undertake displacement activities in an attempt to calm themselves when the owner is away – a common activity in these circumstances is overgrooming. At first, the cat grooms as a normal part of its everyday behaviour and to relieve tension. However, this does not relieve all the tension, because much of it is caused by the absence of the owner. It grooms more in an attempt to put the situation right and it becomes an obsession. Often these cats have bald patches where they have licked all the hair off.

Another problem that occurs with active cats kept indoors is redirected aggression. They see another cat or are stimulated by birds or movement out of the window. Their system automatically gets ready to fight or hunt. However, there is no outlet for this behaviour and the cat becomes frustrated. Owners of such cats remark that on certain occasions they were simply walking by when the cat attacked them – sometimes quite nastily. The aroused cat has focused on something moving and pounced. Perhaps because most activity is already focused on the owner it makes sense to aim the aggression in that direction too. Some of these cats also start to control their owners by preventing them getting up the stairs or into a certain room by being aggressive.

The therapy for such cats is to give them something to interest them aside from their owner – to tire them out with play and to make their lives fuller. Sometimes this can involve getting another cat – bearing in mind that it can be very difficult to introduce a new cat into the territory of a totally indoor cat because it is a total violation of its space and it has nowhere to escape to, such as out into the garden. It is not used to dealing with new scents and new situations because its life is totally controlled by its owner, so changes may become difficult. Introductions must be done very carefully (and this is the reason it is suggested that indoor cats should come in pairs).

Some cats can become very sensitive to changes in the household, such as new furniture or even just new items of clothing or even black plastic bags, and can be upset at their presence. One such indoor cat began spraying indoors because its owner brought her bicycle, which she rode to work on every day, into the hall at night. Of course, she had driven through all sorts of smells on the way and had brought them into the cat's safe household.

Rather than try not to upset the cat by keeping everything the same, it is better to desensitise it by adding novelty and helping the cat to get a life of its own. If the owner happens to have a garden (which may not be safe to let the cat out in, as it might escape), fencing it in is an excellent option. By building high metal fencing that overhangs at the top and putting collars on any trees the cat could use to scale, the garden can be made escape-proof. The cat can then have a whole new world open up before it. Owners of houses without gardens or flats above the ground floor will have to work extra hard inside with their cats. Some owners have actually built cat rooms with lots of different shelves, cat-entertainment climbing centres, ropes, etc. to keep their cats amused. If you compare it to keeping an animal in the zoo, the owners are the environmental enrichment when they are around but they have to ensure that the cats have some interest and challenges when they are out too. Owners have to live in their cat's environment. Luckily, human comforts such as beds and soft furnishings are also considered feline luxuries.

BRINGING OUTDOOR BEHAVIOURS INSIDE

We are very happy for our cats to scratch or spray, urinate or defecate outdoors. For many cats, these behaviours go on outside the sphere of their owners and often some or all of them go unnoticed by their owners. It is only when the cats start to carry out these natural behaviours in the wrong place – i.e. indoors – that owners begin to think that there might be a problem. A behavioural problem in a cat is usually a natural behaviour taking place in the wrong place. Occasionally, as in overgrooming, it is a natural behaviour that is taken to excess.

When a cat starts to mark more indoors, either scratching more or spraying, it is a sign that it is feeling under threat or insecure about something and that it is trying to make its indoor territory feel more secure. Some of the things that can make a cat feel insecure are:

- Other cats outdoors becoming threatening, coming near or even into the house.
- A new cat in the house.
- Building or alternation work that upsets the household.

- Decoration or new furniture.
- A new person in the house.
- A new baby in the house.

All of these may threaten the cat's feeling of safety. It is up to owners to try and 'think cat', to find the cause and alter it if possible, while also making the cat feel more secure.
Feelings of security can be improved by:

- Locking the cat-flap if other cats are coming in or letting the cat in and out while chasing other cats out of the garden.
- Using a water pistol to discourage other cats from hanging around in the garden or near the cat-flap.
- Giving the cat high areas around the house to retreat to get away from other cats, dogs or children.
- Giving the cat a regular lifestyle – for example, timing the cat's feeding – so that it knows just what is going to happen and when.

If the cat is urinating or soiling in the wrong place, it could be due to a mixture of security problems and housekeeping problems. This can be improved by:

- Making sure the litter is of a type the cat likes.
- Making sure the litter tray is kept clean enough.
- Putting a cover over the tray in case the cat feels vulnerable.
- Making sure the cat has access to the tray at all times and is not annoyed by children, dogs or other cats when using it.
- Putting the tray in a place where the cat feels safe.

CHANGES IN BEHAVIOUR IN CATS

Sometimes owners become worried because, for example, their seven-year-old cat has suddenly begun to hiss and spit occasionally if they go near it. While they can see no obvious explanation or threat that could have brought on the behaviour, they are worried about their cat. In these circumstances, it is wise to have the cat checked over by the vet. Illness can cause changes in behaviour by changing the chemistry of the body. Changes in behaviour can also result from pain or feeling unwell or confused – all of which makes the cat feel vulnerable. When I read the explanation of a 'field of aggression' in cats, a lot of feline behaviour falls into place. How can a cat be perfectly friendly in one place or one situation and be unapproachable only a short time later? To recap on our earlier discussion of this topic, the 'field of aggression' theory argues that, when the cat is relaxed and happy with the world, its field of aggression is smaller than its body – people can approach it and it will be friendly and calm. However, as the cat becomes stressed, tension builds or it feels threatened, its field of aggression grows – anything that comes within this area around it is likely to be reacted to with defensive aggression. Thus, if the cat is feeling very stressed because it is ill or it knows there is another cat in the vicinity that may appear at any time, it will react accordingly – the field may have a circumference of a couple of metres.

This may explain how cats can switch moods very quickly and sometimes seemingly without reason – a threat needs to be reacted to quickly and when the body goes into defensive mode anything near by may be considered threatening.

Some cats will 'switch' from one behaviour to another with a certain cat but then never switch back. Several owners have described a scenario to me that occurred when they stood on the tail of one of a pair of cats they owned (by accident); the cat made that feline yowl of surprise and pain and the second cat, who happened to be close by, attacked the first cat, much to its surprise. Sometimes these had been cats that had lived together in apparent harmony for many years. However, once the episode and attack had occurred, they never got on again. A similar thing has been reported in cats when one of a pair goes to the vet and presumably comes back smelling of the surgery. The cat that stayed at home reacts to it, hissing and growling. The cats may never get on again as they used to or it may take quite some time to get them to feel relaxed with each other again. I don't think we understand feline psychology enough to explain these episodes in which one small incident can negate years of harmonious co-habitation. It may illustrate the relative importance (or not) of other feline relationships to cats. Perhaps this is another of these feline enigmas and no doubt there is a biochemical explanation. We still need a few more years of study in this area to be able to establish exactly what it is.

PHEROMONES – A USEFUL TOOL

If you have waded your way through this book, by this point you will be well aware of the power of scent for cats and be familiar with pheromones – chemicals that the cat produces which it uses to leave scent messages for itself and for other cats. They have a range of meanings depending on the context in which they are used. When cats are feeling under threat, they often resort to increased marking activities – leaving more scents of various types around to try to feel secure. Recently, researchers have been able to synthetically produce some parts (or fractions) of the scents produced by the glands on the face and they have been using them in different situations to see what effect they have on the cat's behaviour. Cat facial secretions may contain up to forty chemicals. Thirteen of these are common to all cats and apparently no cat secretes all the chemicals at the same time. This would seem to give the cat plenty of scope for producing many and various types of scent. Workers have found five 'functional fractions' (numbered F1–F5) for which they think there are distinct roles. Two of these, F3 and F4, can now be made artificially. The F3 fraction is available commercially as Feliway (made by Ceva Animal Health and available from vets). Studies have shown that using this scent in homes where cats are spraying can reduce the spraying behaviour considerably. It worked with spraying induced by stress, but not by sexual arousal. The pheromones do not work so well where there is actual aggression between cats in the household, which may point to the pheromones being a form of passive aggression in a situation of threat that has not escalated to aggression. Once physical violence is in the equation, there also needs to be some form of behavioural therapy to try to resolve the problem.

The synthetic pheromone has also been used to reduce stress when travelling, by being sprayed into the cat carrier half an hour before travelling; it also seems to help in the veterinary surgery and will relax cats and allow treatment more easily. The cats seem to be able to deal with stress better and it may be useful to help cats recovering from surgery or illness in this way. Sprayed on furniture which is scratched, it resulted in cats finding somewhere else to scratch – a redirection of the behaviour rather than a suppression.

The manufacturers have recently produced the product in the

form of a plug-in diffuser – the type which is used to freshen rooms by providing a continual release of scent. This too seems to have been successful in reducing spraying behaviours.

The F4 fraction (Felifriend) has been found to encourage animals to approach unfamiliar people and adapt to a new environment, and may be useful in introducing cats to a new person or a new house.

HELP IN THE VETERINARY SURGERY

Some forward-thinking veterinary hospitals and surgeries are taking what we know about cat behaviour and how cats react in a stressful situation and applying it to the cats in their care. The Feline Advisory Bureau (www.fabcats.org) has a Cat Friendly Practice Scheme, which provides information for both practices and owners to help make a visit to the surgery less stressful.

Advice ranges from the layout of the waiting room (giving cats a chance to wait away from dogs), to the type of cat basket to use (one with an opening at the top rather than at one end and especially not made of wicker which can provide a great anchor point for claws for the cat reluctant to come out). Knowledge of cat behaviour and giving cats time to settle also makes a great deal of difference.

The sick cat is already trying to deal with a medical problem so it may be feeling pretty stressed already. It then has to go into the veterinary surgery for an operation or investigation – add another stress level. The stressed cat may also stop eating. What could be worse for a body that is in trouble than to remove its fuel? It is forced to break down its own tissues to fuel the work of breathing, heating, moving and all those other activities the body undertakes. Veterinary surgeons and doctors know that the sooner you can get an animal or a person to eat after an investigation or operation (before which they have usually been starved anyway) the faster it will recover. Granny's chicken soup is very necessary to build up strength and help recovery.

One of the first things these veterinary hospitals or surgeries do is to ensure the cats are separated from the dogs. Imagine having an operation and waking to find you are surrounded by members of a different species that you may well have had bad experiences with in the past. They will certainly feel very threatening – could you relax to sleep or eat? Separating cats from dogs allows the cats to relax. Cats start to eat and therefore recover more quickly if practices can:

- Separate cats from dogs.
- Give the cats a cardboard box to hide in (lined with a nice warm bedding, of course).
- Cover the front of the cage with a blanket for very nervous or agitated cats so they can hide.
- Spray inside the cage with Feliway.
- Give more nervous cats a higher cage so they feel safer.

Vets have found that the cats soon snuggle in and start to knead their bedding and begin to eat once they feel happier. This makes their recovery much more rapid, as the body can start rebuilding itself much more easily.

CONCLUSION

Part of the fascination of cats is their mystery. We still don't understand why they do all of the things that they do. They live alongside us so successfully that we almost take them for granted.

Most of the time we get away with this because they get on with their lives while we get on with ours. We interact and enjoy the interaction when either side feels the need. However, on occasion we need to be alert to the needs of our cats because they are feeling stressed or distressed. We have to get to know our own cats – whether they like interaction with us; whether they prefer not to be given attention; whether they need full-on attention all the time; whether they are confident outside as well as in – and so it goes on. If we keep cats in a way in which they have little chance of having some control over their lives, such as indoors, then we have to work at the situation – like the mandatory walking of a dog, we must play with the cats and make time to entertain them and keep them agile in mind and body. If our cats are distressed by things going on outside, then we need to be able to try and help them. If we want to take on more cats, we must be aware of the resultant stress on our original cat or cats. If we are aware of the experiences necessary to kittens to make them able to cope with the human world, then we must ensure that they get this exposure at the right time and in the right amounts. All of these things can make a great deal of difference towards how content our cats are. It can be difficult to notice if they are only mildly stressed – they tend to keep quiet or run away if they can. Veterinary surgeons who are involved with pain control in animals find cats very difficult subjects as it can be almost impossible to ascertain when they are in pain – they cover it well. Only when they start to exhibit obvious behavioural changes do we get the message. Luckily, many owners are finely tuned to their cats and their sixth sense tells them that something is not right. Learning more about our feline companions' normal behaviours and motivations may help us to understand them when they are in distress.

Don't take cats for granted; they are fantastic creatures of poise, elegance and intelligence. We need to admire them for the animals they are and not try and anthropomorphise their behaviours. The relationship between humans and cats has been one of the most successful love stories over the years. A successful relationship needs respect and an ability to give both sides a chance to express their own personalities. Cats have long fitted in with us – we have to make sure that we do not try to change them to fit human needs, but admire them instead for their natural and wonderful feline ways.

A–Z Tips for Feline Problems

AS YOU HAVE read through this book and understood what a cat really is, how it behaves and what it wants, you will be able to apply this knowledge to situations where cats don't behave as we might wish, even though it is probably a very natural behaviour for them. Below are some tips for some of the more common problems we meet in living alongside our cats.

A • AGGRESSION

We all witness aggression in our cats from time to time, though, except in the cases of overexcitement during play, thankfully, it is rarely directed towards us. Cats are, of course, well provided for by Mother Nature with a good set of weapons – at the front and all four corners – but their usage to inflict injury has largely evolved to enable the cat to survive as a predator. But just what is aggression? It isn't only expressed in a predatory form when an animal hunts and kills to survive; it can also occur in social situations, in territorial and other conflicts over resources and in self-defence, to name but a few. Aggression can be described as a hostile, physically damaging attack.

AGGRESSION TOWARDS PEOPLE

Aggression towards people is not common, but most of us have experienced what the Americans term the 'petting-and-biting' syndrome. It occurs in many cats, in some after very short periods of handling, and in others after long periods of affectionate stroking when the cat suddenly attacks the hand that is caressing it. The theory is that when it is accepting handling the cat is behaving as a kitten would with its mother: it relaxes, enjoying the protection and attention. Then it seems that the adult cat, the independent, self-determining predator, takes over, and it suddenly feels vulnerable in this confined position. The cat then lashes out with a display of defensive aggression, biting and sometimes kicking, before (usually) jumping off the owner's lap, trotting a short distance away to establish a safe flight distance, and grooming itself to relax and calm down from its state of confusion.

To come to grips with this undesirable behaviour, it's best to try to predict when this state of confusion is likely to arise, and only to engage in frequent, but short, periods of contact with the cat so it never quite reaches this point. The periods of stroking can be increased gradually. During this period, it is essential not to touch the cat in sensitive areas such as on the abdomen, or around the hind legs, and in some cases it's wise to restrict the handling to stroking the back and the head.

Research suggests that there may be two distinct genetically determined character types in cats – one which has a high requirement for social contact and is likely to be friendly with people, and the other which seems to have a high requirement for social (competitive) play and predatory activity and demands less friendly social contact. This second character accepts friendly social contact when it can initiate it, but may be intolerant or even defensively aggressive if pursued by owners intent on handling or petting. But, with either character, actual unprovoked aggression towards owners is rare.

AGGRESSION BETWEEN CATS

While cats are not as hierarchical in their social relations as dogs, they use the same types of antagonistic behaviour to resolve conflicts over territory, such as when a cat threatens a rival with a stare and hiss in the garden, or to compete with housemates for a favoured sleeping position or food. The social order is highly elastic in cats and there is huge variation in their sociability. Some are happy to live in huge groups, others are intolerant of every other cat. Fortunately, most are capable of tolerating at least one or two others in the house and will form a loose system of social order maintained by body language, combative behaviour as required, and the acceptance of established rank.

Sometimes relations between two cats can break down for no apparent reason. If the cats were previously very friendly, then there will obviously be a better chance of repairing the damage than if they only ever tolerated each other. Unlike pack-orientated dogs, cats don't need to be part of a group – there is nothing to gain from co-operation. Hence, if cats decide not to get along, it can be hard to persuade them otherwise. Try to bring the cats together by feeding them more frequently but with smaller meals and serve the food in separate bowls brought progressively closer to each other. Food can act as a useful distraction in getting them to share each other's space, though following this suggested routine does require time and care.

In a household where cats are tolerant of each other, the chief problem that may arise comes at the introduction of a new individual or when a young cat reaches adolescence and becomes more socially competitive. Success then depends on the basic character type of the cat and its experiences as a social animal in a group of cats, as well as on relative sexual and dominance status. One example concerned a five-year-old, by then spayed, mother Sealpoint Siamese cat and her three-and-a-half-year-old neutered son. They had never fought and had always played, slept and fed together in harmony... until the man of the house accidentally trod on the female's tail. She, naturally, yelled in pain but then fiercely attacked her son. He was severely frightened, of course, but, although the owners separated them and gave them a few hours apart to cool off, the female continued to attack the male on sight at every attempt to get them back together over the next few days. Here, a single traumatic incident had triggered a complete breakdown in all social relations.

In a similar case, this time involving Burmese cats normally kept permanently indoors, a total breakdown occurred between two neutered male cats after one escaped and remained outside for two days. On returning, the escapee may have been regarded and treated as a complete newcomer, but more likely it presented new and challenging smells in addition to its own familiar ones. Other cases, though not always of this 'diverted aggression' kind, have been triggered by certain noises, usually high-pitched sudden sounds of particular frequencies.

Treatment of fighting cats is by no means easy or quick, but good progress can be made by going right back to basics and separating the cats, first of all letting them get used to the scent of the other on bowls or toys, then mixing their scents by grooming and stroking one then the other, before letting them gradually get used to each other without actually meeting, for example, in different rooms separated by a glass door. Associate the smell and sight of the other cat with something nice such as a special food or attention (if that is what the cat likes). What you are aiming to do is to break the cycle of aggression and introduce reward for sharing space peacefully. This process can be further assisted by the owner brushing and grooming both protagonists with a solution of catnip, which helps to rebuild shared scents and makes them more attractive to each other (though catnip affects some cats and not others).

Restoring previous good relations in such cases will probably take far longer than when a new cat is introduced to the home of a long-established resident, irrespective of character type. As with some breakdowns in human and canine relations, there may be no obvious or complete treatment path to follow – it's just a case of doing everything that seems logical and investing a lot of time and patience. If even this fails, rehoming one or other of the former friends, never to see each other again, may be better and kinder for all concerned.

B • BABIES

For many people, the first thing that springs to mind on the subject of cats and babies together in one home is that 'cats sleep on babies' faces and suffocate them'. This notion is so strong that many parents-to-be get rid of a cherished cat prior to the arrival of a baby, and others never fulfil the desire to have a cat because of the perceived risk to their young children. What a pity that is when so many other parents with young babies gain so much from including a cat as part of the family.

Of course, it may happen from time to time that a cat, on discovering this new warm place, does curl up in the cot next to the baby, but the risk of harm is reduced to nil if parents follow the simple rule which applies equally for cats and dogs: never leave any child unattended with a free-ranging pet, or where a pet may gain access to the child, such as through an open window or cat-flap.

This rule applies to the newborn baby, the crawler and the exploratory toddler – indeed, right up to the point, usually at about six to eight years old, where a child understands when and how the family pet can be approached and handled or kindly sent away. Initially, the rule is followed in order to guard the safety of the helpless child, but later the innocent pet's safety also needs to be guaranteed.

Ideally, prospective owners of a new cat should wait until they have produced their human family. A new cat or kitten will then treat them all, adults, babies and children alike, as the norm and accept the rigours of family life more easily than an adult cat would when it suddenly has to cope with a noisy, unpredictable increase in family size. But, of course, babies (or cats, for that matter) are not always planned, so it is important to know how to treat the cat when the baby arrives.

Ensure that the baby and cat learn of each other from the earliest days. Controlled, supervised introductions should be carried out, with the cat held safely and allowed to smell the new arrival and all the things that come with it. Dirty nappies, piles of clean ones, the pram, the cot, the baby wipes, the toys – all are changes within the cat's home too, and it must be allowed to explore them and come to realise that neither the baby nor the accoutrements pose any threat to security.

Next, parents should ensure that a new baby poses no competitive threat to the cat. Most cats won't be bothered, as often they only get attention on demand and they rebuke our advances at other times. Others, particularly interactive breeds such as Siamese or Burmese, are more demanding and may perceive a baby as competition for affection. Here it is important to be more rejecting of the cat's attempts to demand attention before the baby is brought home, so that your responses are not always 'on tap'. The baby's arrival is then less traumatic to the cat as it will continue to receive attention only at the owner's initiation (this practice is important for all members of the family, not just mum). If the cat then receives more attention when the baby is present, but only after the baby has been cuddled and tended to, it will perceive the baby as more of a prerequisite for attention and, importantly, that baby comes before cat. Of course, cat and baby should always be fed separately, as a cat excited at the prospect of dinner, be it its own or the baby's – food is food, after all – is a less controllable and potentially more hazardous creature, quite apart from the hygiene aspects. If it all sounds a bit dog-like, well, it is! Many competitive cats do respond well by being treated – in the nicest possible way – like dogs.

The cat may react by urinating indoors, as Bullet did on the arrival of our new baby. After anointing the duvet twice in the first week (in front of our eyes!), he seemed to get used to the baby's presence and went back to being his normal inscrutable self. So don't panic; reassure the cat and let it get used to the new arrival – most cope very well. Often cats are indifferent to a young baby after the initial curiosity value has worn off. Problems are far more likely to crop up when the baby starts to crawl. Suddenly, all the cat's traditional bolt-holes under the sideboard or on the chair under the dining table, and its resting-place in the sun by the hall window, are subject to periodic gurgling invasions. Many will learn to retreat to higher and therefore safer spots, perhaps on the windowsill or atop a cupboard, but it is important to make sure that the cat has somewhere to use as a childproof refuge in every room, and especially that there is a warm covered bed well out of reach of the rapidly developing grasp of the young child. At this stage in the child's development, it is essential that parents guide the child's hand and encourage him or her to touch the cat and stroke it gently. Short frequent socialisation will start to teach the crawling child the methods of communication he or she can use confidently with the cat and will also make the cat aware of the child's right to approach, under supervision and with increasing competence at doing so.

Hygiene is always important and particularly at this stage, as crawling babies with enquiring fingers may discover the delights of the cat's litter tray. Providing one of those trays that have a top cover or placing the tray off the ground, on a table, say, may help but, better still, keep it in the kitchen and only allow the child to crawl elsewhere. Never is keeping the cat regularly wormed and the baby often washed more important!

Remember, too, another and equally important safety matter: small furry cat toys and cat furniture that may topple over (the scratching post, for example) can be very dangerous to the unco-ordinated crawler, so it would be wise to keep them out of the way while the baby is 'exercised'.

As the baby grows up and starts to toddle, his or her behaviour becomes more co-ordinated and predictable for the cat, which may then respond to the child much more as if he or she were an adult. Also, many of the ground-level dangers, such as the litter tray, lose their interest as the child finds objects on the higher plane of head height to investigate. The cat may need to find even higher escape zones, but, by the time the child can reach the cat on the windowsill, he or she should be well versed in the dos and don'ts of reacting with the cat and be more responsive to mum's instructions if the cat looks threatened.

The young child can also start to learn how to pick up and support the cat properly – here again, short frequent efforts are better, so the cat doesn't have to put up with a prolonged grasp. Also by this stage the child can begin to play a contributory role in the care of the cat, for example, by helping mum to feed it. The socialising procedures of supervised contact should continue as often as possible so that the child not only grows up knowing how to react with the cat, but also learns to interpret the cat's body language and moods and, later, its needs. Then the child may happily become one of the next generation of cat lovers.

C • CALLING

Owners are often very worried when their female kitten starts to make loud distressed-sounding noises and to behave in a restless manner, eating less and urinating more. She may crouch in front of other cats with her tail pulled over to one side and with her rear end raised up, at the same time treading with her front paws and 'crooning'. Facially, she may look angry or fearful, with ears back and pupils dilated. She will also lick the area under her tail frequently. These loud monotone vocal sounds are termed 'calling' and are a sign that the cat has reached sexual maturity and is trying to attract local toms to mate with her. It can happen from as early as three months of age or as late as up to eighteen months, and so may catch out some owners who do intend to spay their kitten but have not yet got round to it. The first season may not last long, or may go on for weeks – during which time the cat must not, of course, be allowed to go out of doors and meet entire toms.

Although veterinary surgeons prefer to spay female cats before or after a season (the period when they come on heat) usually before the first one at four or five months of age, they can be spayed while on heat and this may be the best option if the cat is continually 'calling', driving everybody mad with the noise (especially if it is one of the Oriental breeds) and causing herself distress at not being able to go out and find a mate.

D • DEMANDING ATTENTION

Some cats can be extremely irritating in their demands and seem to change their minds or want one thing after another, one minute asking to be let out and the next demanding to be let in again. While it may be simply that the cat hasn't learned to enjoy outdoor life, usually such behaviour occurs because the cat discovers that by calling out its owner will quickly appear and offer the comfort of his or her physical presence or, better, will provide actual contact and petting. From the cat's point of view, having its owner around is better than being alone and either resolves the conflict of whether or not to go out or offers instant reassurance if it feels worried. Night-time is when a cat is likely to feel most vulnerable, but once you have been trained to get up at the sound of its calls there is no further need for it to worry! If you are, understandably, unwilling to endure the noise, it is vital that the cat's calling no longer meets with success in order for you to 'un-train' it. Endure it if you can (have a stiff nightcap before retiring and with any luck you may even sleep through it). Alternatively, you could let the cat sleep in the bedroom with you, of course, but then it will probably demand that you stay awake all night or at least get up early to serve its breakfast.

E • EATING – PECULIAR HABITS

Cats are obligate carnivores – they must eat meat and are not usually interested in much else. A few do indulge in the occasional piece of cake, cheese or even chocolate, but others enjoy a rather more bizarre side-dish to their main course.

WOOL-EATERS

Why some cats should want or need to eat wool, and indeed other fabrics, is not understood. That they do is beyond doubt as many owners of clothes, carpets and furniture-covers with holes in them can testify. Although the behaviour was noted in the 1950s, it was thought to be a trait restricted to certain strains of the Siamese breed. The results of a survey on the problem carried out by the cat behaviourist Peter Neville revealed that the problem is more widespread, and occurs in Siamese, Burmese and cats of mixed parentage, including moggies.

Some fabric-eaters do stick to consuming wool, and where this is the case perhaps the smell or texture of wool acts as the initial trigger to the behaviour. But the majority broaden their appetite and will consume all fabrics, from wool to cotton and synthetics. Items of clothing, preferably worn, bed linen and towels are especially popular.

When eating any fabric, the cat appears to be totally engrossed in its activities and sometimes in a trance-like state. Intervention by hissing or yelling or even throwing water at the cat may cause it to stop, but often it will simply go straight back to the item or look for another in a quieter place. The cat will often take in the wool with its canine and incisor teeth but, having obtained a good mouthful, will start to grind it up using its shearing molars at the back of the mouth. The volume of fabric consumed by some cats is truly remarkable, the more so when one considers that it usually passes through the cat unaltered without causing any harm. Some do unfortunately suffer blockages in the stomach or further down the digestive system and, sadly, for a few euthanasia must be carried out because of the resulting damage. Others manage to live long healthy lives, eating wool or other fabric every day without any repercussions.

A few more are destroyed because they are too expensive in their habits for owners to live with. Some have damaged dresses worth hundreds of pounds and, in other instances, furnishings worth thousands. The average gauged from estimates in the survey is £136 per fabric-eater! Most of those owners who replied to the survey said they had learned to live with the problem and would not dream of parting with the offender; nor would they be deterred from having a cat of the same breed in the future.

One theory as to the origins of fabric-eating has it that, like wool-sucking, the behaviour is linked to a continuing infantile disposition in what are traditionally sensitive breeds which are well nurtured and cosseted by their owners.

The best treatment for cats that eat wool or fabric only in their owners' absence, but which are often clingy and dependent when they are around, may be to encourage them to grow up, to exchange any continuing infantile reactions with the owners for more adult reactions, and to keep affection to short doses at the owners' initiation. Wherever possible, these cats should be encouraged to go outside in order to further their level of stimulation, reduce the importance of owners and home for activity and help establish a less dependent relationship with the owners. Often the problem does appear to resolve, though how many cats are finding fabric sources in the homes of neighbours or from their washing lines is difficult to say. Edible fabric must be made as inaccessible as possible for all fabric-eaters, and sometimes simply that denial for a few weeks causes the behaviour to cease. Direct negative conditioning by ambushing the cat with a water pistol while it is in mid-chew has helped some, though often such tactics only produce a secret fabric-eater. Indirect tactics using taste deterrents applied to specially laid towel baits can have a sufficiently dramatic effect as to put the cat off eating any fabric ever again, though the choice of deterrent is crucial. The traditional tastes of pepper, mustard and chilli or curry paste are invariably useless: they simply broaden the cat's desire for a more exotic normal diet. Aromatic compounds such as menthol and oil of eucalyptus do seem to be more successful and have reformed some ardent fabric-eaters, but need to used with care.

The best chance for curing the problem, however, seems to lie with dietary management. Most fabric-eaters have a perfectly normal, healthy intake of their proper food and their appetite is usually unaffected by having a stomach full of nylon sweater or woollen scarf. By providing a constantly available source of dry cat food in addition to offering the usual diet, the desire to eat fabric can be redirected towards more nutritional targets, and apparently without risk of weight gain. Most cats simply snack all day on the dry food and cut down voluntarily on the intake at usual mealtimes. Sometimes it helps to cease mealtimes altogether and instead simply leave a never-ending supply of dry food for the cat.

If keeping the stomach constantly active and partially full eliminates the need to eat fabric in some sufferers it may be due to the pleasurable, comforting feeling of having food in the stomach rather than to the switch to an alternative form of intake. This may explain why adding fibre, which helps pad out the volume and passage time of traditional canned diets through the cat's system, can help prevent fabric-eating. Such padding can be achieved up to a point, by adding fibre sources such as bran to the usual diet, but most cats will not accept too high a proportion. Instead, adding small lengths of finely chopped undyed wool or tissue to the diet may be more acceptable to the cat. This is, admittedly, a form of giving in, but it's a lot less expensive than letting the cat select its own fabric from the wardrobe. Other owners have resolved the problem of indiscriminate fabric-eating by providing the cat with a towel or scarf to chew at dinnertime. The cat takes a few mouthfuls of food, then chews and swallows a portion of towel – a truly bizarre spectacle, but the method is extremely effective in some cases.

With some fabric-eaters, the time taken to ingest food seems to be relevant to the frequency and severity of their fabric-eating at other times. In the wild, cats would have to stalk, capture, overpower and kill their prey before consuming it. The process of consumption itself would take some time as the fur or feathers have first to be chewed or ripped in order to get to the flesh. Such gory necessities are not preliminaries to eating in the case of the pet cat, but forcing it to invest more time in processing its food may prove to be beneficial. This certainly seems to be the case with some fabric-eaters that spend much time chewing at the gristly meat and indigestible sinew attached to large bones rather than enjoying soft free meals on a plate.

PLANTS

Most cats eat more plant material than we realise, probably in an effort to obtain a quickly digestible source of vitamins, minerals and roughage. Some regurgitate grass with or without a portion of their dinner and this is believed to be a natural method of self-worming or of helping the ejection of hairballs. In general, cats are very fastidious about what they eat. Most are at liberty in gardens and houses and do not eat any poisonous plants. However, cats kept indoors permanently, and inquisitive kittens, may sample house pot plants out of a need for vegetation or just out of boredom or curiosity. Indoor cats should be provided with a tub of seedling grass sprouts to munch on, to discourage the consumption of houseplants. These tubs of grass are available from pet shops and, being more attractive to cats than most houseplants, are readily consumed in preference. If you do have an indoor or partially confined cat which seems fond of chewing plants, check carefully that there are no poisonous plants in the house or cat run – the Feline Advisory Bureau has a list of poisonous plants – see www.fabcats.org.

OTHER BIZARRE DIETS

The apparently self-limiting behaviour of chewing electric cables is obviously potentially fatal to the cat and dangerous to property, and is even less well understood. Obviously, the habit must be stopped at almost any cost. Encouraging play indoors with a range of toys, perhaps laced with catnip, or letting the cat spend more time outdoors may help divert its attentions. Make cables as inaccessible as possible and other wires as unappetising as possible using eucalyptus oil – and unplug them from the mains when not in use.

F • FEEDING

Feeding time is one of those moments when your cat will be most responsive to you. It can be used as an opportunity for learning, as well as simply providing dinner, and it is an ideal time for strengthening the bond between you. Behaviourists advise that when you take on a new cat or kitten you feed little and often, each time calling the cat and letting it encourage you to hand over the food. Later, you can feed the cat less frequently or leave the food for it to eat ad lib.

You may notice your cat's pupils dilate with excitement and anticipation as you fill its dish. It may mew or purr and wind its tail around your legs and rub against you as it did as a kitten trying to encourage its mother to hand over her catch.

A cat that seems to have lost its appetite should be investigated. There can be many reasons, from illness to bad teeth, for this lack of enthusiasm for food. Watch its behaviour carefully; if it shows enthusiasm as you fill the bowl but stops eating after a few mouthfuls it may be that its teeth or gums are diseased and eating is just not worth the pain it causes. Veterinary surgeons can do a great deal now for tooth problems, so a visit to the surgery is called for. They may also offer advice on diet, in order both to improve general health and maintain the health of the teeth. Like people, finicky cats are often created rather than born. We make the mistake of pandering to their desire for certain foods instead of trying to feed a balanced diet, and it is often difficult to encourage a cat addicted to, say, fish to eat anything else. When changing the cat's diet to a new type or when trying to wean it off a certain flavour, try mixing in a little of the new food with the old and gradually increasing the proportion of the new content. This allows the cat to get used to the new taste and its body to become accustomed to the new food with less of a surprise to the system. Veterinary surgeons say a cat will usually eat what is offered after three days, so persist at least for this long if you are trying to switch your cat on to a more healthy diet.

Cats do lose their appetites after accident or injury and it is important to get them eating again so that the body's system is restrengthening itself rather than breaking down tissue to keep its vital functions going. Heating food to body temperature will release aromas and may encourage the cat to investigate their source. Small pieces of cooked liver, which has a strong smell, may well get the cat interested in food again. Even baby food can come in useful after a cat has had an operation as the patient can lap it up without difficulty and the flavour may be appetising. Tender loving care is vital when nursing such a cat: keep encouraging and talking to it as you offer food. Make sure new food replaces any that is rejected – cats are very sensitive to the smell of rancid food and will be put off immediately.

Cats are commonly believed to like and even to need milk – but, when you consider it carefully, adult animals drinking milk made by a different species is quite extraordinary. Most animals never have the chance to benefit from this bountiful liquid after weaning from their own mother. For this reason, the enzyme in the stomach that breaks down milk sugar is not produced after weaning. While many cats have no problem in drinking milk during adulthood, in others it actually causes upset, as undigested milk passes into the large intestine and ferments, producing gas and diarrhoea. Many veterinary surgeons now advise that adult cats are not given milk. If cats are on a balanced diet, there is no need for extra calcium, and water is a perfectly satisfactory fluid for them to drink.

G • GROOMING DISORDERS

Many longhaired cats are difficult to groom and quickly learn the success of using their claws to avoid such an imposition. Of course, frequent gentle grooming while they are still kittens accustoms them to the practice. Owners must try to make grooming a positive and rewarding experience rather than a battle. Choose a treat which the cat finds hard to resist (prawns are usually a good bet!) and put a tiny bit on your finger and feed the cat. As it concentrates on the food and licking your finger, groom it a little with your other hand. Put on some more prawn and groom a little more. If there are matts, either cut them out with round-ended scissors or, if they are not too tightly matted, work from the top of the hair downwards very gently. Don't pull, as you want this experience to be pleasant. Go very slowly and be patient. Keep going while the cat still has an interest in the food and stop if you get a negative reaction. Leave it for a while and then try again when all is calm. Associate the grooming with food, warmth, praise and attention. If the cat is very badly matted, then you may have to take it to the vet for an anaesthetic so that the matts can be shaved or cut out. Then, when you have it home, even without hair, start the grooming with the food. There will be no matts and therefore it will be easy to groom gently. Get the cat used to getting excited about the food when the comb (a wide-toothed metal comb is the best tool to use) comes out. Prevention is better than cure!

You can resort to a cat muzzle if all else fails. This is actually more like the hood used to calm birds of prey, or the blinkers on a horse, than the traditional dog muzzle and is made of soft material. The cat usually becomes less active, flattens down its body on to the table surface and is more tolerant of being handled and groomed.

The almost opposite problem of a cat grooming itself too enthusiastically is not very common, but is more often seen in the 'highly strung' breeds such as Siamese, although any breed or moggie can suffer. Cats groom themselves not only to keep the coat clean and waterproof but also when disturbed or upset and may lick away the hair and even damage the skin. This self-directed behaviour is believed to produce an increased state of relaxation. With some cases, the behaviour continues at times even when the cat is apparently not anxious but prefers the relaxed state to being bored. With others, the behaviour is sporadic and occurs more in response to occasional forms of stress, such as being isolated from the owner or other house cats. When the behaviour is relatively continuous, the cat may be unable to cope with the stresses of its lifestyle, or there may be a general pressure in its environment or social group with which it cannot deal. Perhaps the reason is that it does not get on with another cat in the household or is distressed by living with a number of cats. This can be tested by isolating the sufferer for two to three weeks to see whether the behaviour continues, though of course one should not be surprised by an initial worsening of the condition due to the stress of isolation itself. Finding the source of the stress is obviously vital to treatment.

H • HOLIDAYS

Many pet owners go on holiday with mixed feelings – relief at leaving work and home pressures behind for a couple of weeks, but sadness and concern at leaving their precious cats in a cattery. Some do not take a holiday at all for this very reason, while others go where they can take the cat too. This latter option can be difficult in many ways unless the cat likes to travel and doesn't mind staying in a hotel (not many will take cats), caravan or holiday home for the holiday period. Even if the cat is accommodating, there are the obvious worries about it getting lost or wandering off and owners must ensure that it is wearing an identity tag with home and holiday phone numbers on it.

Some owners and cats go on holiday together every year without any problems but, for most of us, knowing the cat is in a safe, clean, professionally run cattery is the best option. If you choose your cattery carefully and check it out for yourself, then you can go away with a much clearer conscience and a lighter heart. There may be several catteries in your area, in which case it is best to visit each and ask to look around – if your request is refused, go elsewhere. The proprietors of a well-run cattery with happy residents will be only too pleased to show you their set-up. The Feline Advisory Bureau has a leaflet on what to look for in a good cattery and a list of catteries which come up to their standards of construction and management. Here are some things to look out for (see also www.fabcats.org):

- An overall clean and tidy appearance.
- There should be no smell.
- Cats should look healthy and contented.
- Cats should be housed in individual units (unless they are from the same household). Cats from different households should not be able to touch each other (there should be a barrier called a sneeze barrier, often made of perspex, between runs or a space) or go into any communal areas as this is stressful for cats and is an easy way to spread disease.
- Each cat unit should have an indoor sleeping area with a heater and an outside run.
- Each cat should have its own litter tray and bowls which it keeps for the entire stay.
- There should be a 'safety passage' or double doors on each cat unit so that cats can never just slip out and escape.
- You should be asked to prove with a vet certificate that your cat's vaccinations are up to date.
- You should be asked about your cat's eating habits, illness, etc. and may be asked to sign a consent form for any veterinary treatment which may be required while you are away.
- A longhaired cat should be groomed (you may have to pay more for this) while in the cattery.

Once you have found a good cattery, you will not want to go anywhere else and you will also realise how far ahead you will have to book your place. You can then enjoy your holiday. Most cats soon settle into the new routine and cope very will – in fact, it's almost a personal insult to find on your return that they have been quite happy there, thank you very much!

If you are going away only for a short period, it is probably better if your neighbours or a friend visit your house a couple of times a day to check the cats and feed them. This can work well because it means that the cats do not have to be uprooted but can continue in their normal environment and routines, albeit without you. If your feeders are not reliable or you are going to be away for a week or more, to be sure that the cat or cats get the attention and company they need the best solution is to have a cat-sitter stay in your home. If you can't get a friend to stay, there are several companies which run a pet-sitter service and advertise in the various cat or pet magazines. Obviously, for reasons of security, you should check them out and ask for references or talk to previous customers, but it may be an option to pursue for the cat that just doesn't take to time in a cattery.

I • INTRODUCTIONS

Most cats accept the introduction of a new cat into the household without too much trouble. Plenty of contact when they are young helps cats develop the social language necessary to meet and be around others when older, and the capacity is often retained for life. Those lacking that early experience are less well equipped to deal with other cats later, and it may well be that you can only hope for a tolerant, if slightly distant, relationship rather than a loving, curl-up-by-the-fire-in-a-heap one. The other factor, one that is much more under your control, is how you introduce them. First impressions can be lasting impressions so it is essential that they meet in stages.

Smell is a vital component, and mixing scents by stroking one cat and then the other can help. Do this for several days before the cats meet. It's important to introduce the new arrival to any existing residents and your normal family comings and goings in a controlled manner, so that it is protected from anything frightening while learning to cope. The best way to achieve this is to house the cat or kitten in an indoor cage (when unsupervised) for a couple of days, or, failing this, in its carrying basket while introductions are being made. Protected by the bars of its 'den', it will be able to look out and learn who will be sharing its life and how they behave. Containing the cat will prevent a panic runaway that might trigger a chase from other cats or dogs, and will enable you to keep everything as calm as possible. The cage also protects its occupant when other resident animals or small children make their first, and not always friendly, approaches. The cage should be housed in a well-used area such as the living room or kitchen, so that the kitten or cat is always part of proceedings and gets used to the noises and rhythms of the house.

Expect some 'swearing' when cats first meet, but be persistent as all usually sorts itself out very quickly, provided excitement or a chase are not allowed to escalate out of control. Feeding resident cats outside the cage at the same time as the new inhabitant is feeding inside will help to get them progressively closer to each other. When they have reached the stage where they eat and relax in the same room, try carefully introducing them free of the cage. This usually poses no problem with a new kitten as a resident cat will not yet see it as a rival; introducing older cats may need a little more patience and, again, try distracting them with food for the first few meetings on the loose.

Bring the new arrival out frequently for exploration and play sessions on its own. Gradually and steadily allow more unsupervised freedom in one room and permit contact with other animals when they appear tolerant of the 'invader'. Then allow access to the rest of the house one room at a time, but supervise the first few exposures so that the new cat has the opportunity to learn the geography of your home without much hindrance. Make sure that in each room there are plenty of escape routes, bolt-holes under furniture and safe higher surfaces for the cat to jump on to in case it becomes alarmed. This is particularly important if you own an inquisitive dog. Replace the cage with a normal soft cat bed when the cat is well settled and needs no further controlled exposures.

J • JUVENILE BEHAVIOUR

The very reasons we enjoy our cats, their ability to relax and act like kittens with us, may be the cause of anxiety for some owners. Certain cats just don't grow up and become independent. Most pet cats switch smoothly from one mode to the other, showing kittenish behaviour with us and becoming skilled solitary hunters when outside. However, a few become so bonded to their owner that they continue to suck and knead as they did as kittens and are not able to cope without their owner's presence. You might initially enjoy the behaviour as kittens dribble and suck, often on your neck. However, it can become somewhat annoying, and indeed embarrassing, if the kitten sucks hard enough to leave red marks. This is one of the most difficult habits for owners to curtail because they must necessarily distance themselves from their cat to prevent the sucking. They usually worry that they are being 'cruel' and feel very guilty about pushing their cat/kitten away, but there really is no other way. Mother cats too have to make their offspring independent so that they will cope on their own in the big bad world.

Owners need to make themselves less available in responding to their cat's demands. That doesn't have to mean you must offer less love and attention; it simply means that these should be at the owner's instigation and control, not the cat's. It will soon learn to be more independent and enjoy the new more adult relationship, although there will no doubt be the relapses (of a less severe kind) into kittenhood that all our cats display.

K • KITTENS – WHEN DO THEY BECOME CATS?

We love our cats when they are young – you can't not enjoy their antics. But a kitten grows fast, and by the time it is six to eight weeks old it is the equivalent of an 18-month-old child. By the time the cat reaches its first birthday, it should be considered to be at the same stage as a 15-year-old youth. The comparison is valid as the cat will more than likely have had its first season and, if not neutered, will be able to have kittens.

At the age of two years, a cat can be considered equivalent to a 24-year-old person and then each successive year of its life is deemed to be equal to four human years. On average, the cat lives to twelve years, which makes it sixty-four in human terms, and a life span of twenty years (ninety-six years) is not uncommon. This method of calculating a cat's equivalent age is more accurate than the seven-year one commonly used.

L • LITTER

The cat-litter industry in the UK is worth over £60 million per year – a remarkable fact when one considers that the majority of cats probably never use a litter tray once they are allowed out of doors, except when boarded at a cattery or when confined during veterinary treatment. Indeed, one of the reasons the cat makes such a good pet is its convenient habit of digging a hole in the garden soil for its toilet purposes and then neatly covering up its mess afterwards. But for permanently indoor cats, those kept in overnight or only taken out on a harness and leash, a litter tray has to be provided and replenished with suitable fresh litter as required in order to offer a clean toilet for this, our most fastidious of pets. While young puppies may require several weeks of careful house-training so that they learn not to soil our living areas, young kittens arrive in their new homes already completely clean in their habits. All we have to do is provide a litter tray containing a litter that can be raked and they will use it. It's something that seems to be instinctive in the kitten. Unable to urinate or defecate without stimulation of the anal and genital region by its mother until two or three weeks of age, the kitten through its own movements in exploring and tumbling out of the nest stimulates the process. Providing that easy to dig in material is to hand, it will soon teach itself to use that material for its toilet needs. Of course, it'll play with the litter, scatter it around and possibly actually eat it, but even at such a tender age it is also at the same time house-training itself. It's a training that will serve it for a lifetime.

The cat's ancestors evolved under semi-desert conditions and so it's no surprise that studies have shown that cats prefer a fine material to use as a latrine. While sand is ideal, and fine soil perfectly adequate, the range of modern commercially produced cat

263

litters also suit nearly all cats. There are three main types: Fuller's earth is a clay-based and usually pale-grey granular material and probably the most popular in terms of purchase tonnage. Rising fast in the popularity stakes because of its lighter weight and odour-retention qualities is the wood-chip pellet variety, often pine scented for masking catty smells in our kitchens. There are also 'clumping', fine-grain clay litters which are claimed to offer the benefits of long active life providing that the damp clumps and solids are removed regularly to leave unsoiled litter fresh in the tray. In preference trials, it has been shown that, given a choice, cats go for the litter that is granulated the finest, but the vast majority will use whichever one is provided. If house-training problems do ever arise though, offering a finer-grained litter or sand is often enough to persuade the cat to use its tray consistently again. Some cats will happily use shredded newspaper in a tray – though this may be an unwise choice of material on your part. If your cat finds your daily paper on the doormat before you do in the morning, you may discover that it's left its little comment on your choice of newspaper.

In terms of communication, it's important to remember that the scent of urine and faeces is often used to carry messages. After urinating or defecating, a cat will rake over what it's done, often pausing now and again to sniff the area to assure itself that the right amount of scent is being given off from the deposit. In dry soil or litter, it may rake frequently and endeavour to bury its deposit at a greater depth, while in a heavier or damper litter a lighter cover-up may suffice. In a multi-cat house, a shy cat may try to avoid drawing attention to itself by covering up intensively, while a cat that is trying to boost its own self-confidence or is intent on leaving a dominant sign for other cats may only cover up with a thin layer of litter, or not cover up at all. Such levels of cat talk are all worthy of note, not so much in the case of the well-adjusted and house-trained cat but in individuals presenting some form of behavioural problem. Observing a cat's use of the litter tray (or especially the lack of it!) and the nature of the messages left can help enormously with diagnosis and treatment.

M • MOVING HOME

Moving home can be a very traumatic time for people and cats. Owners have many worries about how their cat will cope and how they can ensure that it does not wander off and get lost in its new environment or, if the old home is within an easy walking distance, that the cat will return there instead of accepting the new house as home. Indeed, this does happen and, since often cats value their territory as much as their owners, they return to their old haunts and try to take up residence with the new people who live there. There are some things which the owner can do to help the cat over the move and to settle into its new home.

It may be wise to board particularly nervous individuals in a friendly cattery before the packing of belongings and stripping of curtains, etc. starts at the old house, and not to bring them to the new house until everything is unpacked and positioned. Outdoor cats with a wider experience of change generally cope better, but should nevertheless be kept in the new home for a week or two in order to learn the geography and smells of their new home base. When finally let out to explore their new outdoor patch and carve out a piece for themselves (temporally or spatially) from that of local resident cats, it's best if they're hungry. Starved of food for twelve hours or so, they will not wander too far from the new home and will readily respond to the call or plate-bashing that signifies 'dinner is served'. Accompanying the cat on its first few excursions into the brave new world will also help, but the cat's adaptability and survival instincts usually serve it well and it soon adopts a similar lifestyle and habits to the ones it enjoyed at the old house.

If the new home is only a few streets away from the old one, it is highly likely that in its explorations the cat will encounter old known routes. It will simply return 'home' along those routes as before and then look confused on arrival to find that all has changed. The bond with the new home is simply not yet well enough established to lure such cats. Some too are inadvertently encouraged by the new occupiers of the old base who provide food, or who are flattered by this strange cat's confident entrance through the cat-flap and willingness to set up home with them. But even when these new occupiers have been warned that the cat might return and they take deterrent action by turfing the cat out, throwing water at it and being generally unpleasant, the bond with the old centre of the territory can persist. The cat keeps returning and will only go to the new home if physically taken there by old owners collecting, or new ones delivering it. Both parties can get tired of the travelling, especially in the remarkable cases where cats have returned to old haunts many miles away.

The first step is to ensure that the new occupiers of the old house do everything to detach the cat from its old home by chasing it away and throwing water at it, and never stopping to say hello or feel sorry for it. Other neighbours, even those previously friendly with the cat, must be asked to behave similarly. The cat should be kept indoors at the new house for about a month, but if it still returns to the old abode after that it should never be taken back to the new home by a direct route. Instead, make as wide a detour as possible, heading off initially in totally the opposite direction and driving, if you have that option, a good few miles before circling round and back. As a last resort, consider boarding the cat for a few weeks in a cattery as far away as possible from either home in order to scramble both its memory of the old home and its homing mechanism. But, once at last at the new house, the tricks of short frequent feeds and plenty of love and attention should help build new bonds. Again, the cat should be starved for at least twelve hours before being let out, and then for the first two weeks allowed out for only one period per day, being called in within half an hour and promptly fed.

The aim is that the new home comes to be perceived as the centre of the new territory and a source of food and shelter (in contrast to the old home, where these things are denied it). It may take weeks and, in some cases, months before the cat can be allowed outside unattended. The moral of the tale is: for the cat's sake, never move to a new home less than five miles away!

If all else fails, encourage the new owners of your old house, or their neighbours, to adopt your cat permanently.

Moving home can be just as traumatic for the permanently indoor cat as obviously this involves a complete change of personal territory and can leave it feeling totally vulnerable in the new house. Slow, careful introductions, one room at a time, and lots of attention will help most cats over the stress of such upheaval within a few days. Taking pains pays dividends, but most owners would agree there are limits. Edward Lear was so devoted to his cat Foss that when he decided to move house he had his new villa built as an exact replica of the old one so that the cat was not upset by the move…

N • NERVOUSNESS AND PHOBIAS

The cat, like every other animal, is born with the capacity to respond to challenge and protect itself from the life-threatening dangers. The responses to such challenges are easily distinguishable from the cat's normal behaviour patterns. The reaction when startled is genetically programmed and even young kittens are seen to arch their back, erect their fur and flatten their ears when alarmed by a loud noise or sudden unfamiliar happening. During the early weeks of life, a kitten, like many other mammals, will run to mum for protection immediately after being startled, if she hasn't already intervened. Gradually, the kitten becomes used to commonly encountered noises or activity, especially if these are never followed by anything harmful or physically painful. In short, as the kitten grows up it learns to adapt and take most things in its stride. Most cats grow increasingly competent and confident on their way through the feline school of life and become good pets.

For others, life is one big fearful experience. They avoid any sort of challenge by hiding in a dark corner or behind the sofa. Any slight noise or movement causes the cat to run away. It never faces what it fears and therefore never learns to cope with even the mildest occurrence. Anxious cats usually have a crouching gait, low carriage of tail, and slow low movements towards a sheltered spot under a table or in a corner. From there, they may peer out, still hunched and with pupils dilated in fear, trying to see but not attract attention. Having found a secure bolt-hole, the cat may avoid facing any challenge altogether and lie still, hoping the threat will disappear. Some even learn to hide themselves under the bedclothes when anxious, a reaction similar to that famous 'head-in-the-sand' method of making worries go away. Others appear withdrawn and take longer and longer to move out into open areas in the house. Whichever course the cat adopts, it is clearly distressed – and it is distressing too for the owner to observe, especially if the cat reacts in such a manner when faced with normal everyday events and never seems to get to grips with life, let alone enjoy it. The signs of its distress are clear, yet it is difficult to comfort the cat at such times without contributing further to its anxiety, because this will draw attention to it and the cat may never learn that our efforts are designed to comfort it. If we push too hard, it may resort to lashing out as a last line of defence when there is nowhere else to run. The threshold of its nervousness may fall even lower as a result. Clearly, such cats are not enjoying life to the full and if the problem is left untreated it will gradually worsen.

Kittens brought up by inexperienced or incompetent mothers are more likely to be less competent themselves at dealing with change, as indeed will those relatively unexposed to challenge during the first weeks of life. When a cat displays a general nervousness, it is often for this reason – having received an inadequate range of experiences as a kitten, it is unable to cope with the flow of challenges as an adult. However, we can rectify this omission by providing fresh opportunities for them to learn to cope with all those happenings by exposing the cat gradually to controlled safe experiences. Nevertheless, in such cases, it is rare to produce a totally competent 'normal' cat as there are always certain things to which the cat can only truly become accustomed while still a kitten. For example, kittens brought up with puppies, or even adult dogs, rarely show nervous reactions in adulthood when dogs approach them to play. By contrast, the adult cat that has had no experience of dogs is unlikely ever to be relaxed about such advances and usually retreats quickly. Some older cats can late in life learn to live with a dog, but it takes an inordinate amount of patience on your part, most only get as far as tolerating dogs and rarely will any social interaction or play develop.

You can, however, build up the confidence of many a nervous cat by providing it with a new den (a kittening pen is ideal), which you place in the main activity room of the house. By this means, normal family life goes on as usual around the cat, which is protected from physical danger by the pen. Most importantly, the cat is also prevented from running away and avoiding the challenges of changes in household members, visits of strangers, noises on the television or movement of furniture going on around it. So it has to face up to them and start to interpret what is happening. The cat is essentially 'in a womb', where it is warm, protected, and provided with all life-support systems of food, water and a litter tray, but is at the same time in a position to get used to all the things that previously induced a fearful, avoiding reaction.

Severe cases can also be helped with certain drug treatments. These can help the cat by letting it learn without panicking. Any drug treatment must of course be under the control of your veterinary surgeon.

AGORAPHOBIA

Agoraphobia is the abnormal dread of open spaces, which includes the outdoors but can also mean open areas within a room. Fortunately, this is quite rare in cats.

The condition can arise from a lack of early exposure to the outdoors, or exposure delayed too long and so not coinciding with a kitten's exploratory phases of development after weaning. In the majority of cases, the agoraphobic cat is unwilling to go out because of a loss of confidence caused by a single traumatic incident, such as a fight with a highly territorial local rival that may even have come into the house. Other causes include major disturbance of access points to the home base during the building of an extension or garage, a chance encounter with a stray dog in the garden or a near miss with a fast car.

The risk of encountering the rival may be present every time the cat wants to go out and its reluctance to do so thus increases steadily. It may lose the ability to cope outdoors with even mild changes such as the sound of leaves rustling or the noise of a car, even if the other cat is not on the scene. Typically, the severity of the cat's reaction is exhibited with all exposures, even on trouble-free days when neither hide nor hair of another cat can be seen. It will be distressed if forced outdoors and a long, long way from enjoying its earlier outdoor lifestyle.

Treatment for agoraphobic cats is similar to that for other forms of nervousness. It involves systematic desensitisation to the stimulus through controlled exposure to the outdoors, perhaps using the carrying basket or, better still, a large secure pen in which the cat can safely spend some portion of its day outdoors. Such treatment is usually best delayed until the cause of the problem is removed. This may mean waiting until building works are completed, or even coming to an arrangement with the owner of the despotic rival about which cat is allowed out at which times, in order to avoid further conflict. Once this has been achieved, the cat can be put outdoors to relearn that it is as safe as before the trauma and that every noise on the wind is not necessarily threatening. Owners and even willing friends should accompany it on a walk round the garden on the first few occasions, making encouraging noises to bolster its confidence. Sometimes it helps to divide the cat's meals into frequent short rations and to move its feeding area to the pen and, later, to just outside the back door. The prognosis for treatment of agoraphobic cats is often very good, depending on the amount of control over the cause of the problem that can be achieved.

Many cats and dogs are afraid of household electrical goods and the vacuum cleaner must be quite frightening from their point of view. Certainly, the noise and sudden movements associated with vacuuming and even with other methods of cleaning, as well as the smells associated with polish, etc. will be challenging to a nervous character. Treatment involves desensitising the cat to these frequent normal household events in the same way as outlined above.

O • OLD CATS

Older cats, like older people, need special care. They sleep more and like peaceful warm corners in which to rest undisturbed by the hubbub of family life. Since joints stiffen up, it is important that your cat has easy access to its bed, litter tray, food and water. Its bed should be warm and preferably by a radiator, and you could perhaps provide another comfortable resting-place in a favourite sunny spot by the window. If these are above floor level, make sure that the cat can get up easily to them in stages – for example, via a chair-arm or side-table to the windowsill – rather than expecting it to leap up in one movement.

Restricting the cat to one or two warm rooms may define a safer, more secure area for it, and, if it is arthritic, offering several litter trays in this area will ensure it continues to able to be clean. An incontinent old cat is usually a very unhappy cat, so pay special attention to its toilet needs and don't expect it to have to go too far when nature calls.

When awake, your cat will require frequent affectionate contact with you. Gentle grooming is relaxing and will help your cat to keep itself clean and maintain its self-respect. It's also important to continue to involve the old boy or girl in family life as much as you or it can manage. While older cats require plenty of rest, they do need to be kept involved and stimulated as well. Even though they may prefer to spend more time indoors, they should continue to be encouraged to go out, perhaps accompanied by you, on warm calm days. Your older cat may become more vocal and seek to initiate contact with you by calling out, especially at night, when it may wake up and feel alone and vulnerable. Don't be cross; it may be time to let your cat sleep by your bed so that it feels more secure at night.

Try plenty of tender loving care. It is perhaps unlikely that acquiring a younger companion will help your cat, though of course older dogs are sometimes given a new lease of life when a new pup is brought home. Cats are more sedate and less able to tolerate sharing their home and family, so instead make time to offer that extra loving care and you'll enjoy the sheer character and affection of your cat in its old age.

Consult your veterinary surgeon about the changing dietary requirements of older cats and be prepared for erratic eating habits. They'll probably prefer frequent small light meals.

Regular check-ups will also ensure that any developing problems, such as kidney disease, which is common in old cats, can be tackled early.

P • PLAY

Kittens seem to play with anything and everything, but especially things that move. Much of their play is about sharpening reflexes and developing the hunting skills of stalk, pounce and despatch, but it is nonetheless a constant source of joy to watch. The best toys for kittens are those that allow the cat to chase. Ping-pong balls, string and tightly scrunched-up paper are cheap and as good as any special toys you could buy. Offer new environments to explore such as newspaper 'tents', paper carrier bags and boxes, which they will love to jump in. Most such games are enjoyed by adult cats too, and if your cat is to live permanently indoors you'll need to offer a steady supply to keep it interested and alert. Beware of toys which your cat could destroy by chewing as removal of swallowed portions may necessitate surgery.

Q • QUIZZICAL CATS

'Curiosity killed the cat' the saying goes, and in some cases it's true – kittens like to get their noses into everything. Bringing a new kitten home may mean that you have to reassess the safety of your home, in the same sort of way you would have to if a small child was coming to stay. Ensure all wiring is safely out of harm's way, that all potentially harmful disinfectants, bleaches and cleaning materials are well out of reach, and check that every window is shut so the new kitten can't escape while making its explorations. Remove breakable items from open shelves as high places are most popular with kittens and, yes, it probably can jump all the way up there. Remember the chimney – many kittens have ventured up these dark tunnels and become stuck, and don't forget to check that the washing-machine door has not been left open and your kitten joined the pile of washing inside.

Kittens soon grow up and out of the overcurious stage, but it's advisable to take care to start with. The more they investigate and learn the more they will want to join in with your activities. Bored, unstimulated kittens may grow up uninterested and even frightened of everyday happenings, so make good use of your kitten's quizzical nature.

R • RECOVERY FROM AN ILLNESS

The wonders of veterinary science mean that our cats can be vaccinated against many killer diseases, be cured using hi-tech drugs and equipment, and given emergency care equivalent to that available to humans. However, any vet will tell you that, no matter how miraculous a job he or she has done in stitching or medicating, the cat's will to recover is determined to a great extent by the quality of nursing it receives.

The cat can be coaxed into wanting to live by giving it good old-fashioned tender loving care, or it can give up the will to live merely because it becomes depressed. You as an owner of an ill cat have a great responsibility to help it pull through. Gentle talk and tending, keeping it warm and away from draughts, encouraging it to eat (warming its food or trying all sorts of tasty tidbits if it has lost its appetite), helping it to its litter tray and generally reassuring with touch can make the difference between life and death. Cats that recover from illness often form very strong emotional bonds with their owners. Perhaps they realise and appreciate the care and love that went into bringing them through.

S • SCRATCHING FURNITURE

As outlined previously, a cat scratches an inanimate object not only in order to remove the old husks from its claws to reveal sharp new points but also as a method of marking territory. A cat scratching furniture may do it for either of these reasons, or both. The sharpening aspect can be diverted from furniture on to a scratching post made by winding string around, or attaching bark to, a wooden pillar. The carpet-covered posts sold by pet shops may merely encourage the cat to use your carpets, so are best avoided. Place the scratching post in front of the area the cat has been scratching and after the cat uses it move the post a little distance to where it is out of harm's and temptation's way. Make sure the post is tall enough to enable the cat to stretch out to full length as it scratches. The height factor is why furniture often suits cats very well and a short post is unlikely to make a satisfactory swap for a tall upholstered chair.

If the cat is scratching to leave a scent mark, it may be that it feels insecure and is trying to enhance its own confidence by having its scent around. This problem should be tackled in the same way as indoor spraying, which is another form of marking, as outlined under 'Urine spraying' in this A–Z section.

T • TOILETING PROBLEMS

Cats are famous for their cleanliness and even young kittens seem to head instinctively for the litter tray when nature calls. Make life easy during your new kitten's or cat's first days with you by placing its litter tray in the cage, or not far from its bed, but well away from its feeding area. Use the same type of litter that was provided at its previous home. Although your cat will be deterred from using the tray if you allow it to become too dirty, you don't have to hurry to attend to it. Cleaning once a day or every two days will ensure that the cat associates its own smell with the tray and perceives it as its latrine.

As the cat gets older and has completed its course of vaccinations and is allowed outside, all toilet procedures should transfer to the garden. You can assist this transition by adding some soil to the tray and moving it a little closer each day to outdoors – first nearer the access door, then on to the step outside

– thereby establishing the indoors as a no-go-toilet zone from then onwards. Tip the used litter/soil mix on to a suitable patch of garden for a few days during the cat's first outdoor excursions to establish the garden as its new latrine.

Remember that sick cats or those unwilling to go out in bad weather will always need a litter tray indoors. It is rare for healthy cats to make mistakes but, if an accident occurs before your eyes, simply pick the cat up and place it in its litter tray. Stroke it and speak kindly; it will soon get the idea. Punishment such as 'rubbing its nose in it' is pointless, particularly after the event, and will only make it nervous and more likely to go in the wrong place again. If you don't catch the cat at it, all you should do is clean it up. If you suspect that the cat is unwell, consult your veterinary surgeon without delay and, if troubles persist, ask him or her to refer you to a professional animal behaviourist for advice.

Treatment of the toileting problem in a cat of any age will depend on the home environment and the degree of learning already established but this set of general principles may help resolve the problem.

1. Choose a suitable small room and confine the cat in a kittening pen with only enough space for its bed and a litter tray. The desire to avoid soiling the bed is an early-established one and the cat should move as far away from the bed as possible to urinate. Since it is confined, this behaviour will have to take place in the litter tray and within seven to fourteen days an attachment to cat litter and the tray as a latrine should be established. The cat when indoors should be kept in this cage at all times when the owner is unable to supervise. After seven to ten days of good aiming, the cat can be allowed out of the cage, but only into the room where it is kept, and the litter tray moved progressively further away from

the bed. Access can then be allowed to the rest of the house one room at a time, and only under supervision, for initial introduction to each room. If the cat is ultimately to be allowed outside, then the litter tray should be moved in stages towards the back door, and then just to the outdoor step. It should be up-ended on to a suitable patch of soil when dirty so as to encourage full transfer of toileting behaviour to the outdoors, and finally withdrawn from service indoors.

2. Before allowing access to a room, all soiled areas should be thoroughly cleaned using a warm solution of a biological washing powder or liquid followed by a light scrubbing with an alcohol such as surgical spirit. The area should be left to dry before the cat is allowed supervised access.

3. A cover on the litter tray provides extra security. Use an inverted cardboard box with a hole cut in for access, or buy one of the proprietary brands of litter tray that come with an integral top.

4. The litter tray should neither be allowed to get too dirty, as this will discourage most cats, nor should it be cleaned too often. Once a day is ideal for singly housed cats (more often when many cats share a tray) as the presence of the cat's own smell on the litter will help it to recognise that the tray is its latrine.

5. Experiment with different types of cat litter such as Fuller's earth granule types, wood-chip pellets, reusable waxed granule varieties and very fine grain litters. If the cat is to be allowed outdoors, the litter should be mixed with up to 50 per cent soil from the garden in order to help the complete transfer of toilet behaviour to the outdoors later.

6. The cat-flap should be closed at appropriate times to help redefine the significance of 'indoor secure/clean zone' as compared with the 'outdoor jungle/toilet zone'. This will also help you to control the cat's access to indoors and aid supervision. It may be wise to put the cat out immediately after feeding, as cats often evacuate their bowels soon after. The cat should be encouraged to spend more time outdoors as the more it is out the more often it will have to go to the toilet in a suitable place and the sooner the garden is recognised as a suitable latrine.

7. Food should never be placed near the litter tray as this deters cats from using the tray and is often the reason behind their selecting other areas in the home for toilet purposes. By the same token, food can be placed at these inappropriate sites to act as a deterrent. Dry food is more hygienic than wet food for this purpose and will help even if the cat is usually fed a canned or meat diet. The food should be stuck down to the dish to prevent the cat from eating it.

8. Cats which toilet indoors should never be punished. Punishment after the event is pointless. Instead, and only if caught in the act, they should be picked up and placed in the litter tray, stroked and calmed. When they do use the litter tray, they should be rewarded with praise and perhaps a treat.

U • URINE SPRAYING

Spraying is a normal act for most cats, be they male or female, neutered or entire. It is a territory-marking behaviour and is usually performed against vertical objects such as fence posts and bushes which rival cats may encounter. It is normally restricted to the outdoors because of competition with local pets. Cats rarely spray indoors because the home is usually secure from rivals and needs no further identification.

The indoor sprayer is therefore usually a cat that is feeling insecure or threatened and is trying to boost its own presence. Redecorating, moving furniture and changes in the household brought about by taking in a lodger, bringing home a new baby, or the death of a family member, for example, may all cause a cat to start spraying. The more cats that share a house, the more likely it is that at least one will spray owing to the presence of competition. Doors, curtains, windows, furniture legs and novel objects such as black plastic rubbish bags are all common targets. However, because owners provide security, spraying is rarely witnessed. The wet smelly deposits are usually discovered some time later.

Spraying and urinating are two different behaviours. Urination is conducted from a squatting position in the litter tray or outdoors in soil. Spraying is not used to empty the bladder, but to direct a small amount of urine on to a cat-nose-high position. When spraying, the cat stands with tail upright and quivering at the tip, which motion is often accompanied by a stepping movement with the back legs; and the spray is directed backwards.

When entire male cats are entering adolescence, the spraying behaviour becomes particularly apparent and the smell very noticeable. The behaviour and the smell are reliably halted by castration at this stage. Entire females often spray to attract mates as they come into season, and such behaviour too is reliably halted by sterilisation. In old age, too, cats of both sexes may feel less secure even in familiar territory and begin to spray to maintain their presence against real or imagined competition.

The spraying posture can sometimes be adopted as a cat strains to urinate. This is a common response in cats suffering from

FLUTD (feline lower urinary tract disease). If such signs of discomfort are observed when urinating or spraying occurs, particularly around the litter tray, the cat should be examined by a veterinary surgeon immediately. Treatment involves trying to make the cat feel secure and breaking the spraying habit. A cat should never be punished for spraying, even if caught in the act, as this will only make it more insecure and spraying more likely.

If changes have been made to the interior of the house or there are new members in the household, the cat should be denied access to most areas unless supervised. Any changed rooms should be explored with the owners present until the cat recognises the area as part of its indoor territory again.

Sprayed areas should be thoroughly cleaned with a warm solution of a biological washing powder or liquid followed by a light scrubbing with an alcohol, such as surgical spirit, to remove fatty deposits. The area should be allowed to dry completely and the cat only allowed back to it initially under supervision.

If the cat has access to the outdoors via a cat-flap, this should be locked shut and the cat let in and out by the owners. Cat-flaps destroy the security of the indoors and could allow other rivals in to compete with the occupant in the very place where it should feel safest. If spraying stops following this measure, a selective cat-flap could be installed later if this would be more convenient. To operate this type of cat-door the cat wears a collar equipped with an electronic or magnetic key that releases the flap lock and allows access only for the wearer.

Confining the cat in an indoor pen or one small room for short periods when it is unsupervised in the home will afford a more predictable area and help the cat feel more secure. A warm covered bed should be provided. As well as being protected by the bars of the pen, the cat will also be unwilling to spray near its bed, as keeping the sleeping area clean and dry is a principle firmly established at only a few weeks of age. If confined for more than two to three hours, a litter tray should be available, sited well away from food and the bed. If the cat stops spraying, you can allow access to the rest of the house one room at a time, but be sure to supervise these first ventures. The aim is for the cat steadily and increasingly to perceive the house as a safe zone shared with protective owners.

Cats rarely spray near their food, so small tubs of dry cat food can be placed at persistently used sites to act as deterrents. Dry food is more hygienic for this purpose and will help even if the cat is usually fed a canned or fresh meat diet. The dry food should be stuck to the bottom of the container to prevent the cat from eating it. Placing uncomfortable walking surfaces such as trays of pine cones or sheets of tinfoil may also deter the cat from standing and spraying at some sites.

V • VEGETARIAN CATS?

Some ardent vegetarians impose their dietary convictions on to their pets, which, if the pet in question is a dog, poses no problems. However, cats must have meat because their bodies cannot manufacture certain essential chemicals, such as taurine, from vegetable matter the way both humans and dogs can. Cats have evolved as hunters and meat catchers so successfully that they have never had to make these essential nutrients from lower-quality materials such as vegetation, and they eat them in the 'purer form' in meat. Dogs and humans, on the other hand, survived on plant material as well and often had to go without the meat, and therefore they evolved making best use of what they could find. So cats cannot be vegetarians, whatever the morals or beliefs of their owners.

W • WILD CATS – TAMING FERALS

There are millions of feral (domestic gone wild) cats in the world – many people first notice them when they holiday at hotels in Mediterranean resorts where the cats congregate for food. There are thought to be over one million feral cats in the United Kingdom alone and many people are involved in their welfare. Some concerned folk take food to their colonies or try to find loving homes for them. This can prove both difficult and dangerous. While a cat that has recently become a stray because it has been lost or dumped from its former home will reassimilate into a new home fairly easily, a wild-born feral will not. As outlined in chapter eleven, a cat needs to be handled by man before it is seven or eight weeks old in order for it to recognise humans as acceptable friends. If not, the cat is unlikely to relax or respond to humans, let alone be able to settle down in a normal home environment.

While it is possible to tame an eight-week-old feral kitten (and even then it may be very spitty and aggressive or very fearful) with patience and care, 'domesticating' an adult feral cat is usually a hopeless task. It may also be an extremely frightening experience for the cat, as any sort of taming requires the animal to learn to live with humans in their environment. Thus, the cat would need to be housed in a pen and quietly and gently introduced to everyday human goings-on. Kittens will usually respond and the younger they are the sooner they become relaxed and friendly. Older cats may simply be overwhelmed by the cage and any attempt by humans to get close. They crouch motionless or hide in a corner and if approached may become fearful and aggressive.

So, if you're thinking of taking on a feral kitten and giving it a loving home, try to be sure (as far as it is possible to tell) that it's under eight weeks old and that you will have the time to be patient with it. Taking on an older feral cat may end in distress for all concerned and it may be best to neuter the adult and return it to a managed colony where it can live out its wild life under the watchful eye of regular feeders.

X • XENOPHOBIA – FEAR OF STRANGE PEOPLE

Some cats which are otherwise untroubled by changes within the house are thrown into turmoil by the arrival of visitors. The problem may not necessarily have been caused by lack of suitable experience with enough different people when young, it could also be brought about by a single unfortunate experience with a particularly noisy, frightening or unkind guest who unwittingly taught the cat to avoid all risk of repetition in the future by running away early.

The first aim of treatment is to block the cat's attempts to escape or avoid exposure to the challenge. Its success in doing so, although protecting it from the danger it perceives, also precludes any possibility of it learning to cope on its own. Instead, the cat is denied the opportunity to avoid visitors either by being restrained on a leash, if it is comfortable wearing a collar or harness, or by being kept in a travelling cat basket for short periods when it is to receive guests. This basket should be placed in the area where guests are invited to relax – usually the living room – before they arrive. The more willing volunteers there are the better, though the cat should first receive 'guests' that it knows, such as members of the family. They ring the doorbell instead of using the key. The cat's first reaction is the usual one of alarm and an attempt to escape, but this is prevented by the basket. Then the 'guest' enters and the cat, seeing that it is a member of the family, quickly calms down. Repetition should help the cat to begin to associate the doorbell with non-threatening arrivals.

Later, visiting guests can be asked to perform the same routine, entering the cat's room with an accepted member of the family and doing nothing more than sitting down some distance from it. It is essential that the cat grows used to their presence in gradual stages. Now its cage serves to protect it from the challenge it has avoided for so long, and it should settle quickly.

Slow progress of extremely nervous cats at this stage can often be speeded up by quelling the cat's overreactions with a little sedative treatment such as valium under the direction of your veterinary surgeon. However, it is essential that the cat's tolerance does not become dependent on drugs. The drug is slowly withdrawn after a few days, so that its tolerance is increasingly learned and decreasingly drug-dependent. The drugs are simply a vehicle for exposing the sufferer to its problem. On or off drugs, with frequent exposure to as many different people as possible under the right conditions, the cat should perceive their arrival and occupancy of the core of its territory as being neutral. More importantly, it learns to accept their remaining inside its flight distance, the space which defines its opportunity to escape.

The next stage of treatment is a little more invasive. Now guests are asked to sit progressively closer to the cat's cage to habituate it further to their presence. This stage can only proceed as fast as the cat can tolerate and guests should certainly not attempt to touch it or even talk to it until it seems confident about their presence. Then the issue can be forced a little. Though it sounds rather unfair, the cat should be starved for up to twelve hours so that it is hungry when pressed into sharing space with its next visitor. The visitor, sitting close by its cage rather than bending down over it which would alarm it, gently proffers a small tidbit or tasty portion of a favourite food through the bars of the cage. Food cements relations far quicker than gentle voices, though the visitor and owner should encourage proceedings by talking gently to the cat while offering food. Thereafter, the cat should be fed frequent short meals for the length of the visitor's stay (or patience) and as many guests as possible, as well as the family, should take part in the process. This steadily brings an increase in the cat's confidence and helps it view all guests as potential providers of food and, later, affection.

The final stage of treatment is to dispense with the cage and restrain the cat on a harness or collar and lead when guests arrive. Ask them to offer food, as before, then hold the cat firmly but gently and take it towards a single known and accepted visitor. This should be done slowly so that the cat doesn't panic as it did before it learned that visitors could be nice. The advance should be slowed down further or halted if the cat starts to look alarmed or struggles. Once alongside, guests can start gradually to stroke it. The process is complete when you yourself have stopped petting it and it is being stroked only by the guest. It may not be possible for guests to hold the cat for some time yet, if at all, because holding is an enclosing action denying escape and thus requires its total confidence. It would only be acting in the same way as a great proportion of cats if it were to restrict this honour to its family alone.

During all contact, guests' hands should initially either approach unseen from the side of the cat, or very slowly from directly in front of the cat so that they can be seen and accepted. Since the cat may regard the advancing hand as very much like a threatening paw, it should be offered very gently indeed. Bear in mind that paws have claws, which are a cat's main armoury, and therefore the approaching hand is likely to cause the cat to be apprehensive in the same way as it would be apprehensive of a swing from a cat's paw.

It may even be a good idea for the visitor to approach the cat at cat level rather than intimidating it unnecessarily by bending over it. If the prospect of crawling along the floor strikes the guest as carrying things to extremes, placing the cat – whether in the basket, on a lead or hand-held – on a table and approaching it face to face could be a dignified and less threatening exercise. Of course, it is important too that all volunteers are safe, so if the cat is at all likely to lash out defensively with a paw it should be in its basket when it receives guests for some time yet.

Y • YELLING

Odd behaviours in older cats have increasingly been coming to light in the past few years. This is probably because behaviour therapy services are now widely available and more owners of pets are encouraged by their vets to look for professional assistance and to seek help when problems crop up. We owners have changed too – we have learned to understand the behaviour of our cats more in recent times and have come to perceive greater value in the individual relationships we share with them. Increasingly, these relationships are based on respect, an attribute of all relationships that improves with the age of both the cat and the owner. Compared with, say, the all-too-ephemeral joys of owning a playful kitten, they are more deeply satisfying and enduring.

In comparison with the young cat of six to eighteen months old, or even the adult up to the age of eight, old cats present very few behaviour problems indeed. The sagacity of age that old people usually acquire through a lifetime of experience applies perhaps even more to the older cat. It has learned how to behave in the human den, when to be part of the social scene and when not, how to let everyone know what it wants, when it wants it, and how to occupy the best spot for snoozing where it won't be disturbed or get into anyone's way. In fact, the older cat gets easier to look after as time goes on. Behaviour problems as such are far more likely to arise as signs of illness of the body 'wearing out' or just through the cat's greater need for company and reassurance. Behaviour problems in young or adult cats stem from inabilities to learn about house-training, or recover from training breakdowns caused by nervousness or conflicts with other cats. They may spray urine, defecate openly or scratch marks on furniture or walls around the house. These are all signs that they are under social threat from the presence of other cats indoors or out, or, most commonly, because they perceive their den to be under some irresolvable challenge because someone has moved the furniture, or had a friend or dogs to stay. Most upset can be caused when the security of the home has been destroyed by installing a cat-flap in the door, so the cat's bed, food bowl and owner's lap are suddenly available to all its rivals.

Without doubt, the most common behaviour problem in older cats is that of the nocturnal yeller. Many owners will report that their cat stared to call out to them for attention and affection since it became an older member of the feline community – and many such calls occur at night. Owners find themselves woken in the night by plaintive cries from their pet. On the first occasion, they leap out of bed to see what has upset their much-loved cat – a sudden illness or afflictions of age. When they find the cat, however, it is often just outside the bedroom door or pacing around downstairs, but looking the same picture of elderly health as it did at teatime.

Usually, owners find that the cat is not in any physical distress at all, and does not even seem to want anything in particular, such as to be fed or let out. Once they have stroked it and asked it what the matter is in a concerned voice, it settles down quietly and goes back to sleep. All it wanted was a little physical reassurance and protection in the lonely silence of the night and to be 'tucked in' again.

However, for the cat, two major events have occurred. First, the ageing animal has conceded to itself that, after years of being independent and perhaps rather aloof, even shunning attention from its owners when it wanted solitude, the time has come when it values their presence. Through feeling lonely or a little insecure, the older cat has now accepted that some of that warm human contact could make everything right. If it can get its owners to be present, the cat can leave all vital decision-making to them for a while.

The second major event to notice is that the clever cat has now trained its owners, in true Pavlovian style and with all the skill of a champion dog handler, to respond to its demands. It has realised that, with one pitiful cry, its owners will leap to its side at any time of the day, but especially at night, to supply heaps of reassuring comfort. So, facing up to making a major decision – such as 'shall I lie next to the radiator or in my favourite sun spot?' – it will utter the same cry. Now the clever cat is assured that its owners will come and help it make up its mind by finding the most comfortable bed or offering the better option of a good cuddle and then being put where it will be most content.

Age brings its own rewards for the cat, especially once it has learned how to use its voice to full effect, when it can no longer physically attract its owners' attention by either jumping on them or rubbing around their legs. As for the night-time problem, some owners place the cat basket next to the bed and deal with waking without having to get out from the warm covers. Others have used a baby communicator and talked to the cat over the intercom when it wakes; others leave on a radio or get a heated pad for the cat to sleep on – better than doing what one lady did every night which was to get up and replace the water in the cat's hot water bottle when it called her! Others, realising there is nothing physically wrong with the cat, have closed their ears, put their heads under the pillows and tried to hold out so that the cat does not learn to do this every night by being rewarded by their presence – they will tell you, however, just how persistent cats can be!

A cat's behaviour pattern varies according to the seasons, the weather, weekends or family activity. It will also vary according to whether food is provided in distinct meals or, as is the case with many dry diets, permanently on offer for free-choice feeding. As the pet gets older, it will tend to sleep more at those times when it would have been out hunting and generally co-ordinate its time in the home with the presence of the owners. Even if it doesn't interact socially with them as much as it used to, the important thing is that they are there, providing security and available for social contact if the older cat feels the need for some affection. The older the animal becomes, the more likely it is that it will look for its owners when disturbed or startled, or if it simply wakes up and finds itself alone, which after all, is most likely to occur at night.

So, if your old cat suddenly becomes a nocturnal yeller, and disturbs your sleep, it may be time to let it sleep in the bedroom and derive comfort from your immediate presence if it happens to wake in the night. But if you don't want to do this, try to ignore the cries for a while. If you get up, remember that you are simply rewarding the cat's lack of confidence and ensuring that it can rely on you even when there is no real need. The longer the cries fail to pay off, the longer the cat will perhaps stay confident and independent and you will get a decent night's sleep again.

Z • ZOONOSES

Zoonoses is the scientific name given to diseases that can be passed from animals to humans. A few potential owners may be put off having a cat or enjoying a close physical relationship with it because of worries about disease. In fact, there is very little to worry about. Rabies is a potential horror, but one we do not have to consider in the UK. Worms can be caught from cat faeces, but the problem can easily be dealt with by worming the cat regularly. Ringworm is not actually a worm but a fungal skin condition which can be caught from many animals, not just cats, and can be treated successfully. It is not common among pet cats but may be present in colonies of feral or farm cats.

Toxoplasmosis is a less visible problem. It is caused by a tiny organism which can be excreted in the cat's faeces. Affected cats show little or no sign of infection and most people who become infected suffer flu-like symptoms at worst. In fact, the organism is more likely to be contracted by eating uncooked or partially cooked meat than from contact with cats. Pregnant women should be especially careful to wash their hands after cleaning the litter tray, as the disease is a risk to the unborn baby. There is really negligible risk of catching diseases from our cats if we keep them wormed and undertake the usual hygiene precautions. The health benefits of pet-keeping are well known, and the small risk of catching a disease is far outweighed by the years of fun and companionship a cat will undoubtedly bring.

For reliable advice on almost anything cat. go to www.fabcats.org.